Resurrection Reconsidered

Gavin D'Costa is Senior Lecturer in Theology in the Department of Theology and Religious Studies at the University of Bristol.

Other books by Gavin D'Costa

John Hick's Theology of Religions
Theology and Religious Pluralism
Ed. *Christian Uniqueness Reconsidered*
Ed. *Faith Meets Faith*

RESURRECTION

RECONSIDERED

EDITED BY

GAVIN D'COSTA

ONEWORLD
OXFORD

RESURRECTION RECONSIDERED

Oneworld Publications
(Sales and Editorial)
185 Banbury Road
Oxford OX2 7AR
England

Oneworld Publications
(US Marketing Office)
PO Box 830, 21 Broadway
Rockport, MA 01966
USA

ISBN 1–85168–113–2

Printed and bound by
WSOY, Finland

Copyright acknowledgement: Jürgen Moltmann's essay is a slightly revised and
expanded version taken from his book, *Jesus Christ for Today's World*, translated by
Margaret Kohl (London: SCM, 1994), pp. 71–87.

Contents

Preface

Gavin D'Costa

*T*here is a cautionary Jewish story found in *b. Baba Mezia* 59b which might well be applied to the resurrection:

> On a certain occasion R. Eliezer used all possible arguments to substantiate his opinion, but the Rabbis did not accept it. He said, 'If I am right, may this carob tree move a hundred yards from its place.' It did so . . . They said, 'From a tree no proof can be brought.' Then he said, 'May the canal prove it.' The water of the canal flowed backwards. They said, 'Water cannot prove anything.' Then he said, 'May the walls of this House of Study prove it.' Then the walls of the house bent inwards, as if they were about to fall. R. Joshua rebuked the walls and said to them, 'If the learned dispute about the Halakah, what has that to do with you?' So, to honour R. Joshua, the walls did not fall down, but, to honour R. Eliezer, they did not become quite straight again. Then R. Eliezer said, 'If I am right, let the heavens prove it.' Then a heavenly voice said, 'What have you against R. Eliezer? The Halakah is always with him.' Then R. Joshua got up and said, 'It is not in heaven' [Deut. 30:12]. What did he mean by this? R. Jeremiah said, 'The law was given us from Sinai. We pay no attention to a heavenly voice. For already from Sinai the law said, "By a majority you are to decide"' [Exod. 23:2].

The resurrection has often been used in the ambiguous manner of Rabbi Eliezer's stunning 'miracles': to try and convince believer and non-believer alike of the truth of Christianity. The argument, crudely put, runs something like this. If Christianity is based on a historical figure called Jesus of Nazareth, and if after a holy life leading to his crucifixion there followed the resurrection of his body from the dead – then Jesus must be who Christians claim that he is: the Son of God, the second person of the trinity, truly God–truly Man. The resurrection acts as proof of these claims. But as the story of the rabbis indicates, such stunning miracles will not always convince even the righteous and holy. The well-known Jewish scholar Pinchas Lapide accepts the resurrection of Christ from the dead, but does not believe that this confirms Christian claims about Jesus of Nazareth. As Rabbi Jeremiah's attitude illustrates, wonderful 'signs' are always interpreted within a particular context and world-view, and therefore one man's holy text may well be another woman's oppression. (This asymmetry is particularly well illustrated by Rupert Gethin's Buddhist response to the resurrection.)

However, to complicate matters further, it is well known that some modern bishops and theologians decidedly deny that any such physical resurrection took place, arguing that God does not and would not work in such a crude fashion, robbing individuals of their freedom to come to faith. Ironically, these theologians still sometimes share the assumption of their opponents: that a physically verifiable resurrection would prove something – usually, the divinity of Jesus Christ and the truth of Christianity. The words 'verifiable' and 'prove' are not incidental, for they are generated as twins by nineteenth-century scientific discourse in establishing the truth of material claims and many moderns have begun to assimilate the resurrection in these terms. This is partly true for Michael Goulder who powerfully argues against the case for a physical resurrection (and is therefore an atheist), and for Dan Cohn-Sherbok who also questions the Christian claim of Jesus' bodily resurrection (and therefore remains a Jew). Goulder also employs intriguing modern psychological explanations in offering his alternative reading of the gospel accounts. Cohn-Sherbok draws from both his Jewish tradition and contemporary science to argue his case. The way in which Goulder and Cohn-Sherbok come to similar conclusions from very different starting points makes for fascinating reading.

However, other theologians question the categories derived from positivist historicism and certain types of scientific rationality in which the truth (or otherwise) of the resurrection is sought. Issues concerning history, truth, strategies for reading the bible, and the nature of language are all explored differently to illuminate the question of the resurrection. Many of these theologians fully realize that if the resurrection is evacuated of all types of physicality, there is then always a danger of obscuring the affirmation of the created world of which Jesus was fully part and of minimizing the embodied and historical nature of Christian discipleship. Most of these theologians are equally suspicious of positivist conceptions of history as the basis of truth, and of historical–critical methods of reading the biblical accounts of the resurrection that rely on historical positivist assumptions. This heated debate (which is well represented in this volume) is like a forest fire; it does not seem to go out and it is difficult to predict the direction in which it will travel, but it has made its mark irrevocably. It has also laid bare much new ground that requires careful regeneration. And last, but not least, it indicates that reading the bible is no easy task. But like all forest fires – it is localized. A collection of essays from those writing and working with 'tribals' in Latin America, or with the poor in the slums of Calcutta, or with battered women in New York would probably produce very different essays. But that is for another book.

This collection begins with John Barclay's masterly survey of the state of New Testament scholarship on various questions connected with the resurrection: the Pauline accounts, the empty tomb tradition and the resurrection accounts in the gospels. Barclay also alerts the reader to the problems of interpreting the texts. Gareth Jones gives a historical introduction to the contemporary context of theologies of the resurrection in an assured inspection of two major modern theologians: Rudolf Bultmann (Protestant) and Karl Rahner (Roman Catholic). In his evaluation of these two influential theologians, Jones brings to light various important questions in theology regarding the status of language and the character of doctrine, showing how our understanding of the resurrection will often be partly shaped by various philosophical assumptions.

Goulder then robustly sets out his case against the historical reality of the resurrection, raising central questions about history and evidence. We find in Wolfhart Pannenberg's essay a careful attempt to rehabilitate the role of historical critical analysis, removed from its positivist assumptions so that it can properly help ground Christian claims to truth in the history of God's action in Jesus. Here the conversation generated between Goulder and Cohn-Sherbok is interrupted and questioned, leaving the reader with a lively sense of some contemporary options. Jürgen Moltmann, also in critical conversation with historical methodology, points to the reality of the resurrection in terms of future hope with its socio-political implications. Moltmann's shifting of the question on to different grounds forms a bridge to the alternative options explored by some of the following writers.

Rowan Williams, David McCarthy Matzko and Gerard Loughlin can profitably be read together for they share the conviction that the church is the proper context for speaking and acting out the meaning of the resurrection. Williams painstakingly and sensitively shows what is at stake in the empty tomb tradition, while simultaneously throwing light on the vexed relationship between historical questions and dogmatic theology. Matzko implicitly undermines much of the basis of the historical–critical debate by approaching the resurrection in what he believes to be the proper way to understand it: in the practice of the saints within the church. The context of the practising church as the locus for learning to share in the resurrected life is the concern of Gerard Loughlin. His view of reading scripture starkly contrasts with Goulder and Cohn-Sherbok as he questions the presuppositions of modernity employed in historical–critical–scientific New Testament scholarship. His employment of postmodern conceptualities (narrative) mark one possible future direction in the debate.

In the light of these many voices and differing options the reader should be constructively bewildered. I say 'bewildered' because all these essays indicate that the question of the resurrection is closely related to clusters of complex hermeneutical presuppositions entertained by different reading communities. The future of theology may rely on the critical, creative and 'constructive' interaction between such different communities. Just such a fruitful and imaginative interaction is to be found in Tina Beattie's essay which employs recent psychoanalytic feminist theory to read afresh the meaning of the resurrection in the light of some deeply perplexing gender questions. Her essay, which takes the engagement of the resurrection into very different worlds, leads into the last four essays which locate the question of the resurrection in the different worlds of other religions.

Christianity in the modern world is inescapably related to religious pluralism and it is fitting that the final section engages with this reality. In my essay I interpret John the Evangelist's theology of resurrection in terms of the gift of the Holy Spirit. I then apply this reading of John to some Roman Catholic teachings that the Holy Spirit is present in the world religions to ask what such language might mean. I argue that we will not finally know what the resurrection means until Christianity has fully encountered the world religions. David Marshall provides a unique study with close Qur'anic exegesis to explore analogies and differences between the resurrection in the New Testament and various Qur'anic themes. Such a reading of the Qur'an suggests new and interesting reading strategies for the future. While I struggle with the question of other religions from within systematic theology, Marshall does so from within the texts of another tradition. The contrast is instructive of different tasks ahead for Christianity.

Finally, Dan Cohn-Sherbok's essay is written from a Jewish standpoint and Rupert Gethin's from that of a Buddhist. Both acknowledge the plurality within their own traditions, but nonetheless their contributions provide succinct and pertinent challenges. Cohn-Sherbok, coming from a theistic Jewish perspective, shows the possibility of an overlap in acceptance of a resurrection, but his scientific world-view also calls into dramatic question the reality of such an event. Here, the Christian is called to account, and the debate between Goulder, Pannenberg, Moltmann, Loughlin and the other writers comes back to the forefront. In Cohn-Sherbok one confronts multiple worlds – his particular understanding of history and scientific method being shared by a proportion of Jews and non-Jews alike. But in Gethin we discover the gulf and differences to be far more profound. Gethin sees fruitful Buddhist ways of possibly making sense of the resurrection, all of which he acknowledges fall dramatically short of the more traditional Christian claims. In fact, his Buddhist perspective entirely questions the main terms in which Christian traditional claims are couched. If 'God' is a deeply problematic term, 'resurrection' may seem like an incidental part of the icing on a very elaborate cake. While Christians may certainly think that the resurrection has universal implications, Gethin's essay is a salutary reminder of the fragmented and plural nature of discourse in the contemporary world: the resurrection is a non-question in Buddhist terms.

What I hope the reader will find, if they read right through this collection, is the rich and varied ways in which the resurrection is understood within overlapping and intersecting communities: the church, the secular world, the scientific world, the world of other religions and the New Testament world. They will also see that all these worlds are themselves contested and plural. This collection is testimony to that richness, with all its possibilities and dead-ends! Hence, to ask about the resurrection is at the same time to ask about ourselves and communities, our loves, aspirations, fears and prejudices – and to engage with the promise of new life that so many claim to have found in the resurrection of Jesus Christ.

I finally wish to thank the contributors, both for their contributions as well as for the enjoyable experience of working with them in editing this collection. Novin Doostdar and Juliet Mabey, the publishers, have been a supportive and efficient presence throughout. My thanks to them and to Pascale Carrington, their assistant.

To retain the stylistic particularity and integrity of each contributor, no attempt has been made to systematize capitalization or gender language.

Chapter 1

THE RESURRECTION IN CONTEMPORARY NEW TESTAMENT
SCHOLARSHIP

John M. G. Barclay

Introduction

New Testament scholars do not live in social or intellectual seclusion. While the New Testament forms the focus of their attention, it is inevitable (and appropriate) that they should be conscious of the contemporary context in which these texts take on personal, social and theological significance. Given the long engagement of the Christian tradition with the New Testament, no area of New Testament scholarship is unaffected by such concerns, but the depth and complexity of the interface between text and faith (or unbelief) is nowhere more apparent than in discussion of the resurrection. Belief in the resurrection of Jesus is generally acknowledged to be a cardinal tenet of the Christian faith, in line with Paul's assertion that 'if Christ has not been raised, then our preaching is in vain and your faith is in vain' (1 Cor. 15:14). Thus no scholar can discuss this topic without being aware of touching a central nerve in the body of Christian faith.

New Testament specialists are, of course, not the only people who reflect on New Testament texts, and considerable contributions to this task have been made by some whose primary specialism is systematic theology. The long and fruitful interchange between textual and theological enquiry prohibits a neat demarcation of scholarship, but I take as my primary object for survey the work performed by specialists in New Testament studies in analysis of New Testament texts. Such work is at present highly diverse: critical assessment of the 'historicity' of the resurrection is no longer the predominant mode of enquiry, but stands alongside literary and theological evaluation of the relevant texts *as texts*, for which investigation of what lies behind or beneath is largely irrelevant. It is worth reflecting on the factors which motivate these two modes of enquiry.

The historical investigation of the New Testament

resurrection texts is driven by many factors besides the simple fact that the historical–critical method has dominated New Testament studies since the Enlightenment. In the first place, the fact that the New Testament locates the resurrection of Jesus in a narrative, succeeding the story of his death, has led to the popular assumption that it is offered for belief on the same terms as other aspects of the life of Jesus, which are clearly to some degree rooted in history. Some New Testament authors support this assumption by invoking witnesses to the resurrection as a real event in history: Paul, for instance, cites the living witness of hundreds who saw the risen Christ (1 Cor. 15:6) and Luke appeals to the 'proofs' by which Jesus presented himself alive after his death (Acts 1:3). Secondly, an important aspect of Christian apologetic has been defence of the claim that the resurrection of Jesus can be affirmed as historically true. Matthew's concern to refute contrary explanations for the empty tomb (Matt. 28:11–16) is the earliest example of such an apologetic stance. Reimarus' thesis that the disciples stole the body and fabricated the resurrection message established the battleground at the start of the modern era of New Testament study, and apologetic concerns have motivated believing New Testament scholars down to the present day.[1] Thirdly, quite apart from the apologetic issue, study of the early Christian movement is naturally concerned to elucidate the origins of its foundational belief in the resurrection of Jesus: historians expect to investigate this question with as much rigour as they would any other aspect of early Christianity.

However, many New Testament scholars (and theologians) consider that 'history' is not the best category in which to place the resurrection and its investigation. In general, it is widely recognized that there are no such things as 'naked' historical facts (as the old historical positivism claimed to find), so that even so-called historical investigations are shaped by the scholar's standpoint. More specifically, there is reason to consider the resurrection to be a topic which escapes (or at least transcends) historical enquiry in a peculiar way. On the one hand, it is a miracle created by God which, by definition, breaks the historical nexus of causation and cannot satisfy the historical quest for analogy. On the other hand, it is an 'eschatological event' which establishes a new order of being quite beyond the space–time continuum which our historical methods are designed to investigate. These factors suggest that 'resurrection'

14

is better investigated in terms of 'theology' (talk about God) than 'history', at least so long as the latter is defined by the non-supernaturalist canons of post-Enlightenment historiography.

The competing interests of history and theology affect the interpretation of the resurrection in many ways. At one end of a spectrum lies the insistence that the truth of the resurrection can be affirmed (or denied) by historical enquiry: defenders of the faith thus bolster the authority of the New Testament with harmonization of the discrepant Easter stories, while its detractors expose the fragility of the historical evidence. At the other end stands an affirmation of faith that God raised Jesus, which is unconcerned with the strength or weakness of the historical evidence: it is enough for this faith to establish that the earliest Christians believed that Jesus was raised from the dead, and it is of no consequence how they arrived at this conviction.[2] In between these extremes lie many intermediate points which assess differently the place of the historical elements in the resurrection claim. Divergent views of Christian faith may underly such judgements: some consider it disastrous for faith to be made dependent on insecure historical conclusions, others that it is dangerously docetic for faith to be deprived of its purchase on historical and physical reality.

In what follows we will explore some key elements in contemporary New Testament scholarship, conscious of the influence of such varied presuppositions. After a survey of the main New Testament texts, we will examine in turn the historicity of the empty tomb and the historicity of the 'appearances', as they fare in contemporary New Testament scholarship. Then, turning from historical to theological enquiry, we will outline some typical features in the theological assessment of the New Testament texts.

A Survey of the New Testament Texts

The claim that 'Jesus is risen' occurs in practically all the New Testament texts, in a wide variety of forms (narrative, creed, argument etc.). One may say that the resurrection is foundational for all the New Testament authors (with the notable exception of James).[3] However, there are only five texts, in two categories, which provide extended reflection on the topic: 1 Corinthians 15 and the four gospel narratives. We will examine each category in turn.

1 Corinthians 15

This chapter is of exceptional importance for historical enquiry, both because it is earlier than the gospels (from the mid 50s CE; the earliest gospel, Mark, is not much earlier than 70) and because it has embedded within it a creed which may date from as early as the 30s. It is simple enough to discern in 1 Corinthians 15:3–5 the outline of this four-member creedal confession:

> Christ died for our sins, in accordance with the Scriptures;
> He was buried;
> He was raised on the third day, in accordance with the Scriptures;
> He was seen by Cephas (then by the twelve . . .)

As indicated here, there is some dispute about where the original formula ended: some would close it after the reference to Cephas (or even after 'he was seen'), others would include the twelve, others the reference to the 500, James and the apostles in verses 6–7 (the final appearance to Paul, verse 8, is clearly a Pauline addition).

It is important to observe that in this, our earliest extant witness to the resurrection:

1. There is no reference to the tomb being empty.
2. There is no reference to women either at the tomb or as recipients of resurrection appearances.
3. There is no indication of the location of the appearances.

It is another matter to know what to conclude from such silences. Does silence imply ignorance? Was there no empty tomb story at this early date? It has been argued that an empty tomb is implied by the juxtaposition of 'he was buried' and 'he was raised', on the supposition that a first-century Pharisee like Paul must have regarded resurrection as (at least) the re-use of the body laid in the tomb. In fact, it is hard to be dogmatic about what first-century Jews meant by resurrection, and Paul's own statements on the matter at the end of 1 Corinthians 15 contain some notable ambiguities. The reference to the 'third day' looks like it could establish a link with the gospel Easter stories; but in fact they do not use 'third day' language nor indicate on which day Jesus was actually raised (the women find the tomb already empty). The 'third day' seems to be connected more with Scriptural sources (e.g. Hos. 6:2?) which are here claimed to be fulfilled.

There are further discrepancies between Paul's listed appearances and those recorded in the gospels. In Paul's list there are some (to James and to the 500) which are not recorded in the gospels, and the priority of the appearance to Peter (Cephas) is not otherwise attested (though cf. Luke 24:34 and Peter's role in the dramas of John 20 and 21). In adding himself to the end of the list, Paul is at odds with the Lukan scheme by which the resurrection appearances took place over forty days (before the ascension); for Luke, Paul's vision of the risen Christ (Acts 9) was in a different category from the rest.

It is generally held that Paul's evidence, being earlier, is to be preferred to that of the gospel accounts. Historically that is a reasonable, though not an infallible inference: later material could nonetheless contain primitive tradition, while Paul's early material could be biased by ideological factors (e.g. disinclination to mention women as the first witnesses). Given the brevity of Paul's account, it alone cannot prove the gospel accounts of the empty tomb to be legendary supplements, though for many it at least raises that suspicion.

One other aspect of 1 Corinthians 15 should be noted at this stage. Paul discusses the resurrection in this chapter because he is at odds with certain Corinthian Christians who questioned the notion that the resurrection involved a 'body' (15:35ff.). Paul insists that it is reasonable to think of a resurrection 'body' so long as one distinguishes between a normal 'material body' and a resurrection 'spiritual body' (1 Cor. 15:42–9). There are real difficulties in grasping Paul's meaning here: he insists that 'flesh and blood cannot inherit the kingdom of God' (15:50), but retains the term 'body' in the phrase 'spiritual body' (15:44). Interpretation depends on the sense of the term *sōma*, which normally has physical connotations but could be used in this context in a weaker sense. Some scholars maintain that the use of the term for both present and future existence implies some real continuity between the different 'bodies' (the future one is a transformation of the present physical entity; cf. Phil. 3:20). Others regard the ambiguities of Paul's language as significant: he talks of the resurrection *of the dead* (15:42) not the resurrection *of the body*, and leaves indeterminate what is the 'it' (simply the person?) which is sown perishable, but raised imperishable (15:42–4; cf. Phil. 1:21–4; 2 Cor. 5:8).[4]

The difficulty in determining Paul's meaning at this point suggests that it is unwise to be dogmatic about what he, or other early Christians, understood to be the physical effects of resurrection. It is often claimed that Palestinian Jews held fairly literalist views about resurrection as requiring an emptying of tombs. But the breadth of meaning in the noun 'resurrection' (*anastasis*) and in the verb 'to raise' (*egeirein*), and the jumble of views about the afterlife held by Jews in the first century, caution us against narrowing the options at this point.[5] Since the early Christians altered the Jewish apocalyptic scheme by proclaiming that a single proleptic resurrection had taken place, it would be unwise to insist that they in other respects held to a pre-set expectation of what 'resurrection' entailed. There was also such cultural and theological variety in the early Christian movement (even in Jerusalem) that it would be dangerous to make generalizing statements about 'early Christian belief'.

The Gospel Narratives

The four gospel narratives vary greatly in their accounts of the discovery of the empty tomb and in their narratives of appearances of the risen Jesus. In relation to the tomb, if one poses the questions, 'Who came to the tomb?', 'For what purpose?', 'What did they find there?' and 'What did they then do?', a survey of the four gospel accounts will indicate a wide range of answers. A similar or even greater diversity characterizes the gospel resurrection appearances.[6]

It is widely accepted that of these accounts Mark is the earliest and an important source for both Matthew and Luke; it remains disputed whether John is also drawing on Synoptic accounts or on an independent version (of uncertain historical value). Most scholars hold that Mark's gospel originally ended at 16:8 and was intended to end there: textually and linguistically it is clear that the following verses (16:9ff.) are later additions intended to fill out what came to be regarded as an inadequate ending. Study of the literary and theological characteristics of the gospels has also shown that the various resurrection accounts match well the narrative patterns of their respective authors: the Lukan account is typically Lukan, for instance, and congruent with his emphases in the gospel and in Acts.[7] This does not itself negate their historical value, of course, but it does suggest that some features of the gospel stories may be tailored more to literary and theological design than to the demands of historical reportage. Thus it is widely observed that Matthew's tale of guards at the tomb and of a dramatic angelic appearance is formed out of his apologetic concern to refute rumours of the theft of the body (Matt. 27:62–6; 28:2, 11–15). Similarly, Luke's special emphasis on the physicality of the resurrection body of Jesus (he invites them to handle him, and eats a fish, Luke 24:36–43) is designed to counter suggestions that the disciples saw merely a spirit or a ghost (Luke 24:40). If these aspects of the stories are apologetic or literary accretions, one is entitled to ask how much else is merely legendary.

If our two earliest accounts are by Paul and Mark, it is striking that one has appearances but no empty tomb, while the other has an empty tomb but no appearances. This might suggest that the two forms of witness to the resurrection were originally independent. In any case, empty tomb and appearances constitute rather different forms of witness and can be considered separately in historical enquiry. In their historical evaluation of the evidence we have surveyed, New Testament scholars may be roughly grouped in four categories:

1. A few at the conservative end of the spectrum attempt to harmonize all the material into a single historical account.[8] Most scholars, however, consider this goal impossible and the attempt symptomatic of a misunderstanding of the resurrection stories, which were written not as jigsaw pieces scattered from an original whole but as integral parts of their individual gospel narratives.

2. Those who desist from harmonization do not necessarily doubt the historical value of all aspects of these stories. A number of scholars hold that both the appearance stories and the story of the empty tomb contain a reliable historical core, even if both traditions have been subject to literary embellishments.[9]

3. Moving further down the spectrum of historicity, others consider the story of the empty tomb entirely legendary, but would uphold the veracity of the appearances of the risen Christ, which are taken to provide some basis for the historicity of the resurrection.[10]

4. At the radical end of the scale are those who deny the historicity of the empty tomb accounts and offer entirely naturalistic explanations of the appearances. On this view belief in the resurrection cannot be supported by any historical evidence and is either to be retained as a bare assertion of faith or rejected wholesale.[11]

Obviously there are degrees of certainty among individual scholars in holding their respective positions on this scale; some would consider 'reverent agnosticism' the only appropriate stance. But since evaluation differs to such a degree concerning the empty tomb and the resurrection appearances, these deserve slightly fuller investigation here.

The Empty Tomb

Debaters of the historical value of the empty tomb stories may be divided into two camps, and their chief arguments summarized as follows:

Arguments Against the Empty Tomb[12]

1. The empty tomb stories are a late tradition, unknown to Paul and first attested in Mark 16. Paul's 'he was buried' (1 Cor. 15:4) only confirms Jesus' death (the previous clause): it does not hint at a story of an empty tomb. In fact, Mark's version can be read as an attempt to explain the late circulation of this story. His story ends with the women saying nothing to anyone (16:8): that is meant to indicate why no one has heard of it before.

2. The massive discrepancies between the different gospel accounts is a sign that nothing other than legend is involved. If they have certain common elements (Joseph of Arimathea

at the burial; Mary Magdalene on Easter morning), these represent only the common roots of the multiple legends, not some primitive historical core.

3. It is quite possible to explain why the empty tomb stories came to be told. Those who held purely spiritual interpretations of resurrection (like the Corinthians addressed by Paul) alarmed those who had a more literal view of a bodily event, and the latter felt it necessary to narrate a discovery of an empty tomb to support their theological perspective.

4. In actual fact no one (believer or unbeliever) knew where Jesus' body was. The story of the burial by Joseph of Arimathea has grown in the telling (compare the different gospel versions). It probably has its origins not in fact but in pious denial of the brutal truth that Jesus' body was unceremoniously disposed of, flung into an unmarked common grave. This was, after all, the usual fate of criminals. Since no one could locate his body, there was no question of checking to see if the bones were there. And by the time the empty tomb stories were in circulation (after the Jewish War, 66–70 CE) Jerusalem had been sacked. The Christians could then claim what they liked without fear of contradiction.

Arguments For the Empty Tomb[13]

As we have seen, only the most conservative scholars argue for the reliability of all the gospel traditions. Most who defend the empty tomb will defend only its core element: that the tomb was found empty early in the morning by one or more women. On this side too there are four main types of argument.

1. Although the empty tomb story is first given literary expression in Mark 16, it should not be regarded as having been created by him. It is likely that Mark here, as elsewhere, was dependent on pre-Markan tradition, whose origins go back before 66 CE. Indeed, Matthew's gospel suggests that there had long been disputes between believing and non-believing Jews concerning the reasons for the empty tomb

(resurrection or theft?). Significantly, both sides agreed that the tomb was empty; they only differed about the explanation. Moreover, Paul's silence on the empty tomb can be accounted for easily enough. He is silent about many details in the life of Jesus which historically there is no good reason to doubt, and the formula he cites in 1 Corinthians 15 has too narrow a perspective to mention every historical detail. Some also hold that between the two events 'he was buried' and 'he was raised' Paul must have thought there to have been an emptying of the tomb (see above).

2. It is impossible to imagine Jews in first-century Palestine proclaiming the resurrection of Jesus without wondering what had happened to his body. Since they knew where his tomb was, they could check whether it was intact, and those who challenged their story could do the same in order to refute them. Since we have no evidence that any hostile party claimed to produce Jesus' bones, the tomb must have been empty. As we have seen, Matthew indicates that the dispute was only over the cause of its emptiness.

3. It is hard to credit that anyone would invent a story about such a remarkable event with women as the first or only witnesses. Since women were generally considered intellectually weak, their testimony was held to be unreliable. An invented story would have included a few men to give it greater credence.

4. There is no evidence for veneration of Jesus' tomb, as was common at the tombs of saints. The lack of veneration suggests that the tomb was empty.

Evaluation

It is important to remain conscious that behind these historical judgements may lie strong theological, or anti-theological, commitments. Defenders of the empty tomb may be motivated by theological conservatism (maintaining the authority of the text), or more generally by a desire not to place themselves in opposition to the united witness of the gospels. Theologically, the empty tomb is often seen as necessary to preserve the sense that God is the creator who can bring dead matter to life and whose purposes for the material world are that it should be transformed, not discarded. By affirming that the body was, as it were, re-used in the resurrection, one also preserves the sense that something happened to *Jesus* at the resurrection, not just to the disciples.[14] Those willing to discard the story of the empty tomb as history may also be influenced by theological factors: a distaste for 'objectifying' stories, for instance, or uneasiness with what seems a crude interventionist miracle. They may also judge it unwise to attempt to support faith with physical evidence or insecure historical claims. Alternatively, they may simply regard the whole notion of the resurrection as a fiction.

Of the arguments mounted by each side it is clear that some are stronger than others. That listed fourth under 'Arguments For' completely backfires: the tomb would not have to contain Jesus' bones for it to be venerated (cf. the Holy Sepulchre) and, indeed, the lack of veneration might support the case that the whereabouts of Jesus' burial was simply unknown. The prominence of women is also not as strong an argument as it seems, since it could arise simply from literary necessity: if Mark was working from a source which had only women as witnesses of the burial of Jesus, only they could be responsible for discovering the tomb empty. Of the 'Arguments Against', the case that the story first originates in Mark (1) is not unassailable, and recent literary studies of Mark 16 have provided alternative and more satisfactory explanations for its ending with the silence of the women. While it is possible to postulate a theological reason for the creation of the story (3), it is not necessary to conclude that it came into being *only* to satisfy a theological need. The crucial question appears to be whether the tomb of Jesus was known. If it was not, the argument that people (disciples or opponents) could check the state of the tomb ('Argument For' 2) is nullified. Thus the historicity of the empty tomb story is dependent to a large extent on the historicity of the burial story. It is strange that its defenders have paid so little attention to that matter.

The Resurrection Appearances

As we have seen, some who doubt the historicity of the empty tomb are content to fall back on the evidence of the appearances. These are, after all, a more direct form of witness. The emptiness of the tomb could be variously explained without reference to a resurrection (e.g. by the removal of the body or the mistaken identification of the tomb), while the appearances provide a direct encounter with the risen Christ. The appearance stories are also, as we have seen, of early provenance and multiple attestation (Paul and the gospels). However, they raise a number of historical questions which must be noted before we consider their evidential value.

Comparing the accounts of appearances of the risen Christ, it is clear that these display even more diversity than the stories of the empty tomb. Thus:

1. Within the gospel accounts there is no agreement about whether Jesus appeared to women (one or more) or not, about who was the first to 'see the Lord', or about where such appearances took place (Jerusalem or Galilee). There is evidence to suggest that appearance stories became more elaborate and the object of increasing reflection as time went on (compare the reticence of Mark with the tale of the journey to Emmaus in Luke 24:13–35 or the fishing story in John 21).

2. There are differences between the personnel in Paul's list (1 Cor. 15:5–7) and those in the gospels, and in the order of the appearances. The appearance to '500' is strangely absent elsewhere in the New Testament (unless it is refracted in Luke's account of Pentecost, Acts 2).

3. There are differences between the accounts as to the nature of the resurrection. It is not entirely clear what Paul's 'he was seen' implies (elsewhere he talks of God 'revealing' Jesus 'to/in me', Gal. 1:16). But it seems to imply something rather less physical than the risen Jesus in Luke, who has a tangible body and eats fish. The insistence of Luke's Jesus that 'a spirit does not have flesh and bones as you see that I have' (Luke 24:40) is not easy to square with Paul's conviction that 'flesh and blood cannot inherit the kingdom of God' (1 Cor. 15:50).

Penetrating through these stories to an original core is a difficult business. In fact 1 Corinthians 15 indicates that multiple stories circulated from a very early date. It is generally held that Peter's was the earliest experience and that the initial experiences were probably in Galilee rather than Jerusalem (Mark 16:7). But certainty is impossible to attain here and, in any case, not crucial for the question of the value of these experiences as evidence for the resurrection.

Their evidential value, however, depends on one's assessment of what these experiences imply. From at least the time of Celsus (second century CE), it has been suggested that these 'appearances' were simply 'apparitions', the product of individual or mass psychological delusion.[15] That theory has become more plausible in the light of Jungian psychology and has received significant support in recent years from some New Testament scholars.[16] By analogy with the 'visions' sometimes experienced during mourning or in the course of conversion, it has thus been suggested that the earliest 'visions' of Jesus were the product of psychological trauma. There are also parallels for such visions being reduplicated on a mass scale in certain conditions. In their apocalyptic frame of mind, and in their eager expectation of the kingdom of God, the early believers were ready to interpret such 'apparitions' as signs of the resurrection of Jesus.

Those wishing to defend the reality of the resurrection find such an explanation inadequate and unconvincing. In defending these 'visions' as genuinely 'trans-subjective' or at least veridical (some would wish to claim physical 'sight'; others merely inner revelation of truth), defenders of the resurrection typically point to the following factors:

1. Whatever the case with individuals, it is harder to explain mass hallucination; appearances to groups or even crowds are well attested in the New Testament sources.

2. The moral and personal transformation of the disciples, from cowardly doubters to confident heroes of the faith, points to an 'objective' experience, not one generated by inner psychological forces.

3. There are many surprising features of these appearances which do not match historical parallels or psychological theories. It is strange, for instance, that the early believers should interpret

their visions as of a *resurrected* Jesus, although they could have considered him simply translated to heaven. The notion of an individual resurrection before the general resurrection was unparalleled in Judaism, so far as we know. Whatever Jesus may have said to them before, it appears that this was not how or when they expected to see him again; nor of course did Paul, who had hitherto resisted Christian claims. Many reform movements in Judaism at this time had leaders who met a violent end, but none other made such extraordinary claims about their leader afterwards. Such peculiar phenomena point, it is argued, to a peculiar event as their basis.

How we adjudicate between these different explanations of the 'appearances' of the risen Christ will depend to a large degree on the ideological framework within which we operate. Can one judge another's experiences as visions or hallucinations except on the basis of one's own faith-experiences (or lack of them)? For the sceptic, naturalistic psychological explanations will appear perfectly adequate; for the believer, they will not. The historical arguments outlined above are in fact of varying strength. There almost certainly *have been* historical examples of mass hallucination, and the transformation of the disciples might be attributable to deep conversion experiences which *could* have been accompanied by spurious 'visions'. Thus much will depend on how extraordinary one judges the disciples' resurrection belief and how extraordinary must have been the event which brought it about. Given widespread beliefs in the ancient world about *redivivus* figures (e.g. Nero in the East, John the Baptist in Palestine, Mark 6:14–15) there is perhaps little in this area of belief which can be judged wholly extraordinary. Those who appeal to the resurrection appearances as the chief historical evidence thus depend on the authenticity of the experiences of first-century men and women whose world-view was very different to our own. Judgement of this matter will inevitably rely to a great extent on a prior faith commitment.

Theological Assessment of the New Testament Accounts of the Resurrection

Finally, we may draw attention to some notable trends in the way scholars assess the *theological adequacy* of the New Testament in its witness to the resurrection. Two features in particular stand out.

The Principle that Earliest is Best

By a combination of historical, literary and theological (especially Protestant) preferences, New Testament scholars as a rule prioritize the earliest New Testament accounts of the resurrection. Thus many rank Paul's view of the resurrection higher than that of the gospels: it is historically earlier and more reliable, it is 'clean' of the complications and uncertainties of the story of the empty tomb, its ambiguous concept of the resurrection body avoids the crude physicality of Luke, and it 'represents constructive thought on the Resurrection without the influence of the popular stories'.[17] Similarly, among the gospels, the earlier Mark is generally given theological priority over the later gospel writers who amplified his resurrection story. On the nearly universal view that Mark's gospel originally ended at 16:8, his account of the resurrection is praised for its literary restraint, its enigmatic allusiveness and its understatement. By contrast, the other gospels, with their concern to describe the appearances of Jesus and to provide proofs of the resurrection, can be castigated for their leaden literalism or theological naivety. Resurrection, for Mark, is to be received by faith not sight; that, to many, constitutes a massive theological virtue.[18]

This preference for the earliest can be turned against all the sources, which can together be accused, for instance, of reducing the real importance of the first women witnesses.[19] And it is not, in fact, universally applied: in the comparison between Paul and the gospels, 1 Corinthians 15 is regarded by some with suspicion for its outmoded eschatology. In the recent re-evaluation of biblical narrative, the gospel stories can even be preferred to Paul, precisely because of their narrative format.[20] Moreover, in some recent discussion of the gospel accounts, there is a marked reluctance to play one story off against another, and a concern to incorporate the positive theological contribution of each canonical witness.[21] This may indicate that the 'earliest is best' principle, which implicitly evaluates later sources as polluted or debased, is losing its force under the impact of new literary and theological readings of the New Testament.[22]

The Prizing of the 'Mysterious'

This second theological principle is one factor in the high evaluation of Mark, whose reticence and unwillingness to tie loose ends has gained him a reputation for literary and theological sophistication. More generally, it is possible to make a virtue of the fact that the New Testament witness to the resurrection is so fragmentary and inconclusive, even downright inconsistent. Theologically this can be interpreted as pointing away from the quest for historical proof, as the texts refuse to satisfy our desire to secure our salvation by historical knowledge ('works'). More particularly, one may interpret the fact that none of the gospels describe the actual moment of resurrection as marking this 'event' in a special way as of ultimate and unique significance.[23] The elusiveness of the narratives at this point signals the mystery of faith, the enigma of divine action which human reason cannot comprehend.

It is at this point that the historical and the theological approaches to the resurrection ultimately part company. The theologian and believer may reject the concern to test the resurrection claim by the weighing of historical evidence as a form of 'myopic positivism' (F. Watson), a product of a rationalist agenda whose empiricist methods are bound to misconstrue the essence of the Christian claim. The historian, on the other hand, may demand that this purported event be investigated on the same terms and judged by the same criteria as any other in history, and may consider that to mystify this subject by claims of 'uniqueness' or 'eschatological significance' is merely to pull the wool over our eyes. Thus each side considers the other ultimately unable to 'see'. Although historical and theological enterprises have effected a remarkably fruitful marriage in biblical scholarship, sensitive observers have noted the underlying tensions, at least since the Enlightenment. And nowhere are such tensions more embarrassingly revealed than in discussion of the resurrection of Jesus.[24]

Notes

1. *Reimarus: Fragments*, C. H. Talbert, ed. (London: SCM Press, 1971), pp. 153–200.

2. G. Lüdemann, *The Resurrection of Jesus*, trans. J. Bowden (London: SCM Press, 1994), represents the rigorously historical approach to the subject, in his case questioning the value of the evidence. The opposite pole is represented by W. Marxsen, *The Resurrection of Jesus of Nazareth*, trans. M. Kohl (London: SCM Press, 1970).
3. A comprehensive survey is given by P. Perkins, *Resurrection: New Testament Witness and Contemporary Reflection* (London: Geoffrey Chapman, 1984).
4. For conflicting opinions on this matter see for example R. H. Gundry, *SOMA in Biblical Theology, with emphasis on Pauline Anthropology* (Cambridge: Cambridge University Press, 1976); P. W. Gooch, *Partial Knowledge: Philosophical Studies in Paul* (Notre Dame: University of Notre Dame Press, 1987), pp. 52–84.
5. See C. F. Evans, *Resurrection in the New Testament* (London: SCM Press, 1970), pp. 1–40; G. W. E. Nickelsburg, *Resurrection, Immortality and Eternal Life in Intertestamental Judaism* (Oxford: Oxford University Press, 1972); A. E. Harvey, "'They discussed among themselves what this 'rising from the dead' could mean" (Mark 9:10)', in *Resurrection. Essays in Honour of Leslie Houlden*, eds. S. Barton and G. Stanton (London: SPCK, 1994), pp. 69–78.
6. R. E. Brown usefully tabulates the evidence in *The Virginal Conception and Bodily Resurrection of Jesus* (London: Geoffrey Chapman, 1974), pp. 100, 118.
7. The theological shaping of the resurrection narratives is explored by N. Perrin, *The Resurrection Narratives* (London: SCM Press, 1977) and H. Hendrickx, *The Resurrection Narratives of the Synoptic Gospels* (London: Geoffrey Chapman, revised edition 1984).
8. For example M. J. Harris, *Raised Immortal: Resurrection and Immortality in the New Testament* (London: Marshall, Morgan & Scott, 1983); J. Wenham, *Easter Enigma* (Exeter: Paternoster Press, 1984).
9. See, for example, R. E. Brown, *The Virginal Conception and Bodily Resurrection of Jesus*.
10. See, for example, B. Lindars, 'The Resurrection and the Empty Tomb', in *The Resurrection of Jesus Christ*, ed. P. Avis (London: Darton, Longman & Todd, 1983), pp. 116–35.
11. Lüdemann, *The Resurrection of Jesus*, rejects all the historical arguments for the resurrection but believes that 'Jesus was not given over to annihilation through death' (p. 183). M. D. Goulder, in his essay in this collection, 'The Baseless Fabric of a Vision', finds the resurrection historically without foundation and altogether a false belief.
12. See, for example, Lindars, 'Resurrection'; Goulder, 'Baseless Fabric'; Lüdemann, *The Resurrection of Jesus*, pp. 39–47, 109–21.
13. Besides Harris, *Raised Immortal*, pp. 37–44 and Brown, *The Virginal Conception and Bodily Resurrection of Jesus*, pp. 113–25, see J. D. G.

Dunn, *The Evidence for Jesus* (London: SCM Press, 1985), pp. 63–9.

14. See F. Watson, '"He is not here": Towards a Theology of the Empty Tomb', in *Resurrection*, eds. Barton and Stanton, pp. 95–107; he at least advances these as reasons to retain the *story* of the empty tomb.

15. G. N. Stanton, 'Early Objections to the Resurrection of Jesus', in *Resurrection*, eds. Barton and Stanton, pp. 79–94.

16. Notably Goulder, 'Baseless Fabric' and Lüdemann, *The Resurrection of Jesus*, pp. 49–84.

17. Lindars, 'The Resurrection and the Empty Tomb', p. 133.

18. See, for example, J. L. Houlden, *Backward into Light* (London: SCM Press, 1987); J. Fenton, 'The Four Gospels: Four Perspectives on the Resurrection', in *The Resurrection of Jesus Christ*, ed. Avis, pp. 39–49.

19. See J. Lieu, 'The Women's Resurrection Testimony', in *Resurrection*, eds. Barton and Stanton, pp. 34–44; E. Schüssler Fiorenza, *In Memory of Her: A Feminist Theological Reconstruction of Christian Origins* (London: SCM Press, 1983), pp. 138–40.

20. J. L. Houlden, 'The Resurrection: History, Story and Belief', in *The Resurrection of Jesus Christ*, ed. Avis, pp. 50–67.

21. See, for example, the essays by Morgan, Barton and Watson in *Resurrection*, eds. Barton and Stanton.

22. C. Rowland draws on all the New Testament sources in his political and liberationist 'Interpreting the Resurrection', in *The Resurrection of Jesus Christ*, ed. Avis, pp. 68–84.

23. Watson, '"He is not here"'.

24. For a fine survey of this problem see Evans, *Resurrection in the New Testament*, pp. 170–83.

Chapter 2

THE RESURRECTION IN CONTEMPORARY SYSTEMATIC THEOLOGY

Gareth Jones

Introduction

The resurrection of Jesus Christ is integral to Christianity's self-definition, whatever the church, whatever the context. It is therefore central to Christian theological reflection, whatever the church, whatever the context. There are three reasons for this. First, the resurrection is an eschatological miracle, revealing God's presence in the world; as such, it moves faith beyond the limits of Jesus' death on the cross. Second, the resurrection is a historical event, something foundational for the Church as a community, and therefore something central to Christianity's worship of God. Third, Christ's resurrection is the first-fruits of the last resurrection, and hence the proleptic resurrection of all peoples.

Simultaneously, however, no Christological doctrine suffers from as much confusion as the resurrection. This is both a reflection of modern rational scepticism's refusal to accept the resurrection's miraculous status, and the mystery that surrounds its origins in the New Testament. (The issues here − are the empty tomb and resurrection appearances traditions separate, and do they imply different understandings of Jesus' resurrection? − have coloured much recent discussion, as reflected in this volume.) And it is a confusion that centres upon one crucial question: what happened to Jesus' body? Any essay on the resurrection which fails to consider this question, fails the resurrection.

The present essay answers this question quite straightforwardly: Christian theology speaks of a bodily resurrection, as it speaks of a bodily ascension and as it asserts God's real presence in time, in a very ordinary sense of the word 'time'.[1] To substantiate this answer, however, I want to consider two important discussions of the resurrection in modern theology. First, Rudolf Bultmann highlights the importance of speaking historically of the resurrection, and therefore of its personal reality for Jesus. Second, Karl Rahner establishes a broadly Bultmannian interpretation of history and eschatology in the wider relationship between nature and grace. In dialogue with these two theologians, I want to establish the question of Jesus' bodily resurrection in terms of some basic philosophical and theological principles.

In the second half of this essay this will lead to some considerations of the language used to speak of Jesus' bodily resurrection, and then to the doctrinal implications of an insistence upon that bodily resurrection for other areas of Christology. In this way, finally, I hope to demonstrate the continuing relevance of certain very modern questions to the way in which contemporary theologians discuss the resurrection.

Rudolf Bultmann

It is a common misconception of Bultmann's theology that it maintains solely the tiniest place for the historical (*historische*) Jesus; that, too keen to embrace the kerygmatic, historic (*geschichtliche*) Christ, Bultmann rushes headlong into the arms of a reductive, symbolic Christology. Nothing could be farther from the truth: 'Revelation consists in nothing other than the fact of Jesus Christ.'[2] Indeed, Bultmann's affirmation of the historical Jesus, far from being concerned solely with the fact of Jesus' existence, is an affirmation of fact itself as the locus of God's revelation in the world. For Bultmann it is axiomatic that when God comes to the world, God comes as a historical person, in and of time (again, in an ordinary, empirical sense of the word); that is what makes Jesus' history simultaneously an *eschatological* event. And because it allows of no demonstration, so its origins can reside solely in the mysterious fate of one individual:

> However little we know of the life of Jesus, if we keep in mind that he was finally crucified as a messianic agitator, we shall be able in the light of the eschatological message to understand the fragmentary accounts of the end of his activity.[3]

In affirming the primacy of history as the locus of God's immanent revelation, therefore, Bultmann also affirms the full reality of Jesus' existence: not solely the wood and nails of the cross, so to speak, but the (ontological) completeness of Jesus' time on earth, from annunciation through to ascension. Bultmann does not need to make this explicit at every turn in his argument, because it is an a priori principle of the way he understands God's relationship to the world: since that relationship has solely one Revealer and solely one Mediator, so that revelation and mediation must themselves be complete events, or better, one complete event. For Bultmann completeness is an eschatological quality, because ontology is always an eschatological enquiry (something with which Barth agreed, though he never pursued philosophical reflection as thoroughly as Bultmann).

This makes sense of Bultmann's strong emphasis upon the need for existentialist interpretation, or demythologizing: the Christ event, in all its completeness, is about humanity's *fullness*. Bultmann himself used the terminology of 'authenticity', following the early Heidegger; but one can recognize more generally the *therapeutic* qualities of Bultmann's theology, of the *healing* of the world in its entirety. This is a theme often overlooked in Bultmann's work, but one which has had a strong influence upon subsequent European theology.[4]

The quotation above from Bultmann's *Jesus* book to 'the end of his activity' points the way here to a deeper understanding of Bultmann's interpretation of the eschatological Christ event. As it is mistaken to see Bultmann's Christology as finally reductive and symbolic, so it is mistaken to see the cross as its *sine qua non*; for whenever Bultmann discusses Jesus' status as the Revealer, he always does so by naming him *the risen Lord*. Bultmann's argument at this point is clearly stated in his commentary on John 11:25 ('I am the resurrection and the life'):

Jesus speaks as the Revealer. He is the Resurrection and the Life, since for those who believe in him; i.e., those who acknowledge him as the Revealer of God, life and death as men know and call them are no longer realities. If the Revealer is described as the life and the resurrection . . . it . . . brings to expression that the life is an eschatological phenomenon; i.e., *that it is accessible only in the resurrection.*[5]

Jesus' final activity, therefore, his *eschatological* activity, is epitomized in his resurrection: there, argues Bultmann, rather than on Golgotha, one recognizes the full meaning of what it is to be human in the sight of God. But if Jesus' entire life finds its meaning in his resurrection, then this must have one immediate implication for how Bultmann understands the resurrection itself: it is, axiomatically, a bodily resurrection.

Why a *bodily* resurrection? Because humanity cannot be divorced from its bodies; because historical existence, no matter how existentially interpreted it becomes, remains something which is bodily realized, as Bultmann well knew (cf. here his analysis of Paul's anthropology in his *Theology of the New Testament* I, London: SCM Press, 1955). To separate existence from the body would be to bastardize the scholastic distinction between essence and existence, something which Bultmann's training in historical phenomenology, devolving from Heidegger's influence in the 1920s, would not permit. To speak of Jesus Christ as the risen Lord was for Bultmann the only meaningful way of addressing Jesus' eschatological significance; but that same eschatological significance could only be realized via an encounter between real persons. It is because Bultmann thinks Jesus Christ is *still* a real person, indeed *the* real person, that he must affirm the bodily resurrection of the Revealer; anything else negates Christ's eternal being:

> For Bultmann, the anthropological relevance of theological statements is the criterion of their truth, because for him revelation is constantly an eschatological happening which as such becomes event in an historical 'that'. It amounts to the 'paradoxical identity', that an historical 'that' becomes historically significant as eschatological event.[6]

This shift to anthropology, as Jungel demonstrates and as Bultmann established in his interpretation of Paul, is where one recognizes the wider significance of Bultmann's work. The affirmation of the bodily resurrection is a consequence of faith, certainly; but it is an affirmation of faith which is itself established in a particular understanding of the relationship between nature and grace. For Bultmann, the encounter with the risen Lord has transformative power (cf. 2 Cor. 5:17); eschatologically, it creates new life out of humanity's existence. In the process, however, human nature becomes itself the medium by which God and the world are gracefully related. This occurs really in Jesus Christ, who as Revealer brings together the two natures of divinity and humanity as the Incarnate One; but in encountering Jesus Christ as the *Risen One*, people today participate existentially in that same mediating reality. That this occurs is a miracle, the mystery of faith; but that it can be spoken of theologically depends upon the bodily resurrection of the Revealer. Without that bodily resurrection, as proleptically the bodily resurrection of all peoples, nature and grace remain distinct, torn asunder in Jesus' inhabited tomb.

Many features of this argument remain hidden in Bultmann's theology. Perhaps he did not see the full implications of his position, preferring to emphasize the pastoral implications of understanding faith as encounter, rather than exploring the metaphysical consequences of establishing questions of identity and relationship in what one might call the 'deep immanence' of grace's transformative power. Be that as it may, the important point for twentieth-century theology is that Bultmann, like Barth and Bonhoeffer, maintains the doctrine of the resurrection within the realm of historical reality, so that for the sake of intellectual consistency (not to mention personal and ecclesial faith) he must locate discussion of bodily nature and graceful resurrection on the same level of discourse. Anything else would mean that the status of Christ's human being were in some way qualitatively different from that of any other person – with catastrophic results for Christianity.

It is the doctrine of Christ's two natures and so his full humanity, therefore, which validates the understanding of being and time, of the bodily resurrection *in time*, which I am developing. Just as we all live in time, with a clear (albeit analogical) sense of past, present and future, so Jesus' own life, from annunciation to ascension, must be thought of in the same way. Failure so to do distinguishes Jesus from every other human being, thereby robbing him of full humanity. For the sake of Christian faith, Jesus *must* be fully human, and therefore theology must speak of the bodily resurrection by analogy with time.

These same emphases are not solely to be found in the hidden depths of Protestant dialectical theology, however; they surface in modern Roman Catholic thought, where they also demonstrate certain important additional and characteristic features. To illustrate these, I will now consider the work of Karl Rahner.

Karl Rahner

Rahner's explicit links with Bultmann are unsurprisingly tenuous, and limited to a few comments in the *Theological Investigations*. When people want to write about any intellectual relationship between the two, therefore, they do so by reference to a shared philosophical background; in particular, a generally pervasive Kantianism, a legacy of simply being German theologians, and a shared debt to Heidegger's historical phenomenology. Less often noticed, however, are the strong doctrinal links Bultmann and Rahner share, which focus upon questions of Christology, but then move beyond those limits.

What does this mean? It means that Rahner, like Bultmann, has a strong emphasis upon an event Christology, in which a phenomenological understanding of Christ's eschatological meaning is related in terms of an encounter between historical existence (time) and God's Word of Revelation (eternity); here the influence of Heidegger is most profound, as evidenced by Rahner's second book, *Hearers of the Word*.[7] Related to such a Christology, both theologians ask ontological questions about the nature of human existence; but whereas these remain somewhat obscure in Bultmann's work, for Rahner they become a distinct (though not separate) subject of inquiry, namely transcendental anthropology. Bultmann's anthropology, though present in his thought prior to explicit Christological reflection, becomes extant in his arguments only consequent to the Word of Revelation. Rahner's anthropology, by contrast, is altogether prior to Christology: people are hearers of the Word, certainly, but 'being a hearer' is something that theologians must think and talk about if they are to understand the actions of a God who becomes human.

The discussion here, therefore, is about nature and grace, and therefore about the way in which one understands human existence in its relationship with the presence of God. For Rahner, one can speak of human being both analogically and epistemologically, by drawing upon Aquinas' theories of existence and Kant's conditions of the possibility of knowledge. In this way one arrives at a composite understanding of humanity's *potential* to look beyond the limits of its world. Such a 'looking beyond this world' is what Rahner means by being religious, which in turn is the subject of Rahner's transcendental anthropology, a complex web of concepts and structures, within which the individual recognizes, however dimly, the existence of God.

For Bultmann, by contrast, theologians speak of God's Word of Revelation, grace, because that is how God comes to the world. Certainly, they have an implicit understanding of what it is to be human so that one might 'hear the Word' (and Bultmann probably would not disagree with much of Rahner's anthropology); but Bultmann is far more concerned with what humanity looks like *after* encountering grace than it does *before*. Bultmann's concern is motivated by his overwhelming (and Lutheran) desire to emphasize always the absolute glory of God's action to save the world, which is why anthropological questions are secondary to his concentration upon *Krisis* or judgement.

In short, for both Bultmann and Rahner historical existence is the normative environment or locus in which humanity and divinity encounter one another. Though they have different strategies for approaching the task of speaking of such encounters, finally they agree that nature and grace relate to each other in such a way that grace always determines nature. The difference between them is epistemological, therefore, and not ontological; a point secured by the way in which Rahner implicitly confirms Bultmann's affirmation of the bodily resurrection. Thus, as talk about the resurrection is for Bultmann ultimately talk about revelation, which must be talk about God's complete action within humanity, so for Rahner talk about the resurrection occurs within a context of talk about the relationship between time and eternity, which is revealed through the cyclical journey of the Son from annunciation to ascension.

This idea needs some development. As a theologian who affirms the full humanity of Jesus Christ as the express meaning of the incarnation, Rahner recognizes the impossibility of rejecting the bodily resurrection. The simile here is very much that of a circular journey, where movement from A to C and back to A, eternally, must always move through B, eternally; there is no logical way around this conclusion. So it is for Rahner with the story of God's action in the world as the Son, the second person of the trinity: since that story begins with and always returns to a bodily annunciation, so any talk today of the risen and ascended Lord must by implication be talk of a *bodily* risen and ascended Lord. For Rahner this cannot be a question of material evidence or causal intelligibility; it is a question of God's *will* to be revealed as God *incarnate*. There is, quite simply, no way in which Rahner's theology can be incarnational, and then abandon the body at one intermediate stage in the story of Christ's relationship with the world, which is an ongoing, present reality awaiting its final consummation. Rahner makes this point in an essay on 'The Hermeneutics of Eschatological Assertions', when he writes: 'The Christian understanding of the faith and its expression must contain an eschatology which really bears on the *future*, that which is still to come, in a very ordinary, empirical sense of the word time.'[8] The point here is that since grace's eschatological relationship with nature always involves time, understood causally, so the fulfilment of that relationship must similarly involve a causal moment in time. This much is axiomatic, for faith and theology, Christ will come again. And because Christ's *parousia* is itself continuous with Christ's annunciation – both being, of course, equally revealing of God's eternal will – so too Rahner can assert the *parousia* will be a bodily *parousia*.

Seen from this perspective, Bultmann and Rahner confirm a central theme of much modern theology, certainly in the twentieth century: reason, functioning within time and therefore as part of humanity's attempt to understand its historical existence, elaborates theology's axiomatic foundations, these being its ability to speak of the real and saving presence of God in Jesus of Nazareth, and subsequently in the life of the Church. If one fails to understand this point, as many commentators have, then one fails to understand the motor which drives along the reflection of theologians like Barth and Bonhoeffer, Bultmann and Rahner. The modern predicament, if one can speak of such a thing, is for Bultmann and Rahner not something which questions theology's axioms; it is, rather, something which questions *the way in which one speaks of those axioms*. The pertinent issue, consequently, is the status one gives to theological language. As Rahner correctly argues, the binding epistemological challenge to modern theology is not whether it can demonstrate its foundations, because as axioms they allow for no demonstration. It is, rather, whether it can justify the language it uses to talk about them.

The highwater mark of this form of modern theology was in the 1960s, before Bultmann's eclipse by political theologies in European and American Protestantism, and during Rahner's epochal work at the Second Vatican Council. Since then, however, challenges to their position have emerged with regularity, culminating in that of postliberalism, in which the cultural-linguistic character of reality itself is used to attack many of modern theology's presuppositions. The result, sometimes identified as a shift from modern to postmodern theologies, is an environment in which the epistemological challenge confronting theology has taken on almost baroque proportions. But to what extent is this unavoidable?

This distinction between modern and postmodern theologies can be quite straightforward. Modern theologies, as with Bultmann and Rahner, want to speak of God's real presence in the world, and so use the analogy of time to make sense of what they confess to be real events (e.g. the bodily resurrection). They do this because they have a clear sense of the normative and absolute character of faith, so that grace always determines nature. Postmodern theologies, by contrast, have difficulties with such dogmatic statements, arguing instead that it is no longer possible to identify and thereby advance metanarratives or general theories which make such absolute claims; rather, such issues become linguistic ones, as indeed reality becomes a linguistic phenomenon. In what follows, I want to argue that postmodern theologies risk losing something vital to the Christian faith, and so are to be resisted as *theologies* (whatever their undoubted contributions to socio-cultural understanding).

The Status of Theological Language

Returning to Rahner's comment on the hermeneutics of eschatological assertions, one can take something else from his words:

> The Christian understanding of the faith *and its expression* must contain an eschatology which really bears on the future, that which is still to come, in a very ordinary, empirical sense of the word time.[9]

The point here is Rahner's express correlation between reality and language; i.e. between the event, God's breaking into the world (here as *parousia*) as a causal occurrence, and the theological language used to speak of that event. The dominant analogy at work in Rahner's argument is time, however, not space or matter, a distinction with significant implications for the way one speaks of the *bodily* resurrection.

As has already been argued, it is axiomatic for Bultmann, Rahner, and generations of modern theologians that God's entry into the world is an entry into history; i.e. the realm of human existence, understood temporally. Heidegger gave (in *Being and Time*) the clearest interpretation yet of the specific conditions of possibility of temporal being, and theologians today are still using his ideas to work forward from this position. That historical existence includes bodily extension is always clear, however; there is no sense in any of these writers that one can live historically without living bodily: the body is the vehicle for encounter and relationship, something about which the Heidegger of the 1920s is entirely clear (if not after the war).[10]

Granted this conviction, the argument about the bodily resurrection runs something like this: God enters the world as a certain person, within a specific 'slice of time', understood empirically; God raises up that slice of time into eternity, so that the Son always wills to be Jesus of Nazareth; *ergo, the body within time* comes too. The question which then occurs, correctly understood, is not: 'Where is Jesus' body?', but rather: 'When is Jesus?' (Bultmann would add, 'for me'). Or better: the *answer* which then *should* occur is to a temporal rather than a spatial question: 'now' rather than 'heaven'.

Why is this so? Because the point of the Christ event, from annunciation to ascension and therefore including resurrection, is *identity*; God's identity with the world and everything in it. And the task of a theology, in any given context, is to attempt to make that identifying event accessible. That attempt, so Christians believe and argue, occurs in the power of the Holy Spirit, in and for the Church; but the eschatological given which empowers it is a consequence of God's action in time. This is a general principle, and any theology which does not want to speak of such a general principle is not a *Christian* theology.

It is important to remember here Rahner's comment about correlation, namely that reality and expression need to correspond when one is speaking of eschatological events, something which is most important when one is speaking explicitly of the bodily resurrection of Jesus Christ. The key issue is accessibility, central both to theological language and the reality of God's action in Jesus Christ. Through an event occurring and being understood materially, as an incidence of spatial extension, accessibility is always localized: the only people who can encounter it are those in its immediate, perceptible vicinity. Thus, the only people who experienced the raising of Lazarus in John II as a material event, for example, were those able to witness it, in a crude sense of the word 'witness': they saw, heard, experienced it as a causal sequence of incidents.

With a temporal event, by contrast, anyone or anything simultaneously in existence is affected, because time's essential character is its universality; if one is together with someone else in time, albeit many hundreds of miles apart, then there is an identity *in time.* So it is with Jesus' resurrection; though no person other than Jesus was present at his resurrection, all share (so Christians believe) in its significance because all share *in time.* Again, as a Christian theologian one must emphasize that this was the point of the incarnation: that God in entering time enters *all* time, so that *all* time in consequence enters God. Resurrection and ascension are therefore simultaneously singular and universal events: they are Jesus', but they are ours, too. Asserting Jesus' bodily resurrection is simply a statement of the obvious; i.e. that time for people – Jesus, Mary, you and I – is embodied. This is, consequently, an entirely uncomplicated argument about certain very common factors in people's everyday lives.

The liberating effects of this way of understanding God's action in Jesus Christ, including the bodily resurrection, become ever more apparent when one presses the two themes of identity and accessibility. Granted that theological language here (as always) is functioning analogically, so that talk about God's action is interpreted in parallel with the world's temporal existence, yet that language's effect is to open God's action to access from a very large range of different perspectives. Hence, people anywhere in the world, at any time, can speak of Jesus' resurrection as their resurrection, because God has made their time *God's* time, because *all* time is now present as Christ in eternity. And this analogy works in a way that the spatial one does not; for where space is always localized, time is always universal *and* local simultaneously. In this way, any theology in any situation can avoid the tactical mistake of making a false identity between the material circumstances of Jesus' world and their own (as sometimes in Latin American liberation theology), a mistake which causes unnecessary epistemological difficulties. This weakness can be recognized as early as Leonardo Boff's *Jesus Christ Liberator*, though the difficulties persist in Jon Sobrino's *Jesus the Liberator*.[11] God's kingdom is about time and eternity, not place; but since Jesus, God's time is always *personal* time.

Correctly understood, such an emphasis upon time rather than space becomes the foundation of contemporary theological pluralism, simply because understanding God's action as temporal action means that anyone in time can have a valid perspective (and an invalid one) upon that action. This moves theology towards what is variously called postliberalism/structuralism/modernism, and the apparent impossibility in the contemporary world of establishing a theology in any general theory or metanarrative, because of language's inherent contingency.[12] This is a significant development, as far as it goes; but for the Christian theologian, that is not very far at all.

There are two points to consider here. The first is Rahner's: for Christian theology it is axiomatic that God's action has a real past, a real present and a real future. That is a general theory or metanarrative; it is called eschatological realism.[13] The second is Schleiermacher's: people need general theories, and one of the tasks of the Christian theologian is to demonstrate how and why they should be identified with faith in God's action in the world. Like St Paul on the Areopagus, therefore, one may name God's mystery and argue that there are profound epistemological difficulties with finding *any* language to speak of it rhetorically; but at some point one must identify mystery with Christ. People may not like that, and may choose not to listen; but it is not an optional extra. Truth for Christian theology cannot be relegated to the level of a doxological codpiece, covering for the sake of propriety the hidden dimensions of 'the postmodern world'.

The Character of Doctrine

Such an argument takes us immediately into the world of doctrine, its nature, and most importantly its contemporary character. Questions of theological language, therefore, provoke discussion of the viability of certain grammars and vocabularies in the modern and postmodern worlds; but questions of truth are doctrinal, and consequently matters of consensus and confession. This is an important juncture, at which Christian theories of truth need to be carefully distinguished from philosophical ones.

The bodily resurrection of Jesus Christ is a useful example at this point. From the perspective of a correspondence theory of truth, the proposition that 'Jesus' body was raised from the tomb' should be indicative of a definite state of affairs, i.e., that Jesus came back to life and left behind him an empty tomb. And such a correspondence is indeed axiomatic for the Christian faith; but Christian theology cannot stop here. For theology, the key ingredient to the bodily resurrection is its transformative (because eschatological) character, that is, Jesus after the resurrection is *not the same* as he was before the crucifixion. In the Gospels this is most clearly signalled in the resurrection appearances by Jesus' heightened/transformed consciousness of his natures and purpose. For theology, the important theme here is that Jesus Christ's risen state is conditional: he is risen, in order to be subsequently ascended. This much cannot be demonstrated, because it takes Jesus Christ out of time, and into eternity. There can be no possible correspondence, therefore, solely the confession that Jesus Christ is risen to be ascended, and subsequently some consensus in the early Church that thus is revealed God's will for humanity and the world. This, of course, is what does in fact ensue.

This sequence of events demonstrates something both very interesting and very important for Christianity and Christian theology. So long as such a faith and theology are genuinely incarnational, all subsequent questions of doctrine and language, though complex, are inherently straightforward. Thus, for example, the bodily resurrection of Jesus, though theoretically demonstrable and therefore open to scientific critique and demolition on the grounds of correspondence, becomes an entirely straightforward matter when seen within a greater economy of annunciation through to ascension. What one is then speaking of is God's eschatological will, that is, the revelation in time, with power, of God's will to be one with the world. And of course, anything eschatological by definition cannot be reduced to questions of language and method, because it has a priori status as Christianity's substantive and qualifying faith. Importantly, therefore, the bodily resurrection as a doctrinal question takes theology on to a level where language questions, though formally complex, are ultimately secondary. What, then, is the relationship between language and doctrine, and what is doctrine's character? After Lindbeck, one recognizes doctrine's cultural–linguistic form; so much postliberalism teaches everyone. But no Christian theology can remain satisfied with the status of a cultural–linguistic form, when what it really wants to speak of is an eschatological reality; this much Barth teaches everyone! Thus, seemingly, theology is cast into a paradoxical identity at precisely the point where it appears to need clarity – as Jungel correctly observes with respect to Bultmann's theology.

There would seem to be two possible responses to this situation. On the one hand, with Rahner and Bultmann, one can assert that, yes, there is a paradoxical identity between language and doctrine, and the power behind that paradox is a greater paradox. Such a response preserves doctrine's distinctive character, but at the expense of theology's reputation in an increasingly secular world. On the other hand, with certain postmodern theologians, one can assert that it is impossible to speak of a paradoxical identity between time and eternity, because time itself is its own linguistic paradox, permitting no reference, even analogically, to an eschatological reality. In such a 'theology', as for example, Mark C. Taylor's, the key notion is altarity; and, as with writers like Gillian Rose and John Milbank, the motive force behind altarity is not God so much as formal diremption.[14] On this reading, 'God' becomes a signifier, buried within the differential flux, wherein God's traces are indiscernibly vague. This is undoubtedly a consistent representation of certain difficulties in late twentieth-century understandings of language and society; but it is not immediately apparent that it helps Christian theology speak of God's real presence in the world.

The solution for contemporary theology is obviously to go beyond the two horns of this dilemma; but that is easier said than done. With the first alternative, God's eschatological reality pulls theology towards making a simple claim: no matter how complex and sophisticated theology's cultural–linguistic context, confessed truth is intelligible in, so to speak, words of one syllable. With the second alternative, by contrast, theology as talk about *God* is pulled inexorably down into talk *per se*, that is, language becomes the dominant force in all constructive disciplines. These two poles themselves signify ironically the altarity and diremption at the heart of theology's contemporary self-characterization: *the*ology, or the*ology*?

It is easy to remain on the level of such ironic discourse, and there is a certain integrity in doing so, but issues like the bodily resurrection of Jesus cast theology back upon more profound issues. The bodily resurrection is not a linguistic question. On the contrary, it is simple and straightforward: did Jesus rise from the dead *as* Jesus? If the answer is 'yes', then theology has to find a way of addressing this fact to the world in which it exists, something to which the Christological doctrines bear witness. If the answer is 'no', however, no sleight of hand will alter the fact that theology is then reduced to the level of literary analysis and narration. As theologians like Bultmann and Rahner recognized earlier in the century, if theology is not 'about' God, then it is solely 'about' humanity; but being about God transforms it into eschatological words about the Word. This is not demonstrable; it simply *is*, confessed and believed.

If this begins to sound dogmatic, then I have successfully indicated what I take to be a fundamental lesson from modern and contemporary systematic theology: that such theology is dogmatic theology, and therefore eschatological theology. And if this begins to sound like theological alchemy, then that too is no bad thing – as long as the transformative power is located within God's Word of Revelation. The difference between Ben Jonson's alchemy and Rudolf Bultmann's is simply one of potential or *power*; for, finally, the resurrection of Jesus Christ is confessed as God's power revealed in and of the world. Was it a bodily resurrection? Of course, for how else could God's Word remain in the world, than by the world remaining eternally in God's Word?

Conclusion

Earlier in this essay I used the expression 'deep immanence', thereby indicating a key point for my discussion – talk of the bodily resurrection means bringing the reality of God directly into the texture of our historical existence. God's immanence is deep because it occurs beyond the surface sheen of metaphor; it lies so far within the world's fabric that only analogy can find it. Hence the way in which theologians speak of God's presence in the events of Christ's life on earth, including the resurrection, as embodied grace.

Very few theologians after Bultmann and Rahner have wanted to speak openly of Jesus' bodily resurrection, and those who do still do so from the perspective of scientific discourse. Without that bodily resurrection, however, a chain is broken, for the resurrection is the necessary link between the affirmations of one life, 2000 years ago, and every other life in time. Christian theology makes this assertion not because it is an affirmative narrative of the way in which people use language to speak of themselves, but because it believes it to be true, whatever the church, whatever the context. And it is prepared to speak of what it believes to be true because theology is faith seeking understanding, and therefore finally faith seeking to define itself by witness and testimony.

What is the content of Christian theology's witness and testimony? That God floods the world in Christ, as God previously flooded the world (Gen. 9), and with the same results: new life from oblivion. The resurrection speaks, proleptically to be sure, of life, and as it affirms life, so it affirms the body of God, Jesus' body, our body. Denying the bodily resurrection consequently denies the reality not only of the incarnation, but also of the full variety of creaturely existence. Today, Christian theology cannot afford to pick and choose within that variety; it must recognize everyone and everything. And Christian theology cannot afford to ignore the deep immanence, hidden though revealed, of God's presence as the mystery of the world.

Notes

1. This is a key point for me: time is the most suitable analogue to speak of God's action in the world, both because time as past, present and future is straightforward and therefore accessible, and because time linked to specific events contrasts strongly with what Christian theology wants to say about *eternity*.
2. R. Bultmann, *Glauben und Verstehen* III (Tübingen: Mohr/Siebeck, 1965), p. 2.
3. R. Bultmann, *Jesus* (Berlin: 1926), p. 29.
4. Cf. J. Moltmann, *The Crucified God* (London: SCM Press, 1974), pp. 317–38.
5. R. Bultmann, *The Gospel of John: A Commentary*, trans. R. Beasley-Murray et al. (Oxford: Blackwell, 1971), p. 402; my italics.
6. E. Jungel, *The Doctrine of the Trinity* (Edinburgh: T. & T. Clark, 1976), p. 59.

7. K. Rahner, *Hörer des Wortes: Zur Grundlegung einer Religionsphilosophie* (Munich: 1963).
8. K. Rahner, *Theological Investigations* IV, trans. Kevin Smyth (London: DLT, 1966), p. 326.
9. Ibid., my italics.
10. M. Heidegger, *Being and Time*, trans. John Macquarrie and Edward Robinson, (Oxford: Blackwell, 1962).
11. L. Boff, *Jesus Christ Liberator: A Critical Christology for our Time* (London: 1980); Jon Sobrino, *Jesus the Liberator: A Historical–Theological View* (Tunbridge Wells: Burns & Oates, 1994).
12. Cf. J-F. Lyotard, *The Postmodern Condition: A Report on Knowledge*, trans. Geoff Bennington and Brian Massuri (Manchester: MUP, 1984).
13. Cf. I. Dalferth, 'Karl Barth's Eschatological Realism', in *Karl Barth: Centenary Essays*, ed. S. W. Sykes (Oxford: Blackwell, 1989), pp. 14–46; and Bruce L. McCormack, *Karl Barth's Critically Realistic Theology* (Oxford: Clarendon Press, 1995).
14. On this question, cf. J. Milbank, *Theology and Social Theory* (Oxford: Blackwell, 1990); and G. Rose, *The Broken Middle* (Oxford: Blackwell, 1992).

Chapter 3

THE BASELESS FABRIC OF A VISION[1]

Michael Goulder

The Christians of the New Testament believed in the resurrection of Jesus for two quite distinct reasons: first, a series of people thought that they had *seen* him; and secondly, there were reports of a more concretely *physical* kind – the tomb was empty and his body had gone, or his disciples touched him, or he ate with them, and so on. The evidence for the first basis, the Appearances, is very early – it goes back at least to what Paul was taught when he was converted, a couple of years after the crucifixion. The stories about the empty tomb, the touching and the eating, all come to us from much later – the Empty Tomb is first spoken of in Mark, writing about forty years after the crucifixion. There are excellent reasons for being sceptical about both of these two bases of belief, but they are quite different. The Appearances are to be explained psychologically; the concrete physical details arise from disputes within the Church.

Psychological Explanations

Conversion Visions

If someone tells us they have seen a friend from another world, we may speak of an appearance, if we accept what they say, or an apparition if we doubt it. How do we decide which? Well, we may know of similar events which we think we do understand; and we will follow the general principle that it has proved sensible to trust this-worldly explanations rather than ones with ghosts, demons, etc. Here is a statement by Susan Atkins, who was involved with Charles Manson in a dreadful series of murders in California in the 1970s:

> The thoughts tumbled over and over in my mind. Can society forgive one for such acts against humanity? Can it take this guilt off my shoulders? Can serving the rest of my

life in prison undo what's been done? Can anything be done?

I looked at my future, my alternatives. Stay in prison. Escape. Commit suicide. As I looked, the wall in my mind was blank. But somehow I knew there was another alternative. I could choose the road many people had been pressing on me. I could follow Jesus. As plainly as daylight came the words, 'You have to decide. Behold, I stand at the door and knock.' Did I hear someone say that? I assume I spoke in my thoughts, but I'm not certain, 'What door?'

'You know what door and where it is, Susan. Just turn around and open it, and I will come in.' Suddenly, as though on a movie screen, there in my thoughts was a door. It had a handle. I took hold of it and pulled. It opened. The whitest, most brilliant light I had ever seen poured over me. In the center of the flood of brightness was an even brighter light. Vaguely, there was the form of a man. I knew it was Jesus. He spoke to me – literally, plainly, matter-of-factly spoke to me in my 9-by-11 prison cell: 'Susan, I am really coming into your heart to stay.' I was distinctly aware that I inhaled deeply, and then, just as fully, exhaled. There was no more guilt! It was gone. Completely gone! The bitterness, too, instantly gone! How could this be? For the first time in my memory I felt clean, fully clean, inside and out. In 26 years I had never been so happy.[2]

We may speak of Susan Atkins' experience as a *conversion vision*. Psychologists would say she had hallucinations, both in hearing voices and in seeing things.[3] But the point is that she was able to achieve a deep and satisfying new orientation to life, a conversion, which expressed itself in the form of a vision. We often read about this sort of experience in religious literature – Isaiah's vision of God in the Temple, for instance – but it is also common with non-religious conversions, like Arthur Koestler's conversion to Marxism in 1931.[4]

That is what was experienced by Peter on Easter Day, when he saw the Lord, or by Paul outside Damascus. Paul describes his own experience as a conversion vision in Galatians 1:12–16. He received the gospel 'by a revelation of Jesus Christ. For you have heard of my former way of life in Judaism, that I persecuted the

Church of God exceedingly and ravaged it. And I advanced in Judaism beyond many of my coevals . . . But when he who separated me from my mother's womb and called me by his grace was pleased to reveal his Son in me that I should preach him among the Gentiles . . . ' Paul had been persecuting the Church, and then he had experienced 'a revelation of Jesus Christ', he had been converted and had gone out to convert Gentiles to Christianity. Elsewhere he speaks of the experience as 'he appeared to me' (1 Cor. 15:8), or 'Have I not seen Jesus our Lord?' (1 Cor. 9:1). Of course, like Susan Atkins, he thought that Jesus was 'really there', but it is characteristic of such experiences that they occur at deep crises of life and seem intensely real. Paul, like Susan, knows it is Jesus although neither of them had ever seen him. Luke, who was Paul's close friend, describes the occasion three times (Acts 9, 22, 26), and never speaks of an appearance of Jesus at all; each time it is 'a [bright] light from heaven' – again as with Susan. We speak of the conversion of Paul, and we might well speak of the conversion of Peter, for Jesus said to him, 'When you are converted [epistrepsas], strengthen your brethren' (Luke 22:32) – he was no longer a boastful, sleeping, denier of his Lord, but a courageous champion of the faith, to martyrdom.

Psychologists have suggested various theories to account for such conversions, the cognitive dissonance theory, for instance;[5] but we do not for the moment need to claim that we fully understand such experiences; it is enough that we see the general thrust of what is happening. Faced with such a bleak future, Susan Atkins found a resolution which enabled her to see herself in a different light and lose her burden of guilt.

Guilt may quite often be associated with such dramatic conversions.[6] Koestler had been moving towards Marxism in 1931, but he had not joined the Communist party. He was making a good living, but one Saturday lost three months' salary at a poker party. It was December, and when he emerged his newly mended car had burst its radiator in the cold. He was offered a bed for the night by a woman he did not care for, with foreseeable consequences. In the morning, he says,

Pacing up and down in my bedroom, I had the sudden impression that I was looking down from a height at the track along which I had been running. I saw myself with great clarity as a sham and a phoney, paying lip-service to the Revolution that was to lift the world from its axis, and at the same time leading the existence of a bourgeois careerist, climbing the worm-eaten ladder of success, playing poker and landing in unsought beds.[7]

Perhaps Peter had a similar experience on Easter Saturday. He might well see himself as a sham and a phoney, paying lip-service to the kingdom of God which was to lift the earth from its axis, and climbing the worm-eaten ladder of self-preservation. So even if we do not have a full theory to explain conversion, we know what we are talking about; as Starbuck said, 'However inexplicable, the facts of conversion are a natural process.'[8]

Another feature often found in association with conversion is the accumulation of pressures.[9] Susan Atkins has been through the trauma of the trials, and is now facing a life in prison. Koestler had just lost three months salary at poker, found his newly mended car frozen, and gone to bed with a woman he disliked. Peter had been humiliated for his boasting after the Supper (Mark 14:29–31), for his sleeping in Gethsemane (Mark 14:37–41), and by his triple denial in the High Priest's courtyard (Mark 14:66–72) – and then found that Jesus, whom he had thought to be the Christ, had been crucified to death. Paul was making a considerable journey, and it was midday (Acts 9:3, 22:6, 26:13).[10]

Another important consideration is the upheaval of a recent bereavement. It is quite a common occurrence for widows and widowers who have been deeply attached to their partners to have experiences of them soon after their death; a Welsh GP reports that as many as forty-five per cent of his patients recently widowed have seen or heard their dead partners.[11] Peter and the others were certainly very attached to Jesus.[12] Or again violent conversions are correlated with matters like being easily hypnotized,[13] or having had an intense religious upbringing.[14] Both Peter and Paul are reported as having had other visions – Peter at the Transfiguration (Mark 9:2–7) and at Cornelius' visit (Acts 10:9–16), Paul by his own account had 'an excess of revelations' (2 Cor. 12:7). Paul tells us that he had been a Pharisee in his youth (Phil. 3:5).

Of course, not all of these features apply to both Peter and Paul. We know less about Peter as a character, but more about the events immediately before his conversion; the series of blows to his self-image, the guilt, the bereavement, all make a conversion vision a plausible explanation for his experience. We know less about the immediate events of Paul's conversion, but more about him as a character. His upbringing, his intensity, his liability to visions are all testified in his own writing. Furthermore, we know that he was going to Damascus to persecute the Church there, and this level of intense feeling is also correlated with conversion. Carl Gustav Jung writes about Paul:

> Fanaticism is only found in individuals who are compensating secret doubts. The incident on the way to Damascus marks the moment when the unconscious complex of Christianity broke through into consciousness. Unable to conceive of himself as a Christian on account of his resistance to Christ, he became blind, and could only regain his sight through complete submission to Christianity. Psychogenetic blindness is, according to my experience, always due to unwillingness to see; that is, to understand and to realise something that is incompatible with the conscious attitude. Paul's unwillingness to see corresponds with his fanatical resistance to Christianity.[15]

Some New Testament scholars would rather trust Heikki Räisänen than Jung; and he has rightly derided the unwillingness of Pauline scholars to consider psychological motivations.[16] He cites J. C. Beker, 'How could the Christophany have been so traumatic and so radical in its consequences unless it lit up and answered a hidden quest in [Paul's] soul?'[17] He thinks that the passages about the law as a yoke, and of 'not receiving a spirit of bondage to be again in fear' (Gal. 5:1; Rom. 8:15) suggest that Paul had experienced Judaism as bondage and fear himself. My own suspicion is that Paul had had a Gentile friend in his youth, and that the connection of his conversion with his call to evangelize the Gentiles has to do with some such experience. The fact that we cannot provide a full account of a psychic event two millennia ago does nothing to commend theological dogmatism; even if speculative, a natural explanation is to be preferred.

Collective Delusions

We may speak of Peter's and Paul's experiences as primary; they both started from scratch, so to speak – the appearances to the apostles or the 500 brethren which Paul mentions are secondary in the sense that these groups have already heard, and perhaps credited, the reports of Jesus being alive.[18] We have many instances of this kind of experience – large groups of people who have seen the statue of Mary at Knock moving, or UFOs, or experiments with groups where expectation affects perception in ways that can be repeated. I cite here a series of appearances of Sasquatch, or Bigfoot, an eight-foot hairy, evil-smelling monster, over three months in the autumn of 1977 in South Dakota.[19] Sasquatch had been a legend for a century further west, and his exploits were shown in a B film in South Dakota in the summer of 1977. He was then sighted in the area, first by Indian youths, then by white ranchers, then by hundreds of people. His giant footprints were found in the mud. The police went after him. Experts from the Bureau of Indian Affairs were unable to explain the phenomena. Traps were set for him, with recordings of women's voices all night; but Bigfoot was clever. He was reported at length in the local papers daily, and even made national television.

The Bigfoot phenomenon is explained as *collective delusion* by Smelser's value-added theory.[20] Such things cannot happen without (1) a close-knit community in which rumour can spread easily, and which is isolated from the sceptical normal world. This was the case in the settlements in South Dakota, and also in the primitive Church. (2) There has to be structural strain – anxiety, the lack of clear criteria; and the presence of poorly educated people, and women helps. The early Church was anxious; its doors were locked for fear of the Jews; and it was not well educated either. (3) It has to be easy for a generalized belief to become specific. The Sasquatch legend was part of Indian culture, and the film was recent. In the same way many Jews believed the dead would rise when God's kingdom came, and Jesus had recently proclaimed the advent of the Kingdom. (4) There have to be precipitating factors – the film, the media coverage of Bigfoot; Jesus' execution, Peter's conversion vision with the Church. (5) The community has to mobilize for action. There were constant meetings over Bigfoot, the setting of traps, police-hunts, etc. The Church met constantly for prayer in Acts 1.

Finally (6), there has to be a pay-off for the sightings. If you sighted Bigfoot, you were the centre of attention; people spoke about you; the press sought you out. If you sighted Jesus, you confirmed the Church's hopes, and your own. You were an approved member of the Kingdom of God. Instead of accepting that you had been totally mistaken, that all Jesus' talk of the Kingdom had been eyewash, that you must go back to the old life amid the derision of sceptics, another prospect opened. Despite the crucifixion, Jesus was right after all! The end of the world had begun! The first of the dead had been resurrected! It is not difficult to see that such a visionary experience would have an enormous pay-off; and it is easy to parallel cases where people have had similar hallucinations with much less to gain.

I may close this first section with two general points. Apologists have often relied on what Don Cupitt has called the 'beaten-men' argument. From the Thursday night the apostles were beaten men; but from Easter Day they were transformed into bold proclaimers of the gospel, and in time into martyrs for the faith. Something must have happened to change them; and that something can only be Jesus' resurrection. The psychological considerations I have set out above undercut this apology. Peter and Paul (and in a secondary degree the others) experienced conversion visions. So of course they were transformed – that is what conversion means. Their subsequent heroism and martyrdom are sure evidence of the depth of their conversion (which we might have expected from their having had visions, a rare phenomenon); they are no evidence that Jesus was 'really there'.

The other point is a philosophical one. The response of religious people to such explanations as I have offered is usually rather undisturbed. You have shown a possible psychological mechanism, it may be said; but you have not affected the substance of the Resurrection claim. The apostles may have had conversion visions, but the Christian faith is that they were genuine visions of Jesus, alive after his passion; both elements stand. I need to stress therefore that the psychological explanations make the supernatural claims otiose; it is a matter for Occam's Razor.

The point may be illustrated from other areas where we have a natural and a supernatural explanation for the same thing. Hysteria may manifest itself in distressing symptoms, paralysis, tremors, anaesthesia, etc.; and the same symptoms were described in the Middle Ages and ascribed to demons.[21] No one today would say, 'Ah yes, the man has hysteria, which can be cured with such a treatment, but hysteria is caused by demons.' We have a medical and a supernatural explanation *competing*, and we prefer the medical one. When the Armada sailed up the Channel in 1588, the English guns had a longer range than the Spanish, but at the longer range the cannon-balls bounced off the oaken Spanish ships' sides. An English captain commented, 'It is for our sins'; but later, when the range closed, the firing turned out to be quite effective. Here a practical hypothesis, that cannon-balls will only penetrate oak at a short distance, is in competition with the providentialist hypothesis, that God is taking a hand in the battle, and serving out the sinful Protestants. Hypotheses, or explanations, should not be multiplied beyond what is necessary: we do not need both a natural and a supernatural explanation for any phenomenon: experience shows that we should always prefer the natural hypothesis, or we shall fall into superstition. The early Church took a supernatural explanation for its visions of Jesus, being the only explanation on offer. We can see that there will be psychological explanations for them: so we should prefer the psychological hypothesis and abandon the supernatural one.

The Resurrection Controversy: Physical or Spiritual?

For the Empty Tomb, the touching and eating, we move into a different area. At first, it seems, the explanation accepted in the Church for the visions of the first weeks after the crucifixion was that Jesus had risen from the dead (1 Cor. 15:5). But by the middle 50s there were Jewish Christians[22] who said that there was *no physical* resurrection – neither for the dead generally, nor, we must suppose, for Jesus in particular, for Paul asks, 'How is it that some among you say there is no resurrection of dead bodies [*nekron*]?' (15:12). There was *spiritual* resurrection, for they thought it worthwhile to be baptized a second time on behalf of their dead relatives (15:29), but they laughed at the idea of a physical resurrection – 'How are the dead raised?', they asked, 'and with what body do they come?' (15:35). A few years later they were saying that 'the resurrection has already taken place' (2 Tim. 2:18).

The beliefs of Jews on the afterlife were vague and various in the New Testament period.[23] Josephus makes it clear that most Jews – Sadducees excepted – saw the soul as continuing after death, and we find the same in Philo, and implied in the apocalypses. It is usually made clear that the wicked will suffer eternal torment.

Sometimes the righteous become pure 'mind', or in unspecified ways attain immortality;[24] sometimes they go to the Blessed Isles;[25] sometimes they transmigrate into new bodies.[26] The rabbis discouraged speculation on the subject, which may mean that it was rife.[27] Both Josephus and Philo are using Greek terms to clothe Jewish thinking, so we cannot be too confident of how normal people would have thought. But they do not speak about resurrection, only about immortality. Resurrection (of the body) is an *interpretation* of Daniel 12:2, 'Many of those who sleep in the dust of the earth shall awake.' So the idea of the perseverance of the person, of spiritual resurrection if one likes so to speak of it, goes back to the first century, and is likely to have been the norm, rather than a physical resurrection; and it is in fact not far from what many Christians believe today, including Bishop David Jenkins. The significant thing is that *either* interpretation of 'resurrection' was possible, physical or non-physical; but that the Jewish–Christian, spiritual view in 1 Corinthians 15 is in line with Josephus and Philo.

This spiritual theory was not a passing fad. We find it continuing, still among Jewish Christians, in the letters of Ignatius, about 115. Ignatius writes to the Christians in Smyrna:

> For I know and believe that [Jesus Christ] was in the flesh even after the resurrection; and when He came to Peter and His company, He said to them, *Lay hold and handle me, and see that I am not a demon without body.* And straightway they touched Him, and they believed, being joined unto His flesh and His blood . . . And after His resurrection He ate with them and drank with them as one in the flesh, though spiritually He was united with the Father. (Smyrn. 3)

Of course, when debating with those holding the spiritual resurrection theory, it was no good stressing how many people had *seen* Jesus, because they could always reply that they had just seen the risen spirit: what is necessary is reports of touching and eating, because touching and eating require *physical* presence.

Now the stories which Ignatius draws on are from Luke's Gospel, which was written about 90, sixty years after Jesus' death. Such details come in no earlier source, though they are elaborated by John about 100, with the famous story of Thomas. It is Luke who first tells us that Jesus said to the apostles, 'Handle me and see, for a spirit has not flesh and bones', and that he ate some fish. Wasn't that lucky for Ignatius, that he had just the right kind of story to hand, just in time! It seems rather too good to be true that such a story should have been circulating orally for *sixty years* after Jesus' death, and have recently come to light. The obvious explanation is that the Lucan church felt certain that the resurrection was a physical event, and they interpreted the tradition of the visions with the extra details of touching and eating to make the point.

Now exactly the same motive underlies the creation of the Empty Tomb story in Mark, which was written about 70, forty years after Jesus' death. Paul never mentions an empty tomb; though he does record as part of the tradition, ' . . . He was buried . . . ' (1 Cor. 15:4), and Mark may have felt that that was suggestive. No doubt he had a tradition that Jesus had been buried by Joseph of Arimathea, and that Mary Magdalene and other women had meant to anoint the body, but had not been able to. But his story supplies the exact need of a Pauline church which believed in a physical resurrection. The women come with their spices, and are met by an angel who says, 'You seek Jesus of Nazareth, the crucified one; he is risen, he is not here – *behold the place where they laid him*' (Mark 16:6). So Mark has solved the problem of how to make clear in narrative (and so, memorable) form the error of the spiritual resurrection theory: the women saw the place where he had been laid, now without the body – so he had been raised *physically*.

This view of the Empty Tomb story as the creation of the Marcan church is not just the speculation of a sceptic; there is a contradiction built into the story which gives it away. Mark says the angel told the women to give the message to Peter and the others to go to Galilee, where they would see Jesus; so the congregation is led to think that all is smooth – the disciples got the message, they suppose, and went to Galilee, where the resurrection appearances took place. But now Mark thinks of a difficulty. What are people going to say who hear this story for the first time in 70 – especially Jewish Christians holding the opposition view in 1 Corinthians 15:12, who will be deeply sceptical of physical resurrection stories? Will they not say, 'I've been a Christian for forty years, and it is the first time I have heard such a tale? Why have I never heard this before? It is a pack of lies.' So Mark thinks of an answer to this problem. He ends the tale, 'And [the women] went out and fled from the tomb, for trembling and astonishment seized them; and they said nothing to anyone, for they were afraid' (16:8). You know what women are like, brethren: they were seized with panic and hysteria, and kept the whole thing quiet.[28] That is why people have not heard all this before.

The only trouble with Mark's ingenious solution is that he is left with the problem of how the apostles got the message to go to Galilee; and he solved this by putting the same message in Jesus' mouth in 14:28. There Jesus is prophesying, 'You will all be offended, for it is written, I will smite the shepherd and the sheep shall be scattered', and Peter replies, 'Though all shall be offended, yet will not I': 14:28 has been inserted, and breaks the thread, 'But after I am risen, I will go before you to Galilee.' So even though this makes the angel's similar instruction pointless, Mark has covered his tracks; and Matthew and Luke complete the job by suppressing the women's silence in their accounts.

Belief in Jesus' resurrection does not rest on a fraud. Peter and Paul and the others had genuine conversions which they experienced as visions; in the circumstances of the time, when there was a widespread belief that the Kingdom of God was coming, and that the dead would be raised, these were quite naturally interpreted as evidence that Jesus had risen from the dead. At first people accepted this without much question; but from the 50s and for perhaps a century, two theories were competing in the Church. The Paulines, Mark, Luke and John, elaborated the traditions of appearances with an empty tomb story, and the details of touching and seeing. But it is now obvious that these were interpretative additions to counter the spiritual theory; and that neither the eating and touching stories nor the empty tomb story have any basis in the most primitive tradition.

So there was no resurrection of Jesus. Psychological explanations are available for the early, appearance traditions; and known intra-ecclesial controversies about the nature of the resurrection explain the Gospel additions. So the Pauline, physical theory is without basis. But the psychological explanations also take the ground from under the feet of the Jewish Christian spiritual resurrection theory too – Peter and James just had conversion visions like Susan Atkins. Such a conclusion presents the Church with a paradox. Paul's own faith was entirely dependent on the truth of the resurrection of Jesus: 'If Christ has not been raised, your faith is vain and you are still in your sins' (1 Cor. 15:17). The historical faith of the Church has been Paul's faith, and it is in trust in his gospel of the cross and resurrection that Christians have died, and killed. Perhaps the sapient sutlers of the Lord may manage without Jesus' resurrection, or reinterpret it; but it will not, I think, be the same religion.

Notes

1. A shorter form of this paper was delivered at a meeting of the British Section of the SNTS at Sheffield in September, 1991, in a debate on the Resurrection of Jesus with Professor James Dunn, and was published in a Festschrift for Leslie Houlden, *Resurrection*, eds. G. N. Stanton and S. Barton (London: SPCK, 1994), pp. 58–68.
2. M. J. Meadow and R. D. Kahoe, *Psychology of Religion* (New York: Harper and Row, 1984), p. 90. I am grateful to my colleague, Dr Carolyn Hicks, who has directed my thinking in various excursions into psychology; but who is not to be held responsible for any errors.
3. Ibid., p. 91.
4. *Arrow in the Blue* (London: Collins, 1952); cited by W. Sargant, *Battle for the Mind* (Garden City, NY: Heinemann, 1957), p. 85.
5. Meadow and Kahoe, *Psychology*, 101f.; L. Festinger, *A Theory of Cognitive Dissonance* (Stanford, CA: Stanford University Press, 1957). Sargant (note 4) works with a theory of Transmarginal Inhibition.
6. F. J. Roberts, 'Some Psychological Factors in Religious Conversion', *British Journal of Social and Clinical Psychology* (1965), pp. 185–7, reports that sudden conversions among 43 theological students showed no higher incidence of reported guilt than among gradual converts; but such samples do not include mass murderers like Susan Atkins, or people driven to psychological blindness like St Paul.
7. See note 4.
8. E. D. Starbuck, *The Psychology of Religion* (New York: Scribner, 1903), p. 143.
9. Sargant, *Battle*, passim; Meadow and Kahoe, *Psychology*, pp. 99f.
10. It is to be noted that Paul himself does not mention the location of the experience at all. For this we are entirely in the hands of Luke; although Luke is not to be thought of as on a par with a modern historian, he has earned a rather high reputation over other ancient historians; cf. M. Hengel, *Acts and the History of Earliest Christianity* (London: SCM, 1979), especially pp. 81–91 for this story. Compare C.

K. Barrett, *The Acts of the Apostles* (Edinburgh: ICC, T. & T. Clark, 1994), I, 443, 'In essentials the three Acts narratives agree with one another, and with the evidence of the epistles.'

11. Dr W. D. Rees, *British Medical Journal*, 4 (Oct. 1971), pp. 37–41, cited in Timothy Beardsworth, *A Sense of Presence* (Oxford: Religious Experience Research Unit, 1977), pp. 12f. Beardsworth stresses that the patients were mostly English.

12. Whereas Peter, James and John are conspicuously absent from the crucifixion, the women are there; but then women were not likely to be arrested for leading Messianic rebellions as men were, so their presence is understandable. Care is necessary in treating the Gospels as objective accounts of the facts. Luke, who wants a united Church, whitewashes the Jerusalem leaders, while Mark, who is promoting the Pauline gospel, never spares them.

13. D. Gibbons and J. DeJanrette, 'Hypnotic Susceptibility and Religious Experience', *Journal for the Scientific Study of Religion*, 11 (1972), pp. 152–6; G. Matheson, 'Hypnotic Aspect of Religious Experiences', *Journal of Psychology and Theology*, 7 (1979), pp. 13–21.

14. W. H. Clark, *The Psychology of Religion* (New York: Macmillan, 1958), p. 204; G. E. W. Scobie, 'Types of Christian Conversion', *Journal of Behavioral Science*, 1 (1973), pp. 265–71.

15. C. G. Jung, *Contributions to Analytical Psychology* (New York: ET, Harcourt, Brace; London: K. Paul, Trench, Trübner, 1928), p. 257.

16. *Paul and the Law* (London: SCM, 1982), p. 232.

17. *Paul the Apostle* (Philadelphia: Fortress, 1980), p. 237.

18. Paul cites in 1 Cor. 15:5–7 a list of the accepted appearances of Jesus which he had 'received' at his initiation – Cephas (Peter), the Twelve, five hundred 'brethren', James, all the apostles. There are no women, except those included among the 'brethren'. Mark and Luke record women as seeing the empty tomb (see below), but not as seeing Jesus. The appearances of Jesus to Mary Magdalene (and others) described in Matt. 28:9f. and John 20:11–18 are variously evaluated for historical reliability; but the Matthaean incident seems just to be an expansion of the preceding incident, and John's story has a strong Johannine theological feel.

19. J. R. Stewart, 'Sasquatch Sightings in South Dakota', in G. K. Zollschan et al. eds., *Exploring the Paranormal* (Bridport UK: Prism; New York: Avery; Lindfield, NSW: Unity, 1989), pp. 287–304. I am grateful to Dr Mark Fox for the reference.

20. N. J. Smelser, *Theory of Collective Behaviour* (London: Routledge, 1962), pp. 12–22.

21. Ernest Jones, *The Life and Work of Sigmund Freud* (Abridged version, London: Pelican, 1964), p. 205.

22. That they were *Jewish* Christians is indicated by their exposition of the

two men of Gen. 1:27/2:7, a technical piece of Jewish scriptural exegesis known to us from Philo, and countered by Paul at 1 Cor. 15:45ff.; and by their devotion to *the Law* (1 Cor. 15:56). The view that Paul was a total obsessive, who attacked the Law whatever the topic being covered, like Cato on the destruction of Carthage, is quite without foundation. Where is the evidence for such an obsession elsewhere?

23. There is a brief but authoritative outline of the evidence in E. P. Sanders, *Judaism; Practice and Belief 63 BCE–66 CE* (London/Philadelphia: SCM/Trinity, 1992), pp. 298–303. For fuller discussions see H. C. C. Cavallin, *Life after Death* (CB New Testament 7:1, Lund: Gleerup, 1974); G.Sellin, *Die Streit um die Auferstehung der Toten* (FRLANT 138; Göttingen: Mohr, 1986).

24. Philo, *Moses* 2.288; Josephus, *Antiquities* 18.14,16,18, *War*, 1.650, 2.165, 7.343–6, *Apion* 2.218.

25. Josephus, *War*, 154f.

26. Josephus, *War*, 2.164, 3.374f.

27. Sifre Deut. 356.

28. Mark's Gospel finished at 16:8, and the women's silence was a scandal. Both Matthew (28:8) and Luke (24:9) have the women go forthwith to tell the disciples; and an early 'editor' added a spurious ending to Mark (16:9–20) to cover the difficulty.

Chapter 4

HISTORY AND THE REALITY OF THE RESURRECTION

Wolfhart Pannenberg

The Christian proclamation of Jesus' resurrection from the dead continues to be met by derision and unbelief. Nor should this be otherwise, for it is in line with the New Testament witness itself. The reason is that the general resurrection of the dead – or at least of the 'righteous' ones – which the early Christians expected to happen soon in the line of Jewish apocalyptic expectations, is still a matter of the future, to say the least, if one does not prefer to speak of a falsification of that hope after a 'delay' of two thousand years. The resurrection of Jesus was experienced and proclaimed as the beginning of that final future of God's kingdom in his creation. Calculations concerning the general possibility (or improbability) of any such resurrection in the midst of history depend largely on the assumption or rejection of that future, and they depend on belief in God, the one who might bring about such a future and in whose power it would be possible to let such an event occur in the midst of our human history. In other words, the Christian belief in the event of the resurrection of Jesus Christ presupposes an outlook on reality in general that is not shared by everybody.

According to Christian expectation and hope, there will be a time when doubt will not be possible any more that dead persons indeed have been raised to a new life. This will be the case when a general resurrection of the dead will have occurred. But we do not live as yet in such an epoch. Therefore, on the basis of present everyday experience, it seems extremely unlikely that any dead person will be raised to a new life. This present experiential situation also informs our historical judgements. Consequently, the Christian proclamation of Jesus' resurrection is met by a great deal of disbelief and suspicion. There are strong a priori prejudices against the possibility of such an event as well as against any affirmation of its actual occurrence. They precede any examination of the historical evidence for the early Christian proclamation of the event of Jesus' resurrection. In the words of David Hume, the greater the rarity of the kind of event in question, the more overwhelming the evidence must be, if we are to accept the real occurrence of such an event. In the case of a resurrection of a person from death, however, the event is so rare that Hume judged the assumption of its real occurrence to be contrary to the regularities of all our human experience. For similar reasons, any claim affirming the occurrence of such an event will be judged impossible by many people, and they will be inclined to accept almost any alternative explanation of the course of events, no matter what the historical evidence might be, whenever claims to such an occurrence are raised.

The Christian proclamation of Jesus' resurrection has been met by reactions of this type since the time of the apostles, and it is quite understandable that this controversy will continue until the end of time. Not so understandable, however, is such a reaction on the part of Christian theologians who happen to work in the capacity of historical exegetes of Biblical literature and of historians who investigate and reconstruct the course of early Christian history.

Admittedly, in the historical interpretation of early Christian literature and in their judgements on issues concerning historical fact in early Christian history, the Christian historian has to apply the same criteria and tools employed elsewhere in the critical analysis of traditional texts and in historical judgement; not only on their claims concerning matters of fact, but also in the critical reconstruction of the actual course of events which finally emerges from historical analysis. There is a problem, however, in that the criteria and tools of historical judgement are not beyond dispute. Modern historical method has been in the process of development since the origins of modernity. In principle, each and every technique that helps analyse and evaluate texts in such a way that a critical judgement can be formed on their historical background and context as well as on their own truth claims concerning matters of fact is part and parcel of the historical critical method.

In the early decades of this century, there was heated debate as to whether form criticism should be recognized as part of the historical method. The debate resulted, however, in widespread acceptance of the claim that the identification of certain literary forms in traditional texts allows for conclusions concerning the truth claims of statements that occur within such a text. If a story is identified as a fairy tale or legend, the statements occurring in such a story should not be treated as claims to historical fact. So far, there should be no controversy about the legitimacy of applying historical criteria (including form criticism) in Biblical exegesis and about the appropriateness of drawing consequences from the results of such an analysis in historical judgement. A case in point is the Biblical story of the Virgin Birth of Jesus. If it is correct that this story shows the marks of a legend, then it can no longer be used as evidence for the claim that the Virgin Birth occurred as a historical fact.

There are deeper issues, however, in connection with the use of the historical method. These issues are especially connected with the historical task of finally providing a reconstruction of the actual course of events, and here Christian historians – like any other Christians – are called to engage secular history in a controversy concerning the nature of reality at large. Historical reconstruction of the course of events is habitually based on analogy with present experience of reality or, in more general terms, with presently accepted views on the nature of reality. This principle is important in providing plausibility of historical reconstructions. But in view of the avowedly secularist character of public assumptions on the nature of reality at large in our contemporary Western society, Christians have to claim exemption at this point. They cannot subscribe to a conception of reality that a priori excludes God from the understanding of it.

The decision to exclude God from the public understanding of reality is of course not a specifically historical issue. It is not among the tools of historical critical method. But it impinges upon the use of that method, and it does so by way of looking at the course of events as they actually *may* have happened, in the light of contemporary assumptions on the nature of reality at large. This, in the present situation, excludes God from the understanding of historical processes, and it also excludes the very possibility of a (in whatever sense) 'bodily' resurrection of a dead person.

This fact amounts to a prejudice in dealing with the textual evidence of the early Christian Easter tradition. The negative judgement on the bodily resurrection of Jesus as having occurred in historical fact is *not a result* of the historical critical examination of the Biblical Easter tradition, *but a postulate* that precedes any such examination. There are many examples from contemporary literature on the Christian Easter tradition that show how the historical examination of the textual evidence and the reconstruction of the course of events based on the results of such examination, aims from the outset at a description of the textual evidence and a reconstruction of the events that provide, with some plausibility, an alternative explanation of early Christian history. Reconstructions of this type are not done in bad faith, but rather in assuming that such is the task of the historian, including the Christian historian, in applying the historical method to this story. But precisely at this point a historian who happens to be a Christian should take exemption from a procedure that for a priori reasons imposes upon the Christian story a secularist reading.

It is good to remember that in the development of the modern historical method God was not always excluded from scholarly accounts of historical processes. When in the eighteenth century Johann Lorenz von Mosheim proposed his 'pragmatic method' of explaining the sequence of events in history by human actions rather than divine interventions, he at the same time assigned to the historian the task of demonstrating in the course of history the design of divine providence. A century later, the German secular historian, Gustav Droysen, in his very influential book on historical method, dealt with the task of a theological interpretation of history as part and parcel of the general historical method. It is only since the rise of historical positivism around the turn of the century that reference to God was completely excluded from the public interpretation and presentation of history. Hence it does not seem essential to the historical method in general to omit all reference to God with regard to historical events.

The case of the resurrection is different since the mechanistic world-view of science seemed to exclude the very possibility of events that escape mechanistic explanation. But such a view has now become obsolete. Though the idea of miracles as breaking the rules of natural law is still excluded by the very concept of natural law, that concept does not preclude the impact of contingency and hidden parameters that in particular cases may influence the actual occurrence of events without violating the presently known natural laws. When the American physicist Frank Tipler discusses the possibility of a general resurrection of the dead in the final future of the history of our universe in the recent book *The Physics of Immortality*,[1] it is no longer beyond the imagination of scientists to conceive of the possibility of such an event even in the midst of human history, because that history is to be seen in the light of the final future of the universe.

For theological purposes it is not necessary to consider conjectures like Tipler's as established facts of science. It is enough to take into account that considerations of this kind are no longer completely foreign to the range of scientific thought nor hostile to the spirit of science. In this situation, the decision on the issue of resurrection of Jesus as an event in the history of humankind is again a matter of purely historical examination of the early Christian tradition and of specifically historical judgement and not of a priori determination. In the historical discourse among Biblical exegetes, unfortunately, such an a priori attitude continues to dominate the scene. But the verdict on the issue of Jesus' resurrection should not be presented as resulting from historical scrutiny of the Biblical evidence, but as what it is: a prejudice that precedes all specifically historical examination of the tradition.

So far, in this argument, the kind of event in question has not yet been discussed. In any judgement on the historicity of Jesus' resurrection, however, this issue is important, even essential. If we talk about 'resurrection' in terms of a metaphor for some sort of spiritual encounter with dead persons, or with their image, after their death, it is a very different matter from talk about a bodily resurrection of a person, though the idea of body itself is open to a range of different interpretations. In one sense, bodily resurrection can be taken to mean the revivification of a corpse as we have it in John 11:43ff. It can also mean, however, the transformation of the dead body into a different form of bodily life, and this seems to be indicated in many places in Paul's letters. It can also mean, finally, that the spirit of the dead is invested with a different body, and then there might arise different opinions on the extent to which this new body is related to the former one.

All these ideas of resurrection and others are open to the imagination. It is a matter of historical judgement, however, what conception of resurrection applies to the early Christian Easter tradition. It is possible, of course, that in different strands of that tradition different conceptions of resurrection were used. This seems to be true enough on comparison between Paul's experience on the road to Damascus (Acts 9:3ff.) and certain stories from the gospels reporting encounters with the risen Lord.

What idea of resurrection belongs to the earliest forms of the Christian Easter tradition? The visionary experiences of the risen Lord reported by Paul in his list of the sequence of witnesses in 1 Corinthians 15:5–8 are generally considered to contain the original core of the Easter tradition that began with the appearance of the Lord to Peter. Since Paul claimed a similar appearance to have occurred to himself – a claim that apparently was accepted by the Jerusalem community – and since his experience is reported to have occurred as a visionary encounter with the exalted Lord in a light from heaven (Acts 9:3), it is often assumed that the earliest appearances to Peter and others were visionary experiences (*ophtè*) of a more or less similar character. On that basis it could be conjectured that the reality of Christ that was perceived in those early experiences was of a spiritual nature without any necessary connection with the dead body of the crucified Jesus.

Now Paul's own idea of resurrection and of the new life issuing from the raising of the dead was connected with some idea of bodily existence though with a different kind of such existence (1 Cor. 15:35–49). There can be little doubt that Paul conceived of the existence of the risen and exalted Lord in a similar way, since he put so much emphasis on the parallel between Jesus' resurrection and the resurrection that the Christian hope is looking forward to (1 Cor. 15:13–23). But how is the bodily existence that Paul called 'spiritual body' (ibid. 44) related to the present bodily reality of human life in the form of the 'flesh'?

Two different indications for an answer to that question can be found in the letters of the apostle. The first is the idea that in the final resurrection our present earthly life will be 'transformed' into the new imperishable life that has become manifest first in Jesus' resurrection (1 Cor. 15:52). Here a continuity from the old life to the new one is suggested, a continuity that consists in the process of transformation itself. The old body will not be replaced by a different one, but 'this perishable nature must put on the imperishable, and this mortal nature must put on immortality' (15:53).

The same idea occurs in 2 Corinthians (3:18, cf. 5:4) and Philippians (3:21). But there is also, sometimes in the same context, the idea of a new type of body replacing the old one. It occurs in the lengthy passage of 1 Corinthians 15:35–44, a passage that deals with the different types of body God is able to provide. It is also present in 2 Corinthians 5, where the reader is told that when this earthly tent – an image for the human body – will be destroyed, another eternal home is waiting for us in heaven (5:1ff.).

According to the apostle, in this life we are afraid to be found naked, when the vestment of our mortal flesh will decay. But then there will be another one so that we shall be 'further clothed' (5:4). The image of the body as a dwelling place slides into that of a vestment that may be exchanged for another one or, as the apostle suggests in the last place, that may be put upon the other so that the mortal body 'may be swallowed up by life' (5:4). Here the sentence ends again with the idea of transformation. Paul, then, does not seem to have sensed an important difference or even contradiction between the idea of one form of body replacing the other and the idea of a transformation of the present body into another form of life. But, taken by itself, the idea of replacement is different from transformation. It would allow for the mortal body to decay in the tomb while another one will be provided by the creator God in the future.

The application of this conception of bodily resurrection to the interpretation of Jesus' resurrection is also clear – Jesus could be understood to have been 'raised' to a new, 'spiritual' form of existence that would have nothing to do with his former body decaying in his tomb. This interpretation of bodily resurrection recommends itself, because it would render it possible to conceive of Jesus' resurrection and of the one the Christian believers look forward to in strictly parallel terms. For in the case of the Christians there is no doubt that their dead bodies are decaying in their tombs. If it was otherwise in the case of Jesus, his case would be an exception to the general rule rather than the model for what will occur to his believers. The Pauline reference to the risen Lord as 'the first born from the dead' (Col. 1:18; Rom. 8:29; cf. 1 Cor. 15:20) suggests a closer similarity between Jesus' resurrection and the future of his believers.

Unfortunately, the historical evidence complicates the issue. The early Christian proclamation of Jesus' resurrection started from Jerusalem, where Jesus had been tried and executed, and in the Gospel tradition the stories about experiences of encounters of his disciples with their risen Lord are told in connection with another story about the discovery of his empty tomb. The literature on the early Christian Easter tradition is full of attempts at discrediting this story of the empty tomb of Jesus and the tomb tradition of the gospels generally. The story about the walk of three women to visit Jesus' tomb on Easter morning has been dismissed time and again as a later legend. But it has turned out difficult to establish this case by exegetical and historical argument. It is not possible here to enter into the details of that discussion. It must be sufficient to refer the reader to the now classical treatise of Hans von Campenhausen on the subject, first published in 1952[2] and quoted in my book *Jesus – God and Man*.[3]

The lasting importance of Campenhausen's essay consists in the way he exposed the prejudiced treatment of this story in the exegetical literature. Whether his own conclusions on the historical value of the tomb tradition are accepted or not, in any event the story is to be taken more seriously than has been often the case until the present day. In addition, however, there is a general historical consideration suggesting the historicity of the empty tomb. In those days, the prevailing Jewish understanding of resurrection from the dead presupposed that the tombs would empty, the earth would 'return' the dead bodies, etc. It seems inconceivable, under such circumstances, to imagine the situation of the earliest Christian proclamation of Jesus' resurrection at Jerusalem, the place of Jesus' crucifixion, without assuming that all parties knew that his tomb was empty.

Of course, this fact was open to all sorts of different explanations: perhaps Jesus was not really dead, or the disciples could have stolen the body. The empty tomb never provided the decisive evidence of Jesus' resurrection. But without the empty tomb, the Christian proclamation of Jesus' resurrection *at Jerusalem* of all places would have been in serious trouble, because it could have been easily falsified by just pointing to the place where Jesus had been buried.

Modern exegetical literature has tried all sorts of devices to evade that conclusion. Especially, it has been suggested that the burial place of Jesus might have been unknown. But this is a pure invention of modern scholarship without the slightest evidence. Moreover, it does not seem very likely that nobody would have been interested in where Jesus' body had gone when his followers proclaimed his resurrection in that city, and friends and foes of that proclamation would take for granted that there is a connection between resurrection and the dead body. So this is the decisive issue: unless it can be shown that the Jewish community of that time in history could conceive of a resurrection from the dead without being concerned with what happens to the dead body, it must be judged extremely implausible that the Christian congregation at Jerusalem proclaimed Jesus' resurrection while his body was resting in his tomb.

The strength of the interconnection of the two issues – the relationship between Jewish ideas of the time on resurrection and dead bodies on the one hand, and the situation of the earliest Christian proclamation of Jesus' resurrection at Jerusalem on the other – is such that a highly esteemed Roman Catholic exegete some years ago tried to turn the issue around. He proposed that the early Christians had invented the legend of the empty tomb precisely in order to answer the questions concerning Jesus' tomb that their proclamation of the risen Lord would provoke in a Jewish context;[4] as if the early Christians were not Jews themselves and shared the general attitude that there cannot be a resurrection without something happening to the body. If so, how could their proclamation of Jesus' resurrection have started at all without presupposing that his tomb was empty?

The case against the empty tomb tradition, then, is somewhat weak historically, unless one starts from the prejudice that certain possibilities have to be discarded from the outset. Given the fact that the issue of the empty tomb is at best of secondary importance in the overall question of the resurrection of Jesus, because the basis for the Christian proclamation of the risen Christ is provided by his appearances to those who in consequence of that experience became his apostles, the heat of the debate about the empty tomb and the particular bias of criticism against that story is astonishing. It may be understandable, however, with regard to the consequences of the historicity of the empty tomb for the understanding of the resurrection life of Jesus as well as of the nature of resurrection in the Christian hope.

If the Christian proclamation of Jesus has to be accounted for in connection with the emptying of his tomb, the possibilities of spiritualizing interpretations of the Christian Easter message are seriously reduced. Resurrection has to be understood in terms of transformation of the old life into the new one rather than in terms of replacing the perishable body by another one. It is only in the case of Jesus, however, that the two conceptions present a clear alternative, because of the short time between his death and resurrection.

In the case of the Christians whose bodies decayed in their graves and whose earthly lives are preserved only in the eternal memory of God, the issue is different. There, the transformation occurs through participation of whatever is remembered of our earthly lives in the life of God's eternal life, and when a new life of their own is given to them, it will be something entirely new. Hence in any event there is a lack of analogy at this point between the content of the Christian hope and the resurrection of Jesus, supposing it is to be understood as related to his empty tomb. Nevertheless, the Christian hope is to share in the new life that became first manifest in Jesus' resurrection. How that event occurred was not observed by anybody then, according to the Biblical tradition, and it certainly surpasses our imagination at present. But this cannot provide a sufficient reason for objecting to its historicity.

Accepting the affirmation of Jesus' resurrection as an event in history on the one hand, and the role of historical reason on the other, can go together, if the concept of history allows a place for God in the reality of historical processes. God's power can bring about what exceeds the limitations of our human knowledge at a given time. Still this does not mean that affirmations on past events should be accepted without historical examination. If the tools of historical scrutiny of traditions as well as of other kinds of historical evidence remain intact, the task of historical reconstruction would go on more or less in the line described by R. G. Collingwood some decades ago, even when the ideological restrictions imposed upon the concept of reality by the spirit of historical positivism vanish. At present, however, these restrictions continue to be effective in the work of historians, even within the Christian churches. It is at this point that Christian theologians who work in the field of Biblical exegesis should challenge the spirit of historical positivism. As theologians they participate in a contest for a more appropriate understanding of reality, no less than the systematic theologian does.

Notes

1. F. Tipler, *The Physics of Immortality: Modern Cosmology, God and the Resurrection of the Dead* (New York: Doubleday, 1994).

2. Hans von Campenhausen, 'Der Ablauf der Osterereignisse und das leere Grab', 3. Aufl. 1966.
3. W. Pannenberg, *Jesus – God and Man* (Philadelphia: Westminster Press, 1968).
4. R. Pesch, *Das Markusevangelium*, 2nd edn. (Freiburg: Herder, 1980), pp. 519f., 522–40.

Chapter 5

THE RESURRECTION OF CHRIST: HOPE FOR THE WORLD

Jürgen Moltmann[1]

'*I*f Christ is not risen then our preaching is in vain and your faith is in vain' (1 Cor. 15:14). With these strong words Paul underlines the fundamental significance of Christ's resurrection for Christian faith. The Christian faith stands or falls with Christ's resurrection, because it was by raising him from the dead that God made Jesus the Christ and revealed himself as 'the Father of Jesus Christ'. At this point belief in God and the acknowledgement of Christ coincide, and ever since, for Christian faith the two have been inseparable.

Christians believe in Jesus for God's sake, and in God for Jesus' sake. Anyone who draws a dividing line between belief in God and acknowledgement of Christ does not know what the Christian faith is about. Christian faith in God is faith in the resurrection. It is only the pictures and symbols which have anything to do with the mythical world picture of Christianity's early period. In our experience belief in the resurrection is confronted and challenged by death, the fate to which everything living is subjected. Faith in the resurrection is the faith in God of lovers and the dying, the suffering and the grieving. It is the great hope which consoles us and gives us new courage.

This being so, it is a pity that there should be Christians who no doubt believe in a God, but not in Christ's resurrection. For them, Jesus turns into a historical personality who in the process of time sinks further and further into the historical past. It is only a short step to Islam from this liberal reduction of Jesus to history which we can read about in the textbooks. 'God yes, but Jesus no' is not a Christian option.

On the other hand there are Christians who, for various theoretical or personal reasons, feel that God doesn't mean a thing to them, but who still have a certain feeling for 'the man from Nazareth'. This is 'the Jesus of the atheists', the Jesus of the existentialist Albert Camus and the Marxist Milan Machovec. But then why does it have to be just Jesus who is important for humanity? Why not Buddha, Socrates and Gandhi too? 'God no, Jesus yes' is not a Christian option either.

So let us try out another approach, attempting to interpret faith in God and the confession of Christ mutually. We shall begin by looking at the early Christian accounts of the resurrection. Then we shall turn to the modern question about history and the resurrection, seeing what we are permitted to hope for, and what we ought to do. In the third section we shall step outside that paradigm of the modern world whose name is history, and shall move into the paradigm of the postmodern world – into an ecological understanding of history and nature, human history and the history of the earth. We shall ask about the future of the earth in the light of Christ's resurrection, and for this purpose we shall once more take up the patristic church's doctrine of physical redemption, so as to arrive at a new understanding of Christ's bodily nature and our own.

The special character of the resurrection faith

Jesus was crucified publicly and died publicly. But the only people to learn of his resurrection were the faithful women at his tomb in Jerusalem, and the disciples who had fled into Galilee. The disciples then returned to Jerusalem and proclaimed the crucified Jesus quite openly as the Lord and redeemer of the world, whom God had raised from the dead. Those are the relatively well-attested historical facts. And they are astonishing enough. But at the same time, all that can actually be proved about them are the assurances of the women that at Jesus' empty tomb they heard an angelic message telling them of his resurrection, and the assertions of the disciples that they had seen appearances of Christ in Galilee.

Apparently after Jesus' death many of his men and women disciples experienced a great many manifestations in which Jesus allowed himself to be seen as the Christ, who is eternally alive in God. In the earliest testimony to the resurrection we have, in 1 Corinthians, written in the year 55 or 56, Paul cites testimonies that Christ had appeared to Cephas, to the twelve, and then to five hundred brethren at once. At the end he adds himself. Paul's account is especially valuable because it is a personal record of what he himself experienced when Christ appeared to him. According to what he says, Paul 'saw' Jesus the Lord (1 Cor. 9:1), but this 'seeing' evidently took the form of an inward experience: 'It pleased God through his grace to reveal his Son *in* me' (Gal. 1:15f.). The appearance was something that happened to him unexpectedly and completely against his will, for he was a rabbi and had actually been commissioned to persecute Christians in the synagogues. 'I was seized by Christ', he says (Phil. 3:12), and this experience turned his life upside down.

We ought probably to imagine the women's experience of Christ at the tomb and the disciples' experience in Galilee as being not very different from this – if it is possible to enter imaginatively into exceptional visions of this kind at all. The witnesses all agree in reporting that they saw Jesus – the Jesus who had died – as 'the living One'. They all say that he is alive in that eternal glory of God in which he then 'appeared' to them in their earthly lives. They had visions of a supernatural light.

But at this point the interpretations already begin. It is in any case impossible to filter out the substance of these experiences in the form of naked facts detached from their subjective human interpretation. All that would emerge would be unhistorical abstractions. Pure facts are in any case unstatable. In every perception, what is experienced is interpreted with the help of ideas which the people concerned bring with them. Of course these ideas themselves are changed in the process of the perception. And in the case of experiences which turn one's world upside down, this is true to a particular degree, otherwise Saul could never have become Paul. The experiences of Christ being talked about here were apparently experiences which changed the whole of existence. In their disappointment and fear, Jesus' former disciples had fled from Jerusalem to Galilee in order to save their lives; because of these experiences, these same ex-disciples became apostles who returned to Jerusalem and risked their lives there in order to proclaim Christ 'boldly'.

Because the visionary phenomena were evidently linked with ecstatic experiences of the Spirit, they will also have passed into the pentecostal experiences of the early church, and will have continued there – the perception of Christ's presence in his appearances led on to the experience of Christ's presence in the Spirit. The early Christian faith in the resurrection was not based solely on Christ's appearances; it was at least equally strongly moved by the experience of God's Spirit. Paul therefore calls this divine

Spirit 'the life-giving Spirit' or 'the power of the resurrection'. Believing in the risen Christ means being seized by the Spirit of the resurrection.

Paul interprets the christophany he experienced with the word *apocalypsis,* and by doing so he gives the experience a special meaning: God reveals ahead of time something that is still hidden and inaccessible to the ways of arriving at knowledge which are at our disposal in the present aeon, or world time. 'The mysteries of the End-time' and of God's future new world are veiled and impenetrable under our present conditions of knowledge, because the present world of sin and violence cannot sustain the new world of God's justice and righteousness. So this divine justice and righteousness will create the present world afresh. The christophanies were not interpreted as being mystical translations into a world beyond this one. They were seen as the advance radiance of God's coming glory which will shine on the first day of the new world's creation (2 Cor. 4:6). Moreover they are all daylight visions, not dream visions in the night.

If we look at the way these christophanies and Easter visions were interpretatively perceived by the people concerned, we see that their structure has three different dimensions:

1. They were *prospective* visions of hope: the men and women saw the crucified Jesus as the living Christ in the splendour cast ahead by God's coming glory.

2. They were *retrospective* visions of remembrance: the disciples recognized Jesus from the marks of the nails and from the way he broke the bread. The One who will come is the One crucified on Golgotha.

3. They were *personal call* visions: the men and women concerned perceived in this 'seeing' their own call to apostleship: 'As the Father has sent me, even so I send you.'

The resurrection in the perspective of history

It is one thing to see Christ's resurrection in the perspective of history. That inevitably brings us up against the question: is this a historical event or an interpretation of faith? But it is another thing to see history in the perspective of Christ's resurrection. Then the question facing us is the eschatological one – the question, that is, about the end of this world's history of suffering, and the world's new creation.

History: the modern paradigm

In the seventeenth century the concept of 'history', as an all-embracing paradigm for interpreting human beings and nature, and God and the world, began to develop. In the human project of scientific and technological civilization, harmonizations with the laws of the cosmos and the earth were replaced by blueprints plotting progress from an old and obsolete time – the past – into the new time of the future. The more European domination over other peoples was pushed forward, and the more human beings subjugated nature, the more the rich multiplicity of cultural groups gave way to the unity of humanity. That great singular 'History' was born.

It was in the framework of this paradigm of 'history' that the modern science of historical studies also came into being. The historical criticism of legends of rule in church and state developed, and with it the historical awareness that sets the presence in tradition of what is past at a temporal distance, so that the past can be historicized and the present freed from the previous decisions and previous judgements of tradition. 'The true criticism of dogma is its history', said David Friedrich Strauss,[2] and made the historian the ideological critic of religious dogmas and political legends. In historical awareness, events of the past are transformed into past events.

If we look at Christ's resurrection from the standpoint of this modern paradigm 'history', using the categories of the modern historical mind, then – in spite of all the disputes – it makes no great difference whether we see the resurrection as a product of the disciples' imagination, or view it as a historical fact; for as a past event that is becoming ever more past and ever more remote, Christ's resurrection can neither determine the present nor have any relevance for the future. The modern category 'history' has already turned the happening into something past and gone; for anything historical is something that comes to pass, and then passes away.

Ernst Troeltsch certainly no longer has the last word today, even among historians, but his treatise on 'Historical and Dogmatic Method in Theology' had classic importance for the theology of the resurrection in the twentieth century.[3] Troeltsch transferred scientific methods to historical studies and named four axioms for the critical historical method as a way of arriving at soundly established knowledge. We shall put Christ's resurrection to the question by confronting it with these axioms.

1. Historical research can never do more than arrive at assessments based on probability. It can never achieve absolute knowledge. Can theology base the assurance of faith on assessments of historical probability? No.

2. There are interactions between all phenomena in historical life. They are the ontological foundation – the basis in existence – for the connections between cause and effect which apply everywhere. Is Christ's resurrection an exception, and a breach of natural law? No.

3. We can only arrive at historical understanding if we take analogy as our guideline. 'The almighty power of analogy' is based on the homogeneity of all historical happening. Can an event that has no analogy, such as Christ's resurrection, be understood in historical terms? No.

4. Objective historical knowledge, then, is subject to the principles of probability, correlation and analogy. These principles assume that history is made by human beings, not by any obscure powers, gods and demons, and that history can consequently also be known by human beings. Can we talk in a modern historical sense about the activity of a transcendent God in history generally, and about God's raising of Christ in particular? No.

If these principles determining history and historical studies are valid, then Christian theology is brought up against the fundamental question: in what category can it talk about God and Christ's resurrection at all? Troeltsch himself already complained about the schizophrenia of Christians in the modern world, for whom there was a Sunday causality in which God rules and determines history, and an everyday causality, in which all happening has its immanent, this worldly cause. Can a new 'public' theology get over this split consciousness? Or must theology detach itself from the sense of truth publicly and generally shared in modern society, in order to stand by its own truth?

The horizon of expectation and the space of experience

Historical studies do not just have history as their own object of research. They themselves are embedded in history and are part of it. So historical methods and categories have to be fitted into the metahistorical concepts and categories on which they are based. History means interaction and process between people, between human groups, classes and societies, between human beings and nature, and – not least – between human beings and what they consider to be the Absolute.

There is history as long as there is time. Time is perceived only as long as the difference between past and future exists. The difference between past and future is determined in the present presence of both – the presence of the past in remembrance, the presence of the future in hope. It is the difference between 'the space of experience' and 'the horizon of expectation' which determines the awareness of historical time. If there are no longer any expectations of future experiences, then the remembrance of past experiences fades and slips away from us too. If there are no longer any remembered experiences, then there are no expectations either. Remembrance and hope are the conditions for experiencing history. So they are also the conditions for an interest in history, and a concern about it. To experience reality as history presupposes hope for its future. Hope for the future is grounded on remembrance.

So let us look at the fundamental difference between expectation and experience, so as to unfold history in the perspective of Christ's resurrection. 'The resurrection of Christ' is a meaningful postulate only if its framework is the history which the resurrection itself throws open: the history of the liberation of human beings and nature from the power of death. In the framework of history defined in any other way, the resurrection of Christ is not a meaningful postulate at all.

79

History in the perspective of the resurrection

When we talk about Christ's resurrection from the dead we are not talking about a fact. We are talking about a process. We are talking in one and the same breath about the foundation, the future and the practical exercise of God's liberation of men and women, and his redemption of the world. So what we can *know* historically about Christ's resurrection must not be abstracted from the question of what we can hope from it, and what we have to do in its name. Kant made this series of intrinsic relations clear. It is only in the living unity of knowing, hoping and doing that Christ's resurrection can be understood in its true historical sense.

To see history in the perspective of the resurrection means participating through the Spirit in the process of the resurrection. Believing in the resurrection does not just mean assenting to a dogma and noting a historical fact. It means participating in this creative act of God's. If it were merely a historical circumstance, we should simply say: 'oh really?', register the fact, and go on living as we did before. But if it is a creative act of God's, then – if we really know and understand what it is about – we shall be born again to a new life. A faith like this is the beginning of freedom.

If God reveals himself in the resurrection of the Christ crucified in helplessness, then God is not the quintessence of power, as this was represented by the Roman Caesar; nor is he the quintessence of laws, as these are reflected in the Greek cosmos. God is the life-giving energy which makes the poor rich and lifts up the downtrodden and raises the dead. Faith in the resurrection is itself an energy which strengthens and raises people up, liberating them from the deadly illusions of power and 'having', in the perspective of life's future. The proclamation of Christ's resurrection is a meaningful statement against the horizon of the history which it itself throws open: the history of the liberation of human beings and the whole sighing creation from the powers of annihilation and death.

Understood as a confronting event which discloses the future and opens up history, Christ's resurrection is the foundation and promise of eternal life in the midst of this history of death. Paul established this connection quite definitely and explicitly: 'If the Spirit of him who has raised Jesus from the dead dwells in you, he who has raised Christ Jesus from the dead will give life to your mortal bodies also through the power of his Spirit which dwells in you' (Rom. 8:11). He links the perfect tense of Christ's resurrection with the present tense of the indwelling of the Spirit, and the present tense of the Spirit with the future tense of the resurrection of the dead. The raising of Christ is not a phrase describing a past happening. It is the name for a confronting event in the past which in the Spirit determines the present because it opens up the future of eternal life. The present-tense liberating experience of the Spirit is grounded on the perfect tense of Christ's resurrection, while the future 'giving life to mortal bodies' (which is the way Paul describes the resurrection of the dead in this passage) has its objective foundation in Christ's resurrection and is perceived through the experience of 'the life-giving Spirit'. So in talking about Christ's resurrection we have to talk about a *process* of resurrection. This process has its foundation in Christ, its dynamic in the Spirit, and its future in the true new creation of all things. Resurrection does not mean a closed fact. It means a way – the transition from death to life. But what life does this mean?

The formulation about 'giving life to mortal bodies' shows that the resurrection hope isn't concerned with another life. It has to do with the fact that this mortal life here is going to be different. Resurrection is not a consoling opium, soothing us with the promise of a better world in the hereafter. It is the energy for a rebirth of this life. The hope doesn't point to another world. It is focused on the redemption of this one. In the Spirit, resurrection is not merely expected. It is already experienced. Resurrection happens every day. In love we experience many deaths and many resurrections. We experience resurrection through the rebirth to living hope. We experience resurrection through the love which already brings us to life here and now, and we experience resurrection through liberation: 'Where the Spirit of the Lord is, there is freedom' (2 Cor. 3:17).

Because it is the beginning of the annihilation of death and the appearance of eternal life, the raising of Christ from the dead is the fact that changes everything, so it is in itself the revelation of God. As 'the Wholly Other', God is the radical criticism of this world, as Karl Barth said. As 'the One who changes everything', God is the Creator of the new world. The resurrection faith itself is already a resurrection in the energy of life. The resurrection of Christ qualifies world history, making it end-history, and sets the spaces and sectors where we experience history against the horizon of this expectation of the new creation.

Resurrection in the perspective of nature

With the beginning of modern times, the historicity of Christ's resurrection became theology's central problem, because 'history had become the modern world's great paradigm'. By history, people meant the history of human beings, as distinct from nature. Consequently a distinction was made between the humanities and the natural sciences. Nature was supposed to be the realm of necessity, history the realm of freedom. This dichotomy meant that the spirit was thought of as something outside nature, while nature was supposed to be devoid of spirit. Only medicine wavered between the humanities and the sciences. It was not until the beginning of the nineteenth century that in Europe it was finally assigned to the sciences. So are human beings nothing but nature? Are they not spirit too?

Because every woman and man is a unity of body and soul, spirit and nature being inextricably interwoven in their existence, the fundamental modern distinction between history and nature cannot be completely sustained. The paradigm 'history' does not take in the whole of reality; it splits up its wholeness. So we must go beyond this modern paradigm and develop a new one which will grasp nature and spirit, history and nature, as a unity, and will integrate what has been divided.

If we look at Christ's resurrection from this standpoint, we can see that we shall have to transpose modern 'historical' christology, or understanding of Christ, into a new *ecological* christology. This ecological christology brings us back to the patristic church's christological doctrine of the two natures, as a way of integrating nature, because we see that there can be no redemption for human beings without a redemption of the whole of perishable nature. So it is not enough to see Christ's resurrection merely as 'God's eschatological act in history'. We also have to understand it as *the first act in the new creation of the world*. Christ's resurrection is not just a historical event. It is a cosmic event too, as the Orthodox Easter liturgy and our ancient Easter hymns have always known. We have to grasp this cosmic dimension of Christ's resurrection in a new way.

Is the expression 'the raising of Christ' adequate? It is taken from Jewish apocalyptic, and is an eschatological symbol – a symbol that has to do with the end which God will bring about. Here God is the active agent – the 'doer of the deed' – and the dead Jesus is passive. Does the other phrase 'Christ's resurrection' take us any further? Logically, the theological symbol of the divine 'raising' is balanced by the anthropological symbol of the human 'resurrection' – the person who has been woken has to get up. Otherwise the waking has no effect. According to the symbol of raising, the dynamic comes from above; according to the symbol of resurrection it comes from below. Christ was not merely raised up by God. He himself rose.

Are these two symbols, taken together, sufficient for us to comprehend the mystery of Jesus? Both are metaphors for actions, either on God's part or by Jesus. But there are metaphors from nature as well describing what happened to the crucified and dead Jesus. The first is the image of Christ's 'rebirth' from the eternal Spirit of God: through the eternal Spirit Christ offered himself for us (Heb. 9:14), through the Spirit he was 'born again' to eternal life (1 Cor. 15:45).

For this Paul uses the nature image about the grain of wheat: 'It is sown corruptible; it is raised incorruptible' (1 Cor. 15:42). It is only when the grain of wheat falls into the ground and dies there, that it brings much fruit, says John (12:24), meaning Christ's death and resurrection. According to the Letter to the Colossians, Christ is 'the first-born from the dead' (1:18). So we can complement the apocalyptic symbols of God's raising and Christ's rising through the symbol of Christ's 'rebirth' from the eternal divine Spirit. The Orthodox icons make this clear: Christ was born of Mary in a cave hollowed out of the earth; out of a grave in the earth he was born again to eternal life through the Spirit. With Christ's rebirth, the rebirth of the whole cosmos begins, not just the rebirth of human beings (Matt. 19:28). His dying and his 'coming alive again' represent a transition, a transformation, a transfiguration, not a total breach and a radical new beginning.

What images should we use to describe the cosmic significance of Christ's rebirth from the divine Spirit, images from the life of nature? Of course that does not turn Christ's rebirth into a natural phenomenon, as it might be in cellular physiology; for the symbol says that he is reborn to immortal life, not to mortal life. But eternal life is life as well, and rebirth is a birth too. And this makes mortal and natural life open for analogy and also capable of analogy.

From earliest times the Christian church has celebrated Christ's resurrection and the festival of spring together, so that ever since these early times we in Europe have talked about 'Easter'. And it was at the beginning of summer that the church celebrated the experience of the Holy Spirit. The natural analogies from nature were discovered in the morning of the day, the springtime of the year, and the birth of life. So the celebration of Christ's resurrection was joined with joy over the rebirth of nature and the delight of all created beings. Morning, springtime and birth were lifted out of the natural rhythm of nature's growth and decay, its becoming and dying, and were given so enhanced a value that Christ's resurrection meant hope for the redemption of the whole of mortal nature, through the new creation of all things for eternal life.

In the perspective of human history the raising of Christ *from the dead* means that the general raising of all the dead has begun. But that is only the personal side of the hope. In the perspective of nature, the raising of Christ means that the destructive power of death, which is anti-God, is driven out of creation. Death is 'destroyed' (1 Cor. 15:26), and in the new creation there will be no more death. That is the cosmic side of the hope.

What experience of life springs from the resurrection hope? The imaginations of hope always open up the way and experience of life, and also restrict it. If someone hopes for the resurrection of the dead and the new creation in which death will be no more, that person will be possessed by the Spirit of the resurrection and will already experience now 'the powers of the world to come'. That person will be 'born again' to a living hope, to take the phrase used from earliest Christian times.

Because resurrection means the whole human being, body and soul, this living hope must already be a hope for the soul and for the body here and now. But that means that it is confronted by death's negation of everything that lives. The Christian faith maintains that it is impossible to bring life and death into harmony with one another without the resurrection hope. Ought we to accept death as a natural part of life? If so we must do without love, for love desires life, not death. Ought we to renounce the body because it is mortal? If so it would be better not to live at all, for what has never lived can never die either.

But if we affirm life because we love it, we expose ourselves to the pains of death. We can be disappointed and hurt and sad. It is the hope for the annihilation of death and for the resurrection to eternal life which makes us ready to love this life here in such a way that we become vulnerable, mortal and sad. We already experience the power of the resurrection now in love: 'We have passed out of death into life because we love the brethren', says 1 John 3:14 – and we add 'the sisters' too. In the Spirit of the resurrection hope, love can be as strong as death, because in love the victory of life over death is already experienced.

Death thrusts into this life as the violence of separation. The resurrection thrusts into this life as the power of union, and abolishes what death can do. We can experience this not just in relation to other people. We can experience it in relation to our own bodies too. Plato says that in looking forward to the death of the body, the soul elevates itself above the body and distances itself from its needs and frailties. The knowledge that we are going to die already splits human beings into soul and body in this life, and makes the soul try to dominate and repress the body because, after all, it is ultimately of no more value than the corpse buried in the ground.

But hope for what in German is bluntly called 'the resurrection of the flesh' leads to a totally different experience of the body. The *whole* human being, soul and body, is related to the divine, not just the soul; for 'male and female he created them', says the creation account. So it is not just the soul which is to be 'the temple of the Holy Spirit'. It is the body too, as Paul always stresses. But the Holy Spirit is the Spirit of life. Where the Spirit is experienced as present, the body and the soul become a unity once more. The divisions hostile to life and the conflicts addicted to death are overcome. When the fear of death dies, the fear of life disappears too.

In the image of the resurrection of the body, life and death can be brought into harmony in such a way that death doesn't have to be repressed either. In this Spirit of the resurrection I can here and now wholly live, wholly love and wholly die, for I know with certainty that I shall wholly rise again. In this hope I can love all created things, for I know that none of them will be lost.

Notes

1. This is a revised version of Chapter 5: 'The Resurrection of Christ – Hope for the World', in J. Moltmann, *Jesus Christ for Today's World* (London: SCM, 1994), pp. 71–87, translated by Margaret Kohl.
2. D. F. Strauss, *Die Christliche Glaubenslehre I* (Tübingen and Stuttgart: 1840), p. 71.
3. E. Troeltsch, 'Über Historische und Dogmatische Methode in der Theologie' (1898), in *Gesammelte Schriften II* (Tübingen: 1913), pp. 729–53; ET: 'Historical and Dogmatic Method in Theology', in *Religion and History* (Edinburgh: 1991), translated by J. L. Adams and W. F. Bense.

Chapter 6

BETWEEN THE CHERUBIM: THE EMPTY TOMB AND THE EMPTY THRONE

Rowan Williams

*T*his paper is a meditation on images, their connections and their failures. Arguing *from* iconography or patterns of imagery is always dangerous. We can't expect to establish anything very definite from simply noticing convergences in this sort of area, and I am not setting out to *prove* anything in this essay. But convergences can at least suggest paths in to a subject that arguments cannot, and, in an area where arguments – historical, philosophical, dogmatic – can be inconclusive or bitter or both, there is something to be said for coming at the issue another way.

Of course this risks being evasive or self-indulgent. I take it that this is the complaint of Professor Maurice Wiles, when he describes an earlier venture by the present writer as possibly 'shirking' confrontation with the questions of historical evidence or conceptual coherence.[1] I hope this need not be the case. As far as the historical question goes, it is clear that the scholarly analysis of the resurrection narratives, in and out of the canon, has not yielded a single and compelling resolution to the numerous difficulties that the texts pose.

To take two recent examples, the estimates of the historicity of the traditions of Jesus' burial by Crossan[2] and Lüdemann[3] are dramatically at variance: Lüdemann allowing a definite historical substratum to the record of a burial by Joseph of Arimathea; Crossan dismissing the entire tradition on the assumption of anonymous burial in a common grave. Likewise, the two disagree strongly over how the tradition of the women at the tomb is to be assessed – a politically sensitive question these days. Lüdemann regards the women as latecomers to the resurrection proclamation, Crossan seeing the Magdalene tradition as competing on a fairly even footing with other stories, and, like them, functioning as ammunition in a set of struggles for authority in the primitive communities. Elisabeth Schüssler Fiorenza, in her recent essay in feminist Christology,[4] would go further in maintaining that the empty tomb tradition, that is, the tradition of a primitive resurrection proclamation by women, may be more primitive than the apparition stories, which are clearly designed to 'authorize' the male leaders of the community. Those familiar with film and fiction will recognize the dramatically effective use to which something like this last view can be put if they recall the reconstruction of the resurrection in *Jesus of Montreal*, and the account of Mary Magdalene's experience in Anita Mason's exceptional novel, *The Illusionist*.[5]

Nor have we yet a clear consensus about the actual genre of (at least) the canonical resurrection narratives. The attempt to find parallels in the Hellenistic novel seems to have been abandoned; reference to *Chaereas and Callirhoë*, with its striking episode of the unexpected discovery of an empty tomb, seems less interesting when we know (what some who have discussed the parallels seem not to know) that the work is from the second Christian century.[6] Alsup's suggestion that we look to stories of angelic manifestation in the Old Testament for analogues is a good and, I think, sound one. But, while it helps provide a rhetorical and narrative hinterland for the recognition stories (Luke 24, John 20 in particular), it does not take us very far with the origins of the tomb tradition itself.[7]

Now, given this situation in the scholarly world, we have a number of options. It is possible, of course, to decide that one or other reconstruction on the market is the correct one – this is the historian's privilege, and the historian knows that such a decision is vulnerable – as vulnerable in this case as, for example (to turn to a field where I have a little more competence), the decision that the two letters of Bishop Alexander of Alexandria about the beginnings of the Arian crisis in the early fourth century have been put in the wrong order by most twentieth-century scholars (I think they have, but I have not managed to convince the majority of experts in the period . . .). Here one takes a position, knowing that it is contestable, willing to provide a reasonable amount of back-up, but acknowledging that judgements will simply vary. This is fine for the historian; and for someone who has no particular investment in the resurrection narratives, the option for Lüdemann or Crossan (say) as regards Joseph of Arimathea need not be more charged than my options about the correspondence of Bishop Alexander. But, of course, these narratives have a life of their own outside the study –

in liturgy, piety and, indeed, theological construction.

Quite a lot of readers will not want to leave the matter where the historian would. So we could say that the need is to work at the historical material until it becomes clear that there is only one historical judgement that could sensibly or responsibly be made: thus the resurrection becomes a matter of accessible *public* truth, something anyone could in principle know, even if some were just obstinate in refusing to see what was under their noses. Pannenberg's is the name most often associated with this,[8] though in a less sophisticated form it remains the staple of a lot of apologetic writing on the subject by Christians. This strategy has at least two risks, though. By assuming a historical conclusion, it will always be suspect on purely methodological grounds to the uncommitted student: there *must* be a question about the method of a scholar who really does know what she is looking for, who really does know what is to be proved (at all costs); and the identification of belief in the resurrection with acceptance of a set of demonstrable historical facts raises the difficult issue of how 'the resurrection' is being defined. Notoriously, the demonstration of the emptiness of the tomb as a matter of history does not entail the veracity of subsequent visions, missionary commissions, or whatever.

It is possible simply to leave the historical questions unresolved and to settle for a proclamation of the resurrection that regards them as essentially irrelevant. In some sense or other, the work of Jesus is not concluded; the crucified is announced and identified as the risen one, 'risen into the *kerygma*', in the memorable phrase that summarized Bultmann's approach to this.[9] But even here, in what seems to be a bold and clear resolution to the problems of understanding and responding to the scriptural texts, we cannot avoid noticing that there is an implicit option buried in the overt one: if the tomb was empty, there is no substantive theological conclusion to be drawn from that. Whatever we find to say about the resurrection, it will not include anything that depends on the non-availability of Jesus' corpse. This option is not, therefore, quite as agnostic as it looks. It will effectively be claiming that what is vital to Christian discourse about the resurrection can be stated exclusively in terms of what happens to the minds and hearts of believers when proclamation is made that the victim of the crucifixion is the one through whom God continues to act and speak. And, while this is near the centre of what we must say theologically about the resurrection, it leaves us with the conclusion that the narrative form of the New Testament proclamation is pretty incidental to the substance of the proclamation itself. There may be theological as well as literary–theoretical queries worth raising here, if that is indeed what is being suggested.

So I return to the starting point of this reflection. Is there anything in the structure, the patterning of the stories, which might bring us in to the substance of resurrection belief by a different route? My title indicates one such possibility. The angels at the tomb in John's gospel are seated one at the head and the other at the feet of the grave slab. As commentators like Barrett have noted, this is a distinctive addition to the picture given in the other gospels, and, as with other deliberate Johannine narrative expansions, we can reasonably ask what it is doing here.[10] Iconographically, it recalls, of course, the mercy-seat of the ark, flanked by the cherubim.[11] What I want to propose is that – whether or not this is what John had in mind, which would be practically impossible to settle one way or the other – this at least focuses for us the possibility of seeing the empty tomb narratives as saying something about the character of divine presence or action that badly needs saying if we are not to mistake the whole direction of the gospel witness to the resurrection. For the cherubim flanking the ark define a space where God would be if God were anywhere (the God of Judah is *the one who* sits between the cherubim or even 'dwells' between the cherubim); but there is no image between the cherubim. If you want to see the God of Judah, this is where he is and is not: to 'see' him is to look into the gap between the holy images. What is tangible and accessible, what can be carried in procession or taken to war as a palladium is not the image of God but the throne of God, the place where he is not. Whatever the historical origins of the iconography of the ark of the covenant, by the time of the composition of our canonical texts it is clear that YHWH is not capable of being represented definitively or indeed at all except as the one who is invisibly enthroned on the *kapporeth* of the ark. And if John does mean us to catch an allusion here, we must suppose that it is to this non-representable, non-possessable dimension of the paradoxical manifestation of God to God's people; it may even connect with the stories of non-recognition which John and his editor or continuator in the final chapter of the gospel as we have it clearly find so fertile a ground for narrative meditation. But whatever was in the evangelist's mind, the space between the angels is no bad metaphor for a number of features of the tomb tradition that should concentrate our minds theologically.

If we read the resurrection narratives as having to do with the Jewish proscription of idolatry, in a new and distinctive key, not only the empty tomb tradition, but the very confusion and historical uncertainty surrounding it may be of theological import, insofar as both the narrative and the nest of critical questions around it make *closure* so difficult. The stories themselves are about difficulty, unexpected outcomes, silences, errors, about what is not readily accessible or readily understood. We have a variety of stories, not easily reconcilable as regards location or timing or *dramatis personae*, stories which, while they appear to presuppose a background of prophetic anticipation are in fact about laborious recognition, as often as not, the gradual convergence of experience and pre-existing language in a way that inexorably changes the register of the language. In short, it is not a straightforward matter to say what the gospels understand by the resurrection of Jesus; but this seems to have something to do with the fact that the Christian communities of the last quarter of the first Christian century didn't find it all that straightforward either.

The stories as we have them are, as we might now say, ideologically underdetermined; we cannot display the ways in which they are controlled by specific theological interests, though we can, as already indicated, identify with reasonable clarity some of the interests at work (there is no point in disputing the manifest truth that the stories in the gospels and in 1 Corinthians reflect struggles for authoritative status in the communities). The texts are *shaped* by such concerns; but we cannot decisively show how the narrative genre of the tomb tradition in particular is fully *determined* by the political agenda, or even how all the narrative particulars in the various vision stories (particularly the motif of non-recognition) can be anchored in these interests.

This indeterminacy in the resurrection stories is one way of saying what the content of the stories is meant to convey: that Jesus of Nazareth who was crucified is not confined in the past, and that this non-confinement is more than just some sort of survival in the minds or memories of Christian believers. Belief in the resurrection, in Christian scripture and Christian theology, affirms that the action of God in and through the acts of the human subject Jesus continues to be associated with Jesus after his death and to be accessible through his human identity.

What exactly this means is immensely complex, once we start trying to spell it out. It means at least that in the community stemming from that first community of the friends of Jesus, those who had received his announcement of the Kingdom that was available to outcasts and sinners, God continues to do what was done in Jesus' ministry, that is, to re-form a people whose corporate calling was to show the world at large what was the scope and resource of divine love. Yet to say only that would leave us with the risk of identifying the actions of God with the acts of the community, which becomes a dangerous and potentially nonsensical and blasphemous claim when the community's history and administration is so manifestly vulnerable to distortion and betrayal.

Once again, the resurrection narratives themselves insist that the risen Jesus is not grasped, owned or perfectly obeyed by his friends. The Church continues to *attend* to Jesus to discover what it is to be; and it is this attention that constitutes the heart of the oddity and difficulty of resurrection belief. It is not meditation on the teaching of the founder – this can be of much significance, but it hardly exhausts what Christian scripture means by relation with the living Jesus, and it was clearly of variable significance in the early communities, given the uneven state of recollections of Jesus' teaching and the evident freedom taken for granted by the evangelists in reordering or reworking the traditions of Jesus' words. It is not reflection on the inspiring example of a hero; of course, it is common to appeal to the example of Jesus as innocent and non-retaliating victim, but this is not the same as the appeal to a continuing and determinative presence that qualifies the believer's relation to God in certain focal respects. And, although visionary encounter with the glorified Lord had a very important role in the life of the early communities, notably and visibly in something like the Johannine Apocalypse as a guarantee of the authority of the teacher, it is clear that this is debatable territory. It should not be identified as the common ground that might hold together communities as diverse as those addressed by Paul and John.

Jesus is 'in heaven' until the last days; that is one way of putting it. In his earthly life he initiates a redrawing of the boundaries of God's people in such a way that response to his invitation becomes decisive for the relation of persons to God. Response to him remains decisive in just this way (even if, as in Matthew 25, people do not know that it is he to whom they are responding); so that, at the end of time, what is uncovered is the history of the world as a history of response to or rejection of what Jesus offers. He remains 'there' as the point of reference, God's standard of judgement.

Jesus is active as bestower of the 'spirit' that enables us to relate to God as he did; he is the cause of the fact that we can pray as we do (as he did). But he is not the cause of this in the sense of an increasingly remote historical origin; we do not simply continue his practice. Attention to or openness to his presence (faith?) makes possible the receiving of new kinds of prayer and awareness of, or confidence in, God as a *gift*.

Jesus is active in the corporate life of the Church; what he gives to human beings, he gives in significant part through the mediation of the common life, which is itself his 'body', his material presence in the world, though it does not exhaust his identity or activity. To be incorporated into the community by its initiation rite is to become a 'bearer' of what Jesus has to give to other believers, to be entrusted with his renewing or creating agency by means of a ritual setting-aside of 'ordinary' identity. What is distinctive is that this ritual change of identity is not confined to the ritual context, but continues in the practical interactions of the common life. And the further ritual of the 'Lord's Supper' dramatizes all this; the concrete food and drink of the meal is interpreted as the material presence of Jesus, and the conduct, the 'style', of the meal, so Paul argues, is supposed to display the character of the community as itself the body, the material thereness, of Jesus (and when it fails to do this, the community comes under severe, even annihilating, judgement).

We could go on, summarizing and synthesizing the ways in which Christian scripture evokes the idea of continuing personal presence on the part of Jesus. The claim is certainly not that Jesus survived death, or even that he *will* survive indefinitely; it is that he continues to give shape and definition to the act of God initiated in the history of Israel and in his ministry. He is, so to speak, 'held' in the divine action, his identity and human priorities as proclaimer of a Kingdom for the hopeless and impure and materially or morally destitute becoming the channel for God's work of reconciliation. What God did in the ministry is what God still is doing. The mediaeval image of God the Father holding in his arms the cross on which Jesus hangs, displaying him to the onlooker, captures something of this. God's act continues to 'display' Jesus as the form of the divine agency in the renewal of God's people and the universalizing of their calling. We could perhaps express this by saying that the continuity of Jesus' identity as 'other' rests on the action of God, not on the minds of human beings. That Jesus is alive is not a function of the excellent human memory of the Christian community, its profound closeness to the God of Jesus or its vivid evocation of a deceased founder.

The belief that Jesus is alive in any of the senses outlined above amounts to claiming that his 'story' is not over; the narrative of what Jesus did is not a completed thing, as the author of the fourth gospel characteristically reminds us in saying that the whole world could not contain the full record of the acts of Jesus. Thus, controversy in the earliest Church is not, typically, about the 'ownership' and the correct transmission and interpretation of a foundational narrative and set of teachings, but about access to the 'spirit' of Jesus – a far more annoyingly nebulous and irresoluble kind of conflict, as Christian history amply shows – which is no doubt why debates over the sacred text do emerge by the third and fourth Christian centuries as the central form of theological debate.

There is, it seems, an unavoidable untidiness in Christian talk about authority and authorization, in that the foundational texts display a haziness of focus as to the priority of any one claimant among the witnesses of the risen Jesus, and, even more strikingly, what some scholars have seen as a quite deliberate polemic against such claims, in the shape of the original ending of Mark's gospel. This, it is argued, is not to be read as an apologetic explanation of why the empty tomb story did not circulate sooner, but as a conscious splitting-off of the reality of the resurrection from the competing claims of visionaries (whose diverse chronologies are reflected in the awkward juxtaposition in 1 Corinthians 15 of what look like rival accounts privileging Cephas and James respectively). What belief in the resurrection affirms is something other than the authority of witnesses. The risen Jesus is not, for Mark, available for work in the negotiating of the Church's business, and the empty tomb (combined, of course, with Mark's radical scepticism about the wisdom or insight of the Twelve) serves to keep empty the seat of ultimate authority in the Church. In the terms of my governing metaphor, the empty tomb is precisely an empty throne or *cathedra*.

Elisabeth Schüssler Fiorenza's recent treatment of the question offers a similar reading, though it works with a rather undialectical opposition of absence and presence in the stories, and slips rapidly into what might be an over-reductive identification of the Risen One with those involved in the struggle for justice.[12] She argues that, while it is difficult, perhaps impossible, to settle as a matter of historical certainty or even probability whether the story of the women at the tomb or the predominantly male tradition of apparitions came first, it is theologically enlightening to look at the whole question of the significance of the resurrection through a 'privileged' reading of the tomb tradition. This narrative affirms that death, pain and injustice are where God is *not*, at least not in the sense that the experience of these things automatically carries divine meanings (Schüssler Fiorenza here pursues her consistent critique of what she sees as the Christian sacralizing of pain and passivity). It also honours the 'honouring' of the victims of oppression on the part of the faithful women at the cross and the grave; and, above all, it announces that the Risen One is 'going before' into Galilee, into the place where the practice of the new order of God's *basileia* has been initiated.

The empty tomb does not signify absence but presence: it announces the Resurrected One's presence on the road ahead, in a particular space of struggle and recognition such as Galilee. The Resurrected One is present in the 'little ones', in the struggles for survival of those impoverished, hungry, imprisoned, tortured and killed, in the wretched of the earth . . . Jesus is going ahead – not going away.[13]

The contrast is between a Risen One who is present both in the suffering and in those working against injustice for the sake of the Kingdom, and a Risen Lord who has removed himself to heaven, where he may be 'seen' by the privileged and the spiritually gifted. In the latter context, the concrete outrage of crucifixion is increasingly obscured by the treatment of Jesus' sufferings as religiously necessary, and so in a sense removed from their proper setting in a political struggle. To engage properly with Schüssler Fiorenza's passionate critique of a *theologia crucis* would take up far more space than we have here, though I should have to say that I think it suffers from the pressure to construct an 'ideal type' of what she calls 'kyriarchal' theology (theology preoccupied with domination and its legitimacy). But there is a point of substance in her argument as a whole.

The resurrection belief, as laid out in Christian scripture, is ideologically messy. It incorporates major tensions between presence and absence, legitimations and subversions. The empty tomb *is* – and here, I think, Schüssler Fiorenza smoothes out the surface a little – an absence, in the sense that the Risen One is not there for the legitimation of any particular programme. Even the crucially important themes of the identification of God with the powerless and oppressed and the 'honouring' of love and solidarity offered to them do not exhaust what the narrative says, in the sense that the absence at the tomb prevents the risen Jesus becoming simply a heavily freighted code for the needs and dignities of the oppressed. This is an equation that would rob the figure of the Risen One of its 'freedom' to judge and transform, to speak, even in the context of the struggle for the sake of God's *basileia*, for God rather than human enterprise and aspiration. And the 'presence' of the Risen One, even as ascended to heaven and active through visionaries or prophets, is, as I have suggested, a presence other than that of a foundational tradition, other than the beginnings of a succession of leadership, because it ascribes to the Risen One in heaven something like agency and liberty, over against the community and its leaders. This may be obscured and distorted, even in our earliest materials; but it is seldom so straightforwardly a tool of institutional legitimation as a reading of Schüssler Fiorenza might suggest. Reading the apparition stories and the tomb stories together can be one effective way of preserving or highlighting the elements of absence and subversion contained in the tomb stories and allowing them to shape our reading of the apparitions. Once again, Luke 24 and John 21 seem to be working on just this frontier of indeterminacy and destabilization of any simple appeal to legitimating visions.

What I have been proposing is that the empty tomb tradition is, theologically speaking, part of the Church's resource in resisting the temptation to 'absorb' Jesus into itself, and thus part of what its confession of the divinity of Jesus amounts to in spiritual and political practice. Jesus is not the possession of the community, not even as 'raised into the kerygma', because he is alive, beyond qualification or risk, he 'lives to God'. The freedom of Jesus to act, however we unpack that deceptively simple statement, is not exhausted by what the community is doing or thinking – which allows us to say that Jesus' role for the community continues, vitally, to be that of judge, and that those who are charged with speaking authoritatively for or in the community stand in a very peculiar and paradoxical place. The distance from the community that is built into their role has to be something other than a claim to share the kind of distance that exists between the risen Jesus and the community. They remain under the judgement of the Risen One, along with the rest of the community, and their task is to direct attention away from themselves to Jesus, to reinforce the community's awareness of living under Jesus' judgement. The point at which they claim to foreclose the judgement of the risen Jesus is the point at which they occlude the reality of the continuing life or freedom of Jesus. Their rationale is to remind the community of the danger of swallowing Jesus up in its own life and practice; but they have to be aware themselves of the enormous risk of identifying their own 'difference' from the rest of the community with the difference of God. Ideally, the fact that ordained ministry operates with sacramental symbols designed to emphasize the presence of Jesus in his own proper difference ought to be a safeguard against the rampant ideologizing of clerical power. To say that this is not always how it has worked is an understatement of epic dimensions.[14]

The tomb tradition, then, should be the ground of certain kinds of questions put by the Church to itself, especially as regards its attitudes to institutional authority. Just as the focus of Israel's religious integrity in the canonical period was an empty throne, a deliberate repudiation of a graspable image, an absence reflected in the strange formulation of the divine name in Exodus 3, so for the community of the Christian covenant there is a fundamental ungraspability about the source of whatever power or liberty is at work in the community, a quality most easily comparable to that of a contemporary personal other. To vary the metaphor, the silence with which Mark's gospel ends indicates that the speaker of the gospel and the subject of the gospel as a narration is not himself *silenced*. It is not just a homiletic point to say that the 'missing ending' of Mark's text is the response of the reader or community of readers rather than a textual lacuna of some sort.[15] The narrative of Jesus is not finished, therefore not in any sense controlled, even by supposedly 'authorized' tellers of the story; his agency continues, now inseparable from the narrative of God's dealings with God's people, and so his story cannot be simply and decisively told.

The telling of the story of his life and death is, as in Mark above all, but also in the other gospels in varying degree, a process designed to bring the believer to the point of recognition that this is not a life exhausted in any text or ensemble of texts, in any performance or ensemble of performances. Jesus remains subject of his history. What 'controls' what can be said of Jesus is the record of his own historical and political practice, in life and death – his historical acts and sufferings, which specify the kind of thing it makes sense to say of him (proscribing, for example, any discourse about Jesus that leaves him identified with uncriticized power, systemic exclusion, resentment or violence); not just anything may be said of Jesus, but the determination of that 'not just anything' does not lie with a Church into which the life of Jesus has been absorbed without remainder. In this sense, the empty tomb serves to mark in the Church's reflection the unfinished business of the historical Jesus: he is not a dead founder, but neither is he a heavenly Lord whose power and very identity is untrammelled by any record of historical acts and sufferings. The problematic space in which this 'neither/nor' has to work is what the tomb tradition protects.

In short, I should want to claim that the story of the empty tomb is not in fact incidental or secondary in the exposition of what the resurrection means theologically. The form of New Testament proclamation, the *mélange* of stories about the empty tomb, about 'authorizing' apparitions and about misrecognitions and epiphanies in the experience of unnamed or ambiguous figures (Magdalene, the disciples going to Emmaus), is bound up with the substance. Without these narratives, the Church is left with a problem as to how it will avoid making belief in the resurrection simply a belief in its own capacities, making present the Christ who is 'going ahead', not where he has been laid.

But, it will be asked, does this mean that I think belief in the empty tomb as an historical fact is essential to belief in the resurrection? This is a deeply unfashionable conclusion, and immediately runs into the problem of the immense variety of possible conclusions as to the tomb tradition from the point of view of historical and critical enquiry; it may seem to be limiting in advance what such enquiry may turn up. I don't think there is any short cut here; as I have already indicated, I am not happy with either an apologetic colonizing of historical study or a theologically dictated indifference to history. The underlying issue is whether what is so unsatisfactorily called dogmatic theology has any identity or integrity of its own. If the answer to that is yes, if there is a proper and disciplined mode of reflection on the 'grammar' of the assertions of Christian faith, it is open to the theologian *as* theologian to say that there are identifiable moral and spiritual issues for the Church involved in what is said about the character of the resurrection of Jesus, and that a rendering of that belief in primarily 'internalized' terms brings grave difficulties. The empty throne, the space between the cherubim, is filled by identifying Jesus with a dead teacher or a living memory – with a human construct or the object of human mental activity, rather than with the aniconic and paradoxical 'presence' of the God of the covenant.

The catch is that all this would be just as true if we were able confidently to point to a demonstrable historical miracle, a phenomenon that would give us a clearer grasp of what the risen identity is like (i.e. like a resuscitated physical body). To affirm the theological significance, indeed cruciality, of the tomb tradition obliges us to say that the continuing life or presence or agency of Jesus of Nazareth is *material* in the sense that it is not a matter of mental operations on the part of believers. That materiality is associated with the historical realities of community and sacraments and transfigured persons, but it is not completely exhausted in these, nor can the scriptural accounts be translated without remainder into talk about these things. But a speculative confidence about what more is to be said, any pretence at a quasi-scientific discussion of the character of the risen body, takes us back again to a strategy for filling the gap between the cherubim. Is it so intolerable a conclusion for theology that it has to admit what it cannot say here? I believe this is only evasive if it refuses to map out the ways in which the tomb narratives work towards a salutary theological critique of the community of faith. If that is an uncomfortable task, picking a path between 'conservative fundamentalism and liberal existentialism', well, then it is an uncomfortable task.[16]

Dogmatics cannot solve an historical question; the orthodoxies of modern scholarship are correct, and to deny this is to deny the proper integrity of scholarship itself. But where scholarship returns again and again to an historical aporia, the theologian may be pardoned for taking this as matter for reflection. If the issues remain genuinely open, theology may well consider, as suggested earlier, that the indeterminacy of scholarly analysis may be interwoven with the indeterminacy of the various narratives themselves. They do not fall tidily into familiar genres; they do not easily present themselves as fulfilments of prior expectation. (It is worth noting the sharp contrast between the numerous references to fulfilment of prophecy in both infancy and passion narratives and the total absence of such formulae in all the resurrection stories; there are references to the fulfilment of Jesus' prophecies and general appeals, as in 1 Corinthians 15, to the fulfilment of the scriptures, but no correlation of specific incidents as in the other contexts.) They are painfully untidy stories, reflecting sometimes all too plainly the various political interests at work in the formulation of the tradition, yet containing more than those interests can manage. The central image of the gospel narratives is not any one apparition but the image of an absence, an image of the failure of images, which is also an absence that confirms the reality of a creative liberty, an agency not sealed and closed, but still obstinately engaged with a material environment and an historical process. Perhaps we really cannot say much more; not least because, to turn once more to Anita Mason's novel, 'There is a kind of truth which, when it is said, becomes untrue.' The theologian's job may be less the speaking of truth, in a context such as this, than the patient diagnosis of untruths, and the reminding of the community where its attention belongs.

Notes

1. Maurice Wiles, 'A Naked Pillar of Rock', in *Resurrection. Essays in Honour of Leslie Houlden*, eds. Stephen Barton and Graham Stanton (London: SPCK, 1994), pp. 116–27, particularly pp. 122–3.
2. John Dominic Crossan, *The Historical Jesus. The Life of a Mediterranean*

Jewish Peasant (Edinburgh: T. & T. Clark, 1991), particularly pp. 391–4 and chapter 15 passim.

3. Gerd Lüdemann, *The Resurrection of Jesus. History, Experience, Theology* (London: SCM, 1994), pp. 44–5.

4. Elisabeth Schüssler Fiorenza, *Jesus: Miriam's Child, Sophia's Prophet. Critical Issues in Feminist Christology* (London: SCM, 1995), pp. 119–28; see below for some further discussion of this proposal.

5. London: Abacus, 1983, pp. 143–5.

6. The allusion is made by E. Schillebeeckx, *Jesus. An Experiment in Christology* (London: Collins, 1979), p. 341, in the context of a discussion of alleged genres of 'rapture' stories involving the absence of a corpse. The whole account of such a supposed genre or family of genres is badly flawed, and the text of Chariton's novel has nothing at all to do with 'rapture' (the episode is about grave-robbery). Unfortunately, Pheme Perkins repeats the reference in her generally admirable and comprehensive *Resurrection. New Testament Witness and Contemporary Reflection* (London: Geoffrey Chapman, 1984), p. 150.

7. J. E. Alsup, *The Post-Resurrection Appearance Stories of the Gospel Tradition. A History-of-Tradition Analysis* (London: SPCK, 1975).

8. Classically laid out in W. Pannenberg, *Jesus – God and Man* (London: SCM, 1968), particularly pp. 98–106.

9. For a fine summary of Bultmann's perspective, see Gareth Jones, *Bultmann. Towards a Critical Theology* (Cambridge: Polity Press/Blackwell, 1991), pp. 51–62.

10. C. K. Barrett, *The Gospel According to St John* (London: SPCK, 1956), p. 469.

11. This is noted by Westcott, *The Gospel According to St John* (London: John Murray, 1882), p. 291, but is not discussed by most more recent exegetes.

12. Westcott, *St John*, note 4.

13. Ibid., p. 126.

14. I have attempted some discussion of this in 'Women and the Ministry: A Case for Theological Seriousness', Monica Furlong, *Feminine in the Church* (London: SPCK, 1984), pp. 11–27.

15. Cf. N. T. Wright, *The New Testament and the People of God* (London: SPCK, 1992), pp. 140–3 for a comparable picture applied to the Christian scriptures as a whole.

16. Cf. Christopher Morse, *Not Every Spirit. A Dogmatics of Christian Disbelief* (Valley Forge, PA: Trinity Press, 1994), p. 159.

Chapter 7

CHRIST'S BODY IN ITS FULLNESS:
RESURRECTION AND THE LIVES OF THE SAINTS

David McCarthy Matzko

Introduction

*T*his chapter considers the lives of the saints not as singular individuals but as heuristic for the identity of the church. Put simply, the saints are the embodiment of God's grace and people of God's blessed way in the world. This embodied character of grace follows logically from the incarnation, from the resurrection of Christ's body, and from the gift of the Spirit conforming people into the way of God in Christ. The first part of the chapter deals with the resurrection of the body. It takes Paul's treatment of the topic in 1 Corinthians 15 as its point of departure, and focuses on the resurrection as key to God's solidarity with humanity and the (re-)making of the human body in conformity to Christ. The second part of the chapter enquires about the significance and the sanctity of the lives of the saints. In the end, Jacob serves as our representative figure, not because of his virtue, but despite his vice. Regardless of strictly moral questions, Jacob's life is recognized and remembered as part of the lineage of God's promises and presence to the world. Likewise, it is through the saints that we find ourselves heirs of the blessed, holy, gracious way of God.

Resurrection of the Body

The resurrection is both an event of God's incarnation in Jesus Christ and an event in the lives of those who follow, believe and gather in God's name. These two sides of the resurrection cannot be separated, insofar as the Christian doctrine of God's Trinity will not permit the presence of God in Christ to be divided in any substantial sense from God's activity in Spirit. The resurrection of Christ's body is a generative event for the Spirit's incarnation in the church. These two events are inseparable, and the connection between them is the human body – Christ's incarnation, his resurrected body, and the body of Christ, the church. The body is the necessary link because humans do not merely *have* bodies. Rather (barring the reductionism of sociobiology or logical positivism), it is more appropriate to say that humanity is 'bodiliness' and therefore that the body is the only suitable vessel for humanity's reconciliation with God.

For Christian theology, human bodiliness is given its essential character through the incarnation. Christ does not simply wear the cloak of an already-complete humanity; on the contrary, the incarnation of God as human flesh constitutes the human body as reconciled to God. This reconciled humanity reveals humanity in its true form. And the form is not abstract. The incarnation does not bring together general ideas of God or humanity, but is constituted, in the particular, through the story of God's reconciliation in Jesus Christ and the Holy Spirit. The cross and resurrection, along with Jesus' proclamation and ministry, reveal the precise character of God's incarnation in human bodiliness. In this sense, the resurrection of Christ's body necessitates some account of human participation with God as a set of concrete, worldly, bodily events. For the moment, let us call this concrete continuation of bodiliness 'the lives of the saints'.

Our route to a fuller account of sainthood is Paul's discourse on the resurrection of the body in 1 Corinthians 15. In the passage, Paul is answering questions from previous correspondence and rebutting claims that rival the gospel which he has proclaimed among the people of Corinth. But also, in usual fashion, the questions or contending claims are not made explicit in the letter. Do some fear (as the Thessalonians do) that those who have died will not participate in God's coming kingdom? Do the Corinthians believe that the resurrected spirit will be separated from their dying bodies? Are they skeptical of the resurrection of the body because they cannot imagine how (or why) a decomposing corpse would be raised to life? Do some in Corinth believe that their spirits have already transcended their physical bodies?[1] Whatever challenge or enquiry initiates Paul's response, the foundation of his own account is clear. He takes for granted that Christ has been raised from the dead. Paul is concerned not so much to 'prove' the resurrection as to provide what we will call the 'intra-systematic' coherence of the resurrection of the body with the whole of the proclamation of the gospel.[2]

Three aspects of this intra-systematic coherence pertain directly to our topic of the lives of the saints. First, we should note that Paul argues for the integrity of our bodies in terms of the newness of our lives in Christ. From the start, he assumes as self-evident that our bodies are inseparable from our spiritual redemption.[3] He holds that the completeness with which God has established our redemption requires the fullness of our transformation in body and spirit. However, despite his assertions about this psychosomatic unity, Paul does admit that he lacks knowledge about what will constitute our resurrected corporeality. Nevertheless, he is not deterred by the limits of human knowledge. He asserts that we, undoubtedly, will be changed and that our new bodies will be appropriate to the glory that we will share in heaven.

Paul explains his claim through an analogy of the seed, noting the difference between the seed and the grain that grows from it.

> What you sow does not come to life unless it dies. And as for what you sow, you do not sow the body that is to be, but a bare seed, perhaps of wheat or some other grain. But God gives it a body as he has chosen, and to each kind of seed its own body. (1 Cor. 15:36–8)[4]

> So it is with the resurrection of the dead. What is sown is perishable, what is raised is imperishable . . . It is sown a physical body, it is raised a spiritual body. If there is a physical body, there is also a spiritual body. (1 Cor. 15:42, 44)

The significance of the analogy for us is Paul's assertion that our 'bodiliness', however it is constituted, is inextricably bound together with our salvation. The point is entirely consistent with Paul's exhortations elsewhere. In each of his letters, he calls Christian communities to use their bodies in ways appropriate to their new life in Christ. Bodies are important not only in the physical presence of the community as the body of Christ, but also in what its members eat or do not eat, in how they eat together, and in their sexual relations. Paul's claims about the resurrection cohere with his concerns for the integrity of the body of Christ. He calls the Christians in Rome, for instance, 'to present your bodies as a living sacrifice, holy and acceptable to God, which is your spiritual worship' (Rom. 12:1). Our point, then, is that human bodiliness is integral to the fullness of life 'in Christ'.

A second matter of coherence for Paul is that the resurrection is not an isolated event. It is not isolated from Jesus' death on the cross and the soteriological significance of these events for all humanity. While not isolated, we have to admit that Paul's emphasis on the cross and resurrection tends to truncate his account of the gospel.[5] He writes little about the details of Jesus' life and gives infrequent mention of Jesus' teachings. Nevertheless, Paul does provide a wider context for making the resurrection intelligible as God's salvific work. He holds Christ's death and resurrection in focus through his proclamation that they are indeed saving events – set within the long history of God's redemptive activity in covenant with Israel. Jesus Christ, the Son of God, takes on human flesh – is humbled, faithful and obedient, dies and is buried – so that we might be sanctified, set apart for God, and share in the redemptive power of the resurrection. Christ's resurrection is significant, not because a dead body has been revived, but because it is God's action in shaping a landscape through which the world is reconciled to God. The resurrection is not isolated from God's saving activity and human participation in that redemption.

From this soteriological context of the resurrection, a third element of the resurrection's 'intra-systematic' coherence follows: Christ's resurrection provides a 'completed-image' or 'end-picture' of human participation in God's reconciliation. Paul believes that Christ's resurrection hinges on our participation in his resurrected life, and vice versa. This connection is both the first principle of his argument and its conclusion.

> Now if Christ is proclaimed as raised from the dead, how can some of you say there is no resurrection of the dead? If there is no resurrection of the dead, then Christ has not been raised; and if Christ has not been raised, then our proclamation has been in vain and your faith has been in vain. (1 Cor. 15:12–14)

Concerning the lives of the saints, this interdependence between the risen Christ and human participation has a twofold significance. On one hand, Christ's death and resurrection are inextricably bound to our continuing life in the world (since God has made a life of redemption possible through Christ). On the other hand, the resurrection is a condition for the completeness of our resurrected lives in God's coming kingdom.

For Paul, baptism is a centrepiece of participation in God's holy work. Baptism in the one Spirit of Christ is baptism into one body of the people of God (1 Cor. 12:13, Gal. 3:27–9). In this sense, Christ's bodily resurrection is a condition for the church to be a pilgrim people, i.e. the body of Christ on a journey to live into the image of which it is made. From beginning to end, we are conformed to the resurrection. In baptism, we die with Christ, we are raised, and 'we will certainly be united with him in a resurrection like his' (Rom. 6:5). The resurrection points to the end of our pilgrimage and to our complete conformity to the way of God in Christ.

In sum, the three points that we have gleaned from Paul's exposition in 1 Corinthians 15 are: (1) the integrity of the body in the context of resurrected life; (2) the intelligibility of the resurrection when set within a soteriological framework; and (3) the resurrection as a landscape for our conformity to the image of God. These three points provide opportunity to explain the link between the resurrection and the saints. How does the resurrection of the body make possible the lives of the saints? Consider our three points in reverse order.

First, the saints are those who, by the grace of God, have reached the good end of human life – communion with God in a holy community of brothers and sisters where love of God and love of neighbour have come together in their completeness. This 'end-oriented' definition applies particularly when individual persons are identified, remembered, and venerated as saints. Sainthood in this framework is a recognition that St Francis, for example, has entered into community with others in incomprehensible nearness to God. To call Francis or any other person a saint is not to preclude the fact that many unnamed persons have also reached the good human end. To name Francis as a saint is to say that he is one of our best candidates for identifying someone who has completed the journey for certain, and to recognize that he has reached the end puts great weight on the path of life which he has taken.

This 'end-picture' definition may seem to be the primary use of the word 'saint,' especially since it allows us to recognize and set apart particular saintly individuals. But logically, or theologically, this definition depends on a more general account of holiness and sainthood. The general definition emerges from the second point we retrieved from 1 Corinthians 15: Christ's resurrection is inherently soteriological, that is, it is intelligible within the history of God's redemptive activity. Likewise, sainthood is not only the end but also the form and direction of salvation. Because the saints are those who are drawn near to God's holiness, sainthood is nothing other than salvation when considered from the human side. It is the journey for all of us. For instance, 'saints' are those who Paul calls all people of God to be: the communities of Corinth, Philippi and Rome 'together with all those who in every place call on the name of our Lord Jesus Christ' (1 Cor. 1:2). Redemption and redeemed life are inseparable, as well as resurrection and resurrected life, and God's holiness and our holy lives. Sainthood is the path of all Christians.

Finally, Paul's view of the resurrection helps us with the connection between sainthood's particular and general definitions. Appealing to the integrity of bodily resurrection, we are able to say that the call to be saints is the destiny of the human body in relation to Christ's resurrected body. Therefore, when particular saints are identified by the church, they are recognized as the embodiment or the 'human-bodiliness' of God's grace in the world.[6] They are identified not because they are unique or peerless but because they tell us about what we share – or have the potential to share – as human beings in a world graced by God. This final point requires more elaboration.

The embodiment of God's grace in humanity is absolutely necessary for the church to proclaim, given the incarnation of God in Jesus Christ. In Christ, God and humanity are united through the unlikely vessel of the human body. If, indeed, this body shares fully in resurrected life, it follows that the naming of saints is also necessary. Saints are the inevitable outcome of God's trinitarian presence to the world. Saints are the body of grace, given to the world by the power of the Spirit in conformity to Christ. In the economy of salvation, Christ's resurrection is a generative transition from God's incarnation in Christ to his continuing presence to the world, incarnated, that is, *enfleshed*, in the church. In the gospels, Jesus' post-resurrection appearances (in the form of his resurrected bodily presence) are the context for the disciples and others to embark, in a new way, upon the way of God. In Mark, the resurrected Christ sends out, via the disciples, his proclamation of salvation (16:8); in Matthew, he commissions them to make disciples, baptize and teach (28:19–20); in John, the sign of Christ's body, given to Thomas, becomes a sign for those who believe, to do so without seeing Jesus himself (21:29); and in Luke–Acts, Jesus' bodily departure is sealed with the promise of the Spirit's embodiment in the church (Luke 24; Acts 1–2). This embodiment is the indelible bond between Christ's resurrection and the lives of the saints. The 'human-bodiliness' of the incarnation and the resurrection establishes the call of all Christians to be saints and constitutes the necessary task of naming those particular persons in whose lives God's grace is made concrete. According to the particular or broad definition, saints are the continuing 'bodiliness' of God's grace in the world.

The Lives of the Saints

Up to this point, saints have been defined according to God's solidarity with the world. This redemptive solidarity finds its basic expression in Jesus Christ and the people who are gathered by the Spirit in his name. As we have seen, the two are intimately connected through the unity of God's work in Christ and Spirit. The reconciliation of humanity with God is made possible by the resurrection – together with Jesus' death as a martyr, his proclamation of the kingdom, his call for repentance, his teaching and healing, his gathering of Israel, and his continuing embodiment in the church. The resurrection, along with these other events of God's 'human-bodiliness', constitutes a landscape of solidarity where humanity is drawn into community with God. In short, sainthood is a substantive expression of Christianity's trinitarian confession insofar as the redemptive humanity which Christ gives to the world is completed in human bodies which are enlivened by the Spirit.

This statement about God's redemptive solidarity fits with our current definition of sainthood: the saints are the continuing embodiment of grace and the lineage of a redemptive history. We will assume this proposition as a point of departure and ask a more concrete question: 'What, precisely, is saintly about the saints?' The previous section's theological account fits together well with Christian claims about God, but will our interpretation of sainthood continue to hold together when we consider the lives of the saints from the human side? The theological account seems to invoke bold claims about human holiness and the capacity of the human body to be a vehicle for the boundless grace of God. Does the account prove to be too bold when we consider the history of the church, where, all too often, human affairs have been far from holy?

Given human frailty, we might prefer a general definition of sainthood in its most modest form. Avoiding what seems to be an indefensible claim that 'all Christians are saints', we might say that 'all Christians are "called" to be saints'. But, while this definition side-steps the question of empirical 'embodiment', it does not improve our situation. If we hold that Christians are merely 'called' to be saints, with no embodiment of this call, then we have diminished what we believe about God's trinitarian economy. No doubt, we would hear a fiery response from Paul about the logic of human participation in Christ's cross and resurrection. Without our concrete participation, isn't our proclamation of the resurrection in vain? By formulating our reservations about the human capacity for sainthood, we would not be able to hold together the theological side of the argument.

Rather than modify the general definition, we might attempt to deal with the 'human frailty' problem by making the particular definition of saints primary. Yet such a shift from the church to particular individuals will not improve our situation either. Although saints may appear as an avant-garde of the church, we ought to remember that the sanctity of the church is always logically and theologically prior to our recognition that one person or another embodies the church's call to be saints. Saints are those who tell us about the church and about the promises given to humanity in a world graced by God. The sanctity of the saints is always God's holiness rather than a human self-possession, and if particular saints were to glorify themselves, they would not be saints by definition.

For this reason, Vatican II's *Dogmatic Constitution on the Church* locates the saints in a third position behind Christ and after the Church as the sacrament of Christ. The document's seventh chapter, 'The Pilgrim Church', follows the format of the document as a whole by emphasizing Christology and ecclesiology and by introducing saints in terms of the church's eschatological end. By doing so, the writers of the document place our community with saints within the larger story of God's grace given in Christ and the Holy Spirit. The document underlines the point that the saints do not detract from worship due to Christ, but enhance the fellowship of those who give glory to God. The fellowship of the whole people of God is key. The saints are exemplars because they have made their way to our common end. They are signs of God's kingdom and God's presence to us: 'those companions of ours in the human condition who are more perfectly transformed into the image of Christ.'[7] The saints are venerated not for themselves but for Christ. According to the *Constitution*, sainthood marks a continuing relationship of fellowship in Christ, and 'exactly as Christian communion between [men and women] on their earthly pilgrimage brings us closer to Christ, so our community with the saints joins us to Christ, from whom as from its fountain and head issues all grace and the life of the People of God itself.'[8] Here, saints are saints because they are in community with God and with the people who gather in God's name. Their actions or virtues are not separated from their place among us and the history of God's redemption.

Granted that particular saints are conceivable only in terms of the church's embodiment of grace, we still have not settled the question about the precise nature of sanctity. Criticisms directed at the imperfections of the church as a whole can be levied also at those particular persons who have been named as saints. Most saints would probably not measure up to the sanctity which their legends promulgate. Consider, for instance Anthony of Padua, who assists in finding lost things, or Jude, the patron saint of hopeless causes. The cults surrounding these saints have shaped their identities far beyond the character of their own lives on earth. Without legend and a good gloss, who would these saints be? Without their hagiography, who might most saints be? What arrogance, vice or ulterior motives might be lurking behind their stories of virtue?

What is saintly about the lives of the saints? Our question is complicated further by what seems to be the inconsistent character of sainthood when one saint is considered in relation to another. Saints are so numerous and scattered throughout times and places, that they seem to represent contradictory ways of life. Martin of Tours becomes a soldier of Christ and refuses to remain in the military, but Louis of France leads two failed crusades and Joan of

Arc's religious visions lead her to battle as well. Some saints, like Catherine of Siena, are remembered for their roles amid the highest positions of power, while others, such as St Thérèse of Lisieux, assume the lowest, most insignificant place. What definition of sainthood might include these concrete examples? What is sanctity?

More than a few theories can be put forward. One theory appeals to a list of virtues. A saint is a saint only if she measures up to a standard canon of moral perfection. And with a few miracles to add to her purity of thought and action, her sanctity would indeed be verified.[9] Another theory might focus on a single virtue, namely selflessness. Perhaps a saint is a person who gives himself to others and to God completely, without self-serving intentions or covert purposes. While the rest of humanity is self-centred, the saint is a saint because he is other-directed.[10] The other-directed character of the saint might be revealed by a single act, giving his life for others or for the faith. In this sense, martyrdom would be a seal of virtue and a personal achievement of the saint. A third theory might depart from a strictly moral definition and identify a saint's unique religious consciousness, which, of course, would translate into an exemplary life.[11] While the rest of us are absorbed in the trivial matters of our lives, our saint is captivated and transformed by her vision of God or perhaps of love, justice and peaceable human community.

These three theories differ, but they share a great deal. Mainly, all emphasize the saint's moral singularity, her forthright heart, moral perfection or intimate relationship to God in contrast to the rest of us here in the world. Each gives a clear definition, but none resolves the conflict between saints and the gloss of hagiography. Can the saints themselves measure up to the standards which the stories about them represent? Or, put differently, is the idea of sainthood simply superimposed upon less-than-holy lives? One way to resolve this problem is to undercut the moral worth of some saints through a critique of questionable hagiography and unlikely legends. By so doing, we could reduce the number of saints and shore up our standards in the process. This seems to be the inevitable approach of the three theories. When pushed, they will posit criteria independent from those who have been called saints (virtue, selflessness, religious consciousness) in order to judge who belongs and who does not.

But the approach shared by the three theories is ultimately

self-defeating. The three accounts consider a saint's personal character apart from those who tell his story and remember his name. They judge the worth of saints and their stories by moral or religious criteria which have a life of their own. But if we appeal to these independent standards, we would have to entertain the possibility that no one will measure up to them, while our standards, nevertheless, will remain intact. As a result, the saints will be relegated to an illustrative role for moral principles already sustained by the criteria. We might propose that a saint is one who is perfectly self-giving, and then go on to show how this or that saint is, in fact, not a saint. In this way, we could demonstrate, on logical grounds, that no human is a saint because humans by definition are inclined towards self-serving love.

This process of reasoning is the method used by Immanuel Kant to exclude moral exemplars from any significant use in morality. Kant holds that ethics emerges from a reasoning process that is independent from both natural inclination and an empirical knowledge of human nature.[12] If we have a standard for judging who qualifies as a saint, moral significance emerges from the reasonable standards rather than the saints. According to Kant's reasoning, if saints are allowed to proliferate, they will literally crowd out the standards and divert our attention from our real moral sources. For Kant, the saints are not merely a distraction, they block our route to understanding the moral life. Moral reasoning is not 'embodied'. 'Stop depending on others,' he would say. 'Stand on your own two feet, and think for yourself!'

With this end in view, the three accounts of saintliness will contradict their own attraction to the saints. Sainthood implies a conception of the moral life which is entirely different from Kant's. It provides a context for our participation in the lives of others and an absorbing vision of the human end of community with God. So in order to avoid undercutting an account of sainthood, we need to start from a different assumption than our three accounts. We begin with the notion that saints *are* their stories and that there is an intimate connection between the lives of the saints and those who lift up their names. These points will be clearer as we proceed. At this juncture, suffice it to say that standards of virtue and appeals to religious consciousness are secondary. They may prove helpful for describing the details of saintly lives, but they are not definitive for who saints are. In other words, virtue, self-giving or faithfulness may be indispensable, but none makes a saint a saint. In order to advance toward a more basic definition of sainthood, we will fare best if we begin with a story. We will take a look at the story of St Lawrence (f.d. August 10), one of the most widely remembered martyrs of the ancient church.

Lawrence's story offers little about his moral stature; yet the events leading to his death reveal a striking truth about the church. As a deacon in Rome, he seemed destined to follow his Pope, Sixtus, into martyrdom. After the death of Sixtus, Lawrence was confronted by the Roman Prefect. The Prefect smartly cited the adage, 'render to Caesar the things that belong to him,' and required Lawrence to relinquish the riches of the church. The Prefect gave Lawrence three days to perform the task. Lawrence agreed. During the intervening days, he emptied the church's treasury and gave its worth to the poor who had been under the church's care. On the day when he stood before the Prefect, he gathered the poor, sick, blind and lame, and when the Prefect asked for the riches of the church, Lawrence replied that the poor and infirm who were gathered there were, in fact, the riches of the church. According to the hagiography, Lawrence angered the Prefect to such a degree that his martyrdom came as he was slowly baked on an iron grid. While on the grid, Lawrence uttered his famous line, 'Let my body be turned; one side is broiled enough.'[13]

What does this hagiography reveal? Primarily, it tells the church about itself. We are the lame and blind. Our witness, when it is steadfast, has its source in Christ who takes company with us, with the poor, with the feeble. On one hand, the story of Lawrence is about a martyrdom so sweet that he is impervious to the pain that Caesar inflicts, as well as the power Caesar wields. On the other hand, Lawrence calls the church to be intrepid as it stands and suffers with the poor and the infirm. The story of Lawrence reveals more than the virtue of courage. Within the framework of the church's identity, sainthood is more than a moral category. Some saints might function as moral exemplars, but Lawrence does not. If pressed to fit saints into a category at all, we would have to say that their significance is soteriological rather than moral. Lawrence's stand with the poor, lame and blind is significant because it is intelligible when set within the landscape of Jesus' life and ministry. The story of Lawrence makes sense only because God has offered the way of Christ as the path of redemption for the world. God's self-giving in Christ and the Holy Spirit creates the possibility for the story of this saint to be told, and the possibility for it to be told as redemptive.

From one point of view, Lawrence is a stubborn fool. But within the framework of the Christian proclamation about Christ, Lawrence's obstinacy is a mimesis of God's steadfast faithfulness in Jesus – who is humbled, obedient and shows us the way of God's solidarity with the world. In this sense, saints do not fulfill an independent moral standard as much as they populate the history of God's redemption. Apart from this history, saints (à la Kant) are likely to be a moral failure or sheer embarrassment. But the story of Lawrence is the story of a saint because he is an actor on a landscape of action which has been made possible by the life, death and resurrection of Christ. Sainthood is not an award given for personal moral achievement; this is where the three previous accounts of sainthood fall short. Like all gifts of the Spirit, saints are a blessing for building and sustaining the life of the church, and the call to be saints is the call of the church to be a community of God's redemption amid the world. Saintliness is established when the holiness, grace and reconciliation of God become gifts to the whole people of God and to the world. Saints are saints, not when they stand apart from the rest of us, but when their lives are given to us as a people in whom we find God's grace embodied.

Saints' lives are given to others through their stories. For this reason, saints are bound to the telling of their stories, and any clear division between a saint and how she or he is remembered is false. The saints necessarily live among us as stories because we, as the narrators, become agents in their lives. The lives of the saints are a rehearsal of God's redemptive activity, and when rehearsing *their* lives becomes the fabric of *our* lives, we gain access to the landscape of God's way with the world. According to this understanding of saints and their stories, the paradigmatic saint is not someone who has reached moral perfection, but one who is a scoundrel like Jacob.

Jacob appears to be an unlikely candidate. In contrast, his ancestor, Abraham, has exemplary faith, and the writers of the Abraham narratives protect his good standing, even during episodes of questionable behaviour. But Jacob is inclined towards shady dealings. While Abraham and Sarah receive God's promises, Jacob bargains for, and seems to swindle his brother out of, a birthright in return for a bowl of lentils. He tricks his father into giving him Esau's blessing, and he wins a divine blessing through his relentless wrestling with an angel. But in the narratives of Jacob, his personal character becomes insignificant in light of what God accomplishes. In the same way, the saint's story is given over to God's story. Righteousness and faith are not unimportant; Abraham, Sarah, Mary, Francis of Assisi and Thérèse of Lisieux cannot be called lesser saints than Jacob. But these others are fathers and mothers of the faith, not because of their singular achievements, but because their stories are the embodiment of God's presence to the world.

The story of Jacob's life and his ultimate 'reputation' depends upon a community who reads the story of his life as a story about the course of God's covenant promises. It is through his life that readers and listeners discover that they are heirs to a covenant. It is through him that their lives are placed within the narrative of what God is doing in the world. The same can be said about Jude and Anthony, Joan and Louis, Catherine and Thérèse, Francis and Clare. Jacob may be a scoundrel, but when his story is placed between Isaac and Joseph's, he becomes a blessed grandparent of many fortunate children. The blessings of these fortunate 'little ones' are discovered through a vision of God's way. Entrance to God's history is given through grandparents, parents and brothers and sisters of the way. These are the saints. This is the church.

We are now ready for our final definition of sainthood. Saints are those whose lives are: (1) circumscribed by the story of God's redemption and (2) given over to the world as a landscape where others find access to and are defined by this same redemptive story. The first and second points always hang together, as they are two sides of God's continuing embodiment (in the body of Christ) and openness to the world (in the movement of the Spirit). This description of sainthood makes both the general and particular definitions necessary. The church is a community of saints because it is enlivened by and embodies the good word of God's redemption, and particular individuals are often set apart as saints only because their lives become access for the church to name its embodiment on this landscape. Particular saints are possible only in as much as God's way is embodied in a people who call out some of its members to represent and continually remind us about God's holiness and about God's promises of our participation in resurrection life.

Conclusion

The church does not produce saints. God's trinitarian economy does. But sainthood is the necessary form of the church insofar as Christianity's proclamation about God's self-giving in Christ and Spirit is true. In one sense, the saints are the whole church, and in another, they are particular persons whose lives offer witness to the promises of God and access to who the church is called to be. We are called to be saints, and are given holy ones among us to tell us who we are. The self-giving of God in Jesus' life, death and resurrection constitutes our reconciliation with God and establishes a landscape for human participation in the life of grace. Through the enlivening of the Spirit in us, our participation is made possible as a continuing, redemptive way of God's grace embodied in the world.

The calling out and naming of saints is a necessity, not only as an outcome of God's trinitarian economy, but particularly in terms of Christ's bodily resurrection. The import of Christ's resurrection is soteriological; we have been saved and set en route to be conformed into the fullness of resurrected life. The path of conformity is the Christian life and the fate of the human body. From beginning to end, the way of salvation embraces human 'bodiliness': from Christ's incarnation to the life of the community which gathers in Christ's name. Redemption constitutes the body. Likewise, sainthood is constituted by God's continuing embodiment of grace. The saints are the lineage of God's redemptive activity; they are the continuing promise of grace that comes into the world enfleshed; they are the mapping out of God's blessed way. They are evidence that God's promises are true and efficacious for life in the world. The saints are concrete assurance that God's redemption of the world will be made complete.

Notes

1. Kevin Quast, *Reading the Corinthian Correspondence* (New York: Paulist Press, 1994), pp. 88–9.
2. For an account of 'intra-systematic' coherence see George Lindbeck, *The Nature of Doctrine* (Philadelphia: Westminster Press, 1984).
3. Hans Conzelmann, *1 Corinthians*, trans. James W. Leitch (Philadelphia: Fortress Press, 1975), p. 280.

4. All references to Scripture are from the *Holy Bible, New Revised Standard Version* (New York: Oxford University Press,1989).
5. See Leander E. Keck, '"Jesus" in Romans', *Journal of Biblical Literature*, 108, 1989, 3, pp. 443–60.
6. See Karl Rahner, 'The Church of Saints', *Theological Investigations*, 3 (London: Darton, Longman & Todd, Ltd, 1967), pp. 91–104.
7. 'Dogmatic Constitution on the Church, *Lumen Gentium*', *Vatican Council II, The Conciliar and Post Conciliar Documents*, Study Edition, ed. Austin Flannery, O.P. (Northport, NY: Costello Publishing Company, 1986), p. 411.
8. Ibid.
9. See a description of the canonization process in Kenneth Woodward, *Making Saints: How the Catholic Church Determines Who Becomes a Saint, Who Doesn't, and Why* (New York: Simon & Schuster, 1990), pp. 50–86.
10. Edith Wyschogrod, *Saints and Postmodernism* (Chicago: University of Chicago Press, 1990).
11. Lawrence Cunningham, *The Meaning of Saints* (San Francisco: Harper & Row, 1980).
12. See Immanuel Kant, *Foundations of the Metaphysics of Morals*, trans. Lewis White Beck (New York: Macmillan, 1959).
13. *Butler's Lives of the Saints*, 3, eds. Herbert Thurston, S. J. and Donald Attwater (New York: P. J. Kenedy & Sons, 1956), pp. 297–8.

Chapter 8

LIVING IN CHRIST: STORY, RESURRECTION AND SALVATION[1]

Gerard Loughlin

There are Christians so enamoured of death that they want Christianity without resurrection.[2] Like many others in secular society, they believe themselves in love with life, and against mortality. By denying death they affirm life. If death – and resurrection in death – alone gives meaning to life, then life in and of itself has no meaning or worth.[3] This idea offends those who would make their lives their 'own' – monuments to their achievements in the face of adversity. Because there is now meaning only in life, death must be denied, postponed where possible and hastened when inevitable. Death itself must die; and along with death, every one of its metonyms – pain and suffering, decay and disease. When they cannot be eliminated, one must eliminate that which they infect.

The modern euthanaic society, which thinks life and death utterly opposed, refuses death and approves only life. This, however, is to inaugurate a fatal return, for the denial of death is at the same time the denial of life, since life is that which dies. To utterly destroy death one must finally destroy that which alone makes death possible – life. Thus secular culture, which would deny death and affirm only life, becomes, as Pope John Paul II has written, a 'culture of death'.[4] It thinks life is only that which remains, that which does not pass away, so that the 'monument' is more real, because more permanent, than that which it commemorates – life which passes away.[5] But life *is* impermanent and passing; now it is only in the condition of death that there is life.

Christian faith is no friend of death, for it answers to a story that has no end, that knows only the fullness of life. To the culture of death the Church proposes the Gospel of life, the *evangelium vitae* of which Pope John Paul II speaks. Against the culture of death and for a culture of life, a civilization of love, the Church proposes Jesus Christ, whose death – in the condition of life – is a passing away which is at the same time an eternal return, for he is the resurrection

118

and the life – life itself.

The *Gospel of life* is something concrete and personal, for it consists in the proclamation of *the very person of Jesus*. Jesus made himself known to the Apostle Thomas, and in him to every person, with the words: 'I am the way, and the truth, and the life' (John 14:6). This is also how he spoke of himself to Martha, the sister of Lazarus: 'I am the resurrection and the life; he who believes in me, though he dies, yet shall he live, and whoever lives and believes in me shall never die' (John 11:25–6). Jesus is the Son who from all eternity receives life from the Father (John 5:26), and who has come among men to make them sharers in this gift: 'I came that they may have life, and have it abundantly' (John 10:10).[6]

In this essay I seek to suggest how the Church comes to know the resurrection of the Lord, and in his resurrection find that life it calls salvation. I do so against the claim of reasonable religion, that before one can have faith in the resurrection one must have rational certainty that Jesus is raised. Indeed one must, but according to the *ratio* of faith – which is the gift of the resurrection itself.

Reasonable Religion

The modern age insists on certainty, on well-established facts and firm foundations, and on a method that will achieve them and be seen to do so. What counts as a firm foundation and an established fact – as certain knowledge – is what impartial means can publicly demonstrate to a reasonable person. It is the neutral observer, without brief, who can best undertake such a demonstration, a person led by evidence rather than prejudice, who is objective. The scientist is such a person, and scientific rectitude is the quality required for investigating any claim, religious as well as physical. In matters religious it is only after the reasonable inquirer has demonstrated the facts of the case, with whatever degree of probability, that faith can play its part in affirming as true what is reasonably probable.

For the modern believer, the resurrection is the foundation of Christian faith, the fact whose probability must be established by impartial reason for faith. It must be established as a reasonable induction from the historical evidence, and established by an impartial inquirer who does not prejudge the question one way or the other.[7] For the purpose, the question must be addressed as if by someone who *does not have faith*.

Insofar as modern theology of the resurrection conceives its task in the way suggested, it does so from outside faith, albeit for faith. While modern theology seeks to secure the resurrection for faith, it does so by starting from outside faith, and from outside faith there is no way into faith. For faith is neither the conclusion of an argument nor an induction from evidence, but a gift given without necessity. Just as nothing comes from nothing, so nothing other than the world comes from the world. It is for this reason that modern theology, which seeks to move from the world to God, finds only more of the world. Faith, which is finally life in God, comes from God alone.

The objection to reasonable religion is as much philosophical as theological, for it assumes an unreasonable idea of reason, above all a confused idea of 'objectivity'. It assumes that it is possible to have an impartial view of the world, a view from no particular place, since all places limit the view. It assumes a view from nowhere. But all views are from somewhere, otherwise they would not be views. All views are partial, all 'objectivities' subjective. Indeed the viewpoints of science are some of the most subjective of all, since science views the world in highly particular ways, according to protocols rarely applied outside of scientific investigations. A person requires training to see the world from a scientific point of view; dedication to acquire the right sort of squint.

It is thus a philosophical mistake to suppose – as does reasonable religion – that a scientific viewpoint is appropriate for viewing religious matters, such as the resurrection. Reasonable religion fails to notice the partiality of the scientific viewpoint, its limitation and subjectivity. Reasonable religion supposes that it must view the resurrection from the same viewpoint as that of the scientific historian, failing to note that from such a point of view one has a limited field of vision, a highly subjective squint on the world. Where one stands to see the facts determines the facts that one can see.

Viewing the Resurrection

Standing with the scientific historian, squinting as he or she squints, is good enough if you want to see at least some of the things that Jesus did and underwent, but it is doubtful that you will see everything from there. It is doubtful that you will see Jesus heal the sick or raise the dead, or return to his disciples from the tomb. For the scientific historian stands in such a place, and squints in such a way, that such matters are not only unseen but unseeable. Before the scientific historian looks she or he knows that such matters are not to be seen, and she never sees them. This is why Geoffrey Lampe – to give just one example – was unable to accept the tradition of the empty tomb. The body of Christ must have rotted in the grave because decay is the law of all bodies. 'I do not find it possible to believe that bodily corruption, that ultimate negation, as it seems, of all human endeavour, aspiration and hope, can be something from which the manhood of Christ was exempt.'[8]

It is not only a question of from where we look, but of what we look at. While historical science looks in the direction of the New Testament, it does so in order to look through it to what lies beyond it, to the historical facts rather than their imperfect record in the biblical text. Here again we must raise both philosophical (hermeneutic) and theological (faith) objections. The philosophical objection is to the idea that we can have an unmediated knowledge of the past, a knowledge that does not depend on certain presuppositions, that is not already the expression of a contingent and local picture of what the world is like. All historical events come to us in some text or other. There is no event that comes to us from outside of a text, no event that is unmediated by some picture or narrative. It is a fallacy to suppose that one can look through the New Testament to the events behind it, for those events are accessible only as they come to us in the text of the New Testament.[9]

The event of the resurrection is given to us in the narratives of the Gospels. It could not be given to us in the narratives of critical history for the simple reason that such narratives can recognize only analogous events, events that are comparable with others. As Walter Kasper remarks, 'historical phenomena are understood in context and by analogy with other events. Where this understanding of factual reality is absolute, there is no place for the reality of the resurrection, which cannot be explained by reference to context or by analogy with the rest of reality.'[10] For historical positivism all events are in principle repeatable – classifiable as recurring instants under a general category. A unique event, without repeatability or analogy, cannot register in the narratives of historical positivism. This limitation is well stated in Frances Young's conundrum concerning historical evidence for the incarnation of God in Christ. 'If Jesus was an entirely normal human being, no evidence can be produced for the incarnation. If no evidence can be produced, there can be no basis on which to claim that an incarnation took place.'[11] Normality presupposes repeatability and analogy. Moreover, it presupposes the possibilities enshrined in historical positivism's conception of 'normality', which leaves no room for events such as incarnation and resurrection, except as instants of a general category which positivism classifies as merely mythological.

The resurrection is a unique event (though as I shall suggest, it bears a repetition which does not detract from, but rather constitutes, its uniqueness). As Hans Urs von Balthasar says, the resurrection 'pierces our whole world of living and dying in a unique way so that, through this breakthrough, it may open a path for us into the everlasting life of God.'[12] If we are to find our way to this path we must trust to the Gospel story. It is only by finding ourselves in the story of Jesus Christ that our hearts can find their way to the risen life of the Lord.

The form of the story

Historical positivism understands the Gospels as testaments of faith. For positivist historians (and nearly all biblical historians have been and are positivist historians[13]) the Gospels do not testify to Jesus Christ, but to the faith in Jesus of their writers and audiences. This is why the historians have to get behind the Gospels, behind the faith that produced them, in order to determine what 'really' happened. They seek to produce a 'neutral' narrative of Jesus, a story told without faith. In doing so they destroy the 'form' of the canonical story, the four narratives of Matthew, Mark, Luke and John. They seek a single, sensible, coherent narrative, without obscurities, indeterminacies or contradictions. They want clarity and comprehensibility. They want certainty and control.

Happily, the four-fold form of the Gospel story resists positivist control and evades the grasp of the historian. For it is this form, with its obscurities and contradictions, differences and indeterminacies – the very things that positivist reason abhors – that is constitutive of the story. As Hans Urs von Balthasar suggests, it is the Gospel's four-fold form – which is perhaps a 'little divine humour, a little divine irony' at the expense of the historians – which allows the Church to find its way to the resurrection. For the latter cannot be seen from one perspective alone. It can be seen only from many different perspectives.

> The unique and divine plasticity of the living, incarnate Word could not be witnessed to other than through this system of perspectives which, although it cannot be further synthesized, compensates for this by offering a stereoscopic vista. And the divine irony would further suggest that the main fruits to be gathered from the very unfruitfulness and failure of the scientific experiment would be the ever clearer exigency of returning to the one thing necessary. We must return to the primary contemplation of what is *really* said, really presented to us, really meant.[14]

The differentiated form of the story is not simply God laughing at the historians – defeating their attempts to comprehend the mystery of God – but a reminder to all of us that the story is about the mystery of God in the life and death of Jesus. The Gospel narratives mark out, but do not describe, the mystery to which they bear testimony. The mystery of God's life in the death of Jesus gathers to itself many images – including 'resurrection' and 'restoration to life' – which together surround the 'inaccessible mid-point which alone has the magnetic force to arrange around itself, in concentric fashion, the image-garland'.[15] These images are used precisely in the Gospel narratives in order to teach us that we cannot grasp and control the event that is their focus.

The mystery of God's life in the death of Christ requires many descriptions, because no one description is perspicuous of the mystery. It 'engenders a multiplicity of human attempts to express it'.[16]

In the event of the resurrection all previous schemata come to fulfilment and suffer their breakdown at one and the same time. They have to be used in preaching, but the very fact of their cumulative employment shows that each is powerless to contribute more than a fragment to a totality of a transcendent kind.[17]

'Seeing' the unseeable

If the resurrection is the mystery of God's life in the death of Jesus, and as such goes beyond human understanding and discourse – an event that defeats all attempts at rigorous comprehension – how can we think it at all? How can we say it, let alone see it? The mystery withdraws from view at the very moment that the Gospels appear to show it, obscured by the indeterminacies of the narratives. They tell us of Christ's return to his disciples – among the trees of the garden, on the road to Emmaus, by the lake shore – and before that of the empty tomb; but of its emptying they say nothing. The returned Christ is flesh and blood, wounded but able to eat again with his friends. At the same time he must not, and is not touched, and passes through locked doors like a wraith. Some see the risen Christ but do not believe; whilst others believe who have not seen. Some seeing is unseeing, and some blindness insight. And none of this is 'evidence' of anything other than 'faith' – deluded, as it must seem from the 'neutral' viewpoint of positivism, for which death is always terminal.

How is the Church's reading of the resurrection narratives not deluded, how is it able to 'see' the resurrection in its reading of the story? A clue to answering this question is given by the paradigmatic context in which the Church reads the story of Christ's resurrection, the liturgical celebration of Easter. Here the Church not merely reads, but prays the Scripture. Before God the Church calls to mind the story of that first Easter when the women hurried to the tomb, only to find that they were already too late. As always the Lord had gone on before them. The Church not only recalls the story, but ritually enacts it in the solemn joy of vigil and paschal light. It recalls the story before God, not in case God might have forgotten what has passed, but so as to ask God to still make happen what is promised. And, as always, the Church is already too late. The Lord has gone on ahead and is coming to meet it.

The resurrection is known in the Church's prayerful performance of Christ's story. The unseeable mystery of God's life in the death of Jesus is 'seen' through the Gospel narratives in the reading of the Church. The risen life of Christ is present in the gathering of the people who recall before God the promise that they will be called again by him who has already gone on ahead and is coming to meet them, who is already with them in the breaking of the bread and the passing of the cup. This is the way of love to the one who was dead but is alive, who is life itself, now and forever more.

Why Do You Look For the Living Among the Dead?[18]

It is only as the Church comes to know the risen Christ that it comes to know the person of Jesus, for he who was dead and he who is alive are one and the same person – Jesus the Christ who died and is risen. For the theologian Hans Frei, the identity of Jesus comes to its 'sharpest focus in the death-and-resurrection sequence taken as one unbroken sequence'.[19] Earlier in the Gospel story, Jesus's identity is uncertain – 'Who do people say that I am?'[20] But with the resurrection Jesus is manifested as 'who he is, the one who as the unsubstitutable human being Jesus of Nazareth, is not a myth but the presence of God and saviour of man'.[21] Even in the story of the crucifixion, the identity of Jesus is doubtful – 'Are you the King of the Jews?'[22] But with the resurrection there is no longer any doubt *who* he is, though *what* has happened remains obscure.

> Something does indeed take place in the resurrection, but it is not described and doubtless cannot be described . . . The foreground and the stress in the resurrection belong not to the action of God but to its confirmation of Jesus' identity. It is he who is present and none other when God is active. Jesus alone is manifested.[23]

The overall story of crucifixion *and* resurrection – the overall form of the story – holds together both the certainty and uncertainty of identity, the clarity and obscurity of the acts done and undertaken. As the nature of the deeds become dark, the identity of Jesus shines forth. Moreover, Jesus is one and the same person whose identity is obscure on the cross and luminous in the resurrection. It is not just that the resurrection of Jesus shows who he is, but that in following the crucifixion, it shows that he is the one who-was-dead-and-is-risen, the one who cannot be conceived other than as dead-and-raised. 'The Lord has risen indeed, and has appeared to Simon!'[24]

In a sense the synoptic Gospel writers are saying something like this: 'Our argument is that to grasp what this identity, Jesus of Nazareth, is, is to believe that, in fact, he has been raised from the dead.' Someone may reply that in that case the most perfectly depicted character, the most nearly-life-like fictional identity ought also in fact to live a factual historical life. We answer that the argument holds good only in this one and absolutely unique case where the described identity is totally identical with his factual existence. He is the resurrection and the life; how can he be conceived as not resurrected?[25]

In the Gospel story Jesus is identified as he who is alive, he who is life itself: 'I am the resurrection and the life.'[26]

He lives as the one who cannot not live, for whom to be what he is, is to be. But who or what he thus is, is unambiguously Jesus of Nazareth; and as Jesus he is the Son of Man, the one whose history, whose being as self-enactment in his unique circumstances it was to be delivered into the hands of sinful men, to be crucified, and to rise again . . . Who and what he is, what he did and underwent, and that he is, are all one and the same.[27]

To know the identity of Jesus is to know that he is risen from the dead and is now alive in his Church, in the people to whom he always returns. In the same way that St Anselm identified God as that-than-which-no-greater-can-be-thought, the Gospel story – on Frei's reading – identifies Jesus as he-who-cannot-not-live. As with Anselm's identification of God, the Gospels' identification of Jesus as he-who-was-dead-but-is-risen is only an argument to its truth *for faith*. Without faith, such an identification can give only the meaning, but not the truth, of the Gospel story. One may understand that Jesus is the one who died but now lives, who was crucified but is risen, and yet not believe. Without faith it is to know only the identity of Jesus in the Gospel story, it is not to find one's own identity in the story of Jesus – which is faith.

Living in the Story of the Risen Christ

The resurrection is not only part of the story of Jesus, but part of the story of everyone who becomes part of Jesus' story. To enter the story of Jesus is to begin to share in his identity as the one who-was-dead-but-is-risen, the one who-cannot-not-live. And this life in the life of Christ is redemption from slavery to sin, it is salvation.

Soteriology is the theology of salvation, seeking to explain how the story of Jesus transforms life, how 'Jesus saves'.[28] For a story soteriology, salvation is not merely illustrated but constituted by the story of Jesus. Jesus' story is salvation, and the saving relationship between Saviour and saved is a storied relationship, for salvation is being enfolded or inscribed within the story of the Saviour. The task of story soteriology is to say how one becomes part of the story of Christ's resurrection.

Selfhood as Story

In order to understand how one can become part of another's story, it is helpful to consider how a person's identity can be understood as a story. A number of recent writers have suggested that a person's identity is best understood as having a narrative form. Thus Alasdair MacIntyre holds that selfhood 'resides in the unity of a narrative which links birth to life to death as narrative beginning to middle to end'.[29] For MacIntyre, human lives are enacted narratives: 'It is because we all live out narratives in our lives and because we understand our own lives in terms of the narratives that we live out that the form of narrative is appropriate for understanding the actions of others. Stories are lived before they are told – except in the case of fiction.'[30] But we are never fully in control of our own stories, never their sole authors, for 'only in fantasy do we live what story we please'. We are preceded by stories: 'We enter upon a stage which we did not design and we find ourselves part of an action that was not of our making.'[31] Nevertheless, it is because we can understand ourselves as actors within one or more stories, that our lives have some intelligibility. It is above all the sense that our story has some purpose or goal, has an end towards which it is tending, that gives our actions – and finally our lives – some meaning.

> We live out our lives, both individually and in our relationships with each other, in the light of certain conceptions of a possible shared future, a future in which certain possibilities beckon us forward and others repel us, some seem already foreclosed and others perhaps inevitable. There is no present which is not informed by some image of some future and an image of the future which always presents itself in the form of a *telos* – or of a variety of ends or goals – towards which we are either moving or failing to move in the present.[32]

MacIntyre suggests that the story which best gives meaning to life is one in which 'the good life for man is the life spent seeking for the good life for man, and the virtues necessary for the seeking are those which will enable us to understand what more and what else the good life for man is'.[33] MacIntyre's idea of the good life as a quest story allows us to better understand salvation as inscription within a story; but the Church believes that the 'what more and what else' which MacIntyre enjoins us to seek, has already comes to us in Jesus. Christian selfhood is a story whose *telos* is the life of Christ.

Retelling the Story of Christ

To be written into the story of Christ is to have one's story given a new direction, a new *telos*. Indeed, for many, it is to be given a direction or *telos* for the first time. This (re)direction of life begins through entry into the community that retells, and thereby continues, the story of Jesus. For the story of Jesus is a story that continues always; one that, unlike other stories, has no end. The story of Jesus is but the start of a story which continues in the multitude of life-stories that together constitute the story of Christ-become-the-Church. For each Christian life aims to be the life of Jesus in his or her own time and place, a non-identical repetition of Jesus' life. They can be 'non-identical' repetitions because what is repeated is not a discrete and finite existence, a narrative that begins at A and finishes at B, but rather an uncontainable plenitude, which, flowing forth, changes everything and everyone it meets, renewing the world. Jesus is not simply a life, but life itself. The Church's *telos*, the good for which it seeks, is his infinite life, and the virtues necessary for its seeking are those which enable it to repeat his infinity in its finitude. This is possible because the infinite life of God in Christ is given for our repetition, not as an ideal, but as a particular life-story which is at one and the same time the finite instance of the infinite.[34]

The story of Jesus is not just the story told in the Gospel narratives, but the story told in the ever-burgeoning life of the Church. Thus John Milbank suggests reading the Gospels as telling not so much the story of one man, as the story of a 'new kind of community'.

> Jesus figures in this story simply as the founder, the beginning, the first of many. There is nothing that Jesus does that he will not enable the disciples to do: they will be able to cast out demons, heal the sick, raise the dead, forgive sins. And just as Jesus' proper source and place is not contained within this world, so also his followers are to be 'born again', and so somehow exceed their temporal origins – for if birth, like death, is not an event within life, but the opening of life, then a second birth in the midst of life must unite us, in our particular living identity, with that which opens out all life.[35]

One enters the story of Jesus by entering the Church. Through baptism one is written into his life-story; one is written into – born into – life itself. Baptismal imagery is well understood. It marks a transition and transformation from one state to another – a passage through water that is the 'death' of the old and the 'birth' of the new, recalling the journey of Israel from slavery to covenantal life through the parted waters of the sea, the beginning of Jesus' journey to Jerusalem through the Jordan, and his journey to life from death through the silence of the grave. Baptism is a narrative transition that does not destroy one's old life-story, but reorders it towards a new, unforeseen ending, a different unexpected *telos*. The new ending reconstitutes the old story as one of sin-turning-to-salvation.

One seeks the ending of the Church's story by repeating its beginning, and thus opening up the infinite plenitude of its 'middle'. For the promised life of the kingdom is given in the person of Jesus, and it is in the practice of discipleship that the future arrives. The story of Jesus is both the start and the end of the Church's story, its *alpha* and *omega*. Christ is both the beginning and the culmination of the Church's 'middling' practice.

> Not just the seed, but also the fully-grown tree, not just the foundation-stone but also the temple, not just the head, but also the body. Christ's full incarnate appearance lies always ahead of us – if we love the brethren, according to St John, *then* he will be manifested to us.[36] And in what is perhaps the original ending of Mark's Gospel, the risen Christ is not recorded in his visibility, but as 'going before you to Galilee',[37] the place of the original gathering and going forth of the new community.[38]

The story of Jesus is not complete without the story of the Church, and therefore his story waits upon the eschaton for its complete narration. If Jesus is the 'source, goal and context of all our lives', because life itself, we can tell his story only by telling the story of everyone. 'To some extent, the observation of every human "person" follows this pattern, but only in the case of Jesus does an accurate rendering of his personhood involve an ultimate attention to everyone, in so far as their "truth" lies in Christ.'[39]

Exemplary Lives

The Church, in seeking its *telos* in the life of Christ, is aided by stories of the saints' exemplary repetitions of Christ's life. The saints are already gathered into the story of Christ, which they seek to elaborate and extend by repeating his life in their own. Thus the idea of the Church as the retelling or repetition of Christ, is not new, but ancient in the Church. As Edith Wyschogrod notes, a 'background belief of virtually all Christian hagiography is that saints live their lives in the light of Christ's life. *Imitatio Christi* is the apothegm that illuminates saintly contemplation and the command that guides saintly conduct.'[40] In their turn, the lives of the saints inflame their brothers and sisters with a desire for Christ. 'The comprehension of a saint's life understood from within the sphere of hagiography is a practice through which the addressee is gathered into the narrative so as to extend and elaborate it with her/his own life.'[41]

Wyschogrod argues that the saints cannot fully imitate Christ in his divine perfection. The saints undertake both to model their lives upon that of Christ, and to show how impossible it is enact his divinity on earth. But perhaps this is to think Christ's life an ideal which will always be imperfectly repeated in the attempt to repeat it identically. It is perhaps to forget that Christ is repeated perfectly only in and through each non-identical (imperfect) repetition, because Christ is Christ-become-the-Church – which is the mystery of the incarnation. Through the resurrection, Christ is given over to the stories that aim to tell his life in theirs, so that his life is fully told only in the telling of every life. John Milbank reminds us that the Church 'is not founded upon the vision of a transcendent original which we must imitate'.

> Instead it makes its affirmations about the real, and about 'meaning', through the constant repetition of a historically emergent practice which has no real point of origination, but only acquires identity and relative stability through this repetition. And what is repeated is not an insight, not an idea (which is properly imitated), but a formal becoming, a structured transformation. The narrative and metanarrative forms of the Gospel are therefore indispensable, not because they record and point us to a vision which is still available in its eternal 'presence', but rather because they enshrine and constitute the event of a transformation which is to be non-identically repeated, and therefore still made to happen.[42]

It is in the lives of the saints (which finally constitute the life of the Church), that the 'event of a transformation' – which is the risen life of Christ – is 'made to happen', again and again, and each time differently. In the life-story of Jesus we see the overcoming of coercive and selfish power through the refusal of violence, the practice of forgiveness and the transformation of suffering. It is this practice which the Church aims to repeat, and in so far as it does, it is inscribed and incorporated into the very life of the crucified and risen Christ.

> The Gospels . . . narrate Jesus' utter refusal of selfish power, and relate this to a transformation which combines human

words with power over violence and death in the suffering of the body itself. If the suffering body becomes an actively suffering body, suffering for the sake of joy, and a greater joy for all, then it becomes the body that is united with other bodies. And united bodies are the resurrection – the making of words effective and life-giving, because no longer linked to selfish power, which means always the threat to kill, a power of death which in the long run spells the death of power.[43]

The story of Christ-become-the-Church is thus the non-identical repetition of a life which, because it is concrete rather than ideal, is plenitudinous in its telling, different each time it is told. And this telling – which is not recitation but practice – is salvation through the risen life of Christ-become-the-Church.

May the risen Lord
breathe on our minds and open our eyes
that we may know him in the breaking of bread,
and follow him in his risen life.[44]

Notes

1. An earlier version of this essay was read to the Cumbria Theological Association, January 1995. I would like to thank all those who responded so generously on that occasion, in particular John Baron and Myrtle Langley. Some of the themes of this essay are more extensively treated in Gerard Loughlin, *Telling God's Story: Bible, Church and Narrative Theology* (Cambridge: Cambridge University Press, 1996).
2. I am indebted to Catherine Pickstock – in her remarkable essay 'Necrophilia: The Middle of Modernity' (forthcoming in *Modern Theology*) – for showing me that modern necrophobia is best named necrophilia.
3. See Jacques Pohier, *God – In Fragments*, trans. John Bowden (London: SCM Press, 1985), pp. 83–92.
4. Pope John Paul II, *Evangelium Vitae* (Catholic Truth Society, London, 1995), p. 22. But we should not think only modernity institutes a culture of death; rather all culture is death-culture in so far as it seeks an illusory security against death and decay. See further John Milbank, 'Can Morality be Christian?', *Studies in Christian Ethics*, 8:1, 1995, pp.

45–59 (pp. 50–1).

5. Colin Gunton, in his study of modernity and postmodernity – *The One, the Three and the Many: God, Creation and the Culture of Modernity* (Cambridge: Cambridge University Press, 1993) – points to an absurd but telling example of necrophiliac monumentalism in the work of J. D. Barrow and F. J. Tipler: 'From the behavioural point of view intelligent *machines* can be regarded as people. These machines may be our ultimate heirs, our ultimate descendants, because under certain circumstances they could survive for ever the extreme conditions near the Final State [of the universe]'. *The Anthropic Cosmological Principle* (Oxford: Clarendon Press, 1986), p. 615; cited in Gunton, p. 60 note 29. This passage not only represents an 'evasion of death', as Gunton suggests, but also its embrace, since the condition of everlasting survival is the death of the human race: a fundamental misanthropy.

6. Pope John Paul II, *Evangelium Vitae*, pp. 52–3.

7. See Hugo A. Meynell, 'Faith, Objectivity and Historical Falsifiability', in *Language, Meaning and God: Essays in Honour of Herbert McCabe OP*, ed. Brian Davies O.P. (London: Geoffrey Chapman, 1987), pp. 145–61 (p. 146).

8. Geoffrey Lampe in G. W. H. Lampe and D. M. MacKinnon, *The Resurrection*, ed. William Purcell (London: A. R. Mowbray & Co. Ltd, 1966), p. 97.

9. Hans Urs von Balthasar, *The Glory of the Lord: A Theological Aesthetics*, eds. Joseph Fessio S.J. and John Riches, 7 vols (Edinburgh: T. & T. Clark, 1982–91), vol. I: Seeing the Form, p. 32.

10. Walter Kasper, *Jesus the Christ*, trans. V. Green (London: Burns & Oates, 1976), p. 130.

11. Frances Young, 'Can There Be Any Evidence?', in *Incarnation and Myth: The Debate Continued*, ed. Michael Goulder (London: SCM Press, 1979), p. 62.

12. Hans Urs von Balthasar, *Mysterium Paschale*, trans. Aidan Nichols O.P. (Edinburgh: T. & T. Clark, 1990), p. 194.

13. For a rare non-positivist historical approach to the resurrection see J. I. H. McDonald, *The Resurrection: Narrative and Belief* (London: SPCK, 1989).

14. Balthasar, *The Glory of the Lord*, vol. I, p. 32.

15. Balthasar, *Mysterium Paschale*, p. 200.

16. Ibid., p. 191.

17. Ibid., p. 198.

18. Luke 24:5.

19. Hans Frei, *Theology and Narrative: Selected Essays*, eds. George Hunsinger and William C. Placher (New York and Oxford: Oxford University Press, 1993), p. 59.

20. Mark 8:27.

21. Frei, *Theology and Narrative*, p. 74.
22. Matthew 27:11; Mark 15:2; Luke 23:3 and John 19:33.
23. Frei, *Theology and Narrative*, pp. 75–6.
24. Luke 24:34.
25. Frei, *Theology and Narrative*, p. 83.
26. John 11:25.
27. Frei, *Theology and Narrative*, p. 85.
28. Michael Root, 'The Narrative Structure of Soteriology', in *Why Narrative? Readings in Narrative Theology*, eds. Stanley Hauerwas and L. Gregory Jones (Grand Rapids, Michigan: William B. Eerdmans, 1989), pp. 263–78 (p. 264).
29. Alasdair MacIntyre, *After Virtue: A Study in Moral Theory*, 2nd edn (London: Duckworth, 1985), p. 205.
30. MacIntyre, *After Virtue*, p. 212.
31. Ibid., p. 213.
32. Ibid., pp. 215–16.
33. Ibid., p. 219.
34. See John Milbank, 'The Name of Jesus: Incarnation, Atonement, Ecclesiology', *Modern Theology*, 7, 1991, pp. 311–33 (p. 324).
35. Milbank, 'The Name of Jesus', p. 317. See also William J. Lunny, *The Sociology of the Resurrection* (London: SCM Press, 1989), pp. 41–103.
36. John 14:18–23; 13:34.
37. Mark 16:7.
38. Milbank, 'The Name of Jesus', p. 319.
39. Ibid., p. 325.
40. Edith Wyschogrod, *Saints and Postmodernism: Revisioning Moral Philosophy* (Chicago: University of Chicago Press, 1990), p. 13.
41. Ibid., p. xxiii.
42. Milbank, 'The Name of Jesus', p. 319.
43. Ibid.
44. From the Opening Prayer of the Mass for Easter Sunday.

Chapter 9

SEXUALITY AND THE RESURRECTION OF THE BODY: REFLECTIONS IN A HALL OF MIRRORS

Tina Beattie

Now we are seeing a dim reflection in a mirror; but then we shall be seeing face to face. The knowledge that I have now is imperfect; but then I shall know as fully as I am known. (1 Cor. 13:12)[1]

My first childhood visit to a hall of mirrors was an entry into a wonderland of images that were me and yet not me, familiar enough to be recognizable, different enough to be hilarious and a little disconcerting. Years later, when I took my own children to a hall of mirrors, the magic had disappeared. I was struck by how tawdry it was, with its scratched plastic mirrors, peeling paint and smell of sweaty bodies.

With regard to bodily resurrection, we might feel that, like adults in a hall of mirrors, we have outgrown the fascination of earlier generations. But the symbols of faith are made meaningful by our willingness to enter into a story in order to live it anew, and to circumscribe our speculations by a sense of wonder at that which we cannot understand. When considering the resurrection of the body, we glean some idea of what we might look like in the mirrors of revelation, but we also know that the experience of being a body can never be captured in the reflected image. This essay is a theological play on images that takes pleasure in seeing things differently but recognizes that there are as many possible reflections as there are mirrors of theory and discourse. However, I also write in the belief that the fundamental symbols of the Christian faith are not just mirrors in an empty hall, but that they designate the 'body' of truth that is there, a body that cannot know itself fully until the end of time, but that can nevertheless glimpse its likeness in the mirrors of every age. To quote Paul Ricoeur: 'I am convinced that we must think, not *behind* the symbols, but starting from symbols, *according* to symbols, that their substance is indestructible, that they constitute the *revealing* substrate of speech which lives among men. In short, the symbol *gives rise to* thought.'[2]

In what follows I bring Freud's theory of the Oedipus complex into play with the biblical narrative, in order to suggest a feminist reinterpretation of Christian sexual symbols that does not sever the symbols from their archaic significance.[3] I want to ask what sexual difference, and in particular the maleness of Christ, might mean in terms of the resurrection.

Feminist theology argues plausibly that the maleness of Christ has served to legitimate the subordination of women. Rosemary Radford Ruether's question, 'Can a male savior save women?'[4] articulates what many regard as a crucial issue, especially bearing in mind Athanasius's axiom, 'What is not assumed is not redeemed, but what is assumed is saved by union with God.'[5] Elizabeth Johnson claims that 'if maleness is essential for the christic role, then women are cut out of the loop of salvation, for female sexuality is not taken on by the Word made flesh. If maleness is constitutive for the incarnation and redemption, female humanity is not assumed and therefore not saved.'[6]

Many Christian feminists argue that Christ's maleness was a feature of his incarnation into the gendered human species but is not of eschatological significance, emphasizing instead his humanity and his identification with the oppressed. Sandra Schneiders writes that 'Christ, in contrast to Jesus, is not male, or more exactly not exclusively male. Christ is quite accurately portrayed as black, old, Gentile, female, Asian or Polish.'[7] The basis of my argument is that sexual difference is not in the same category as race and age, but that it represents the fundamental likeness of God in human nature, and to minimize the male and female symbolism of the Christian narrative is to impoverish it possibly to the point of incoherence.

From a Catholic perspective, the preoccupation with Christ as the exclusive (male) symbol of salvation is misguided, since Catholic theology has always understood the story of salvation as involving both male and female co-operation at every stage. Catholic doctrine holds that sexual difference is an integral feature of the order of salvation perpetuated in the resurrection. To quote from the 'Declaration on the Admission of Women to the Ministerial Priesthood':

Could one say that, since Christ is now in the heavenly condition, from now on it is a matter of indifference whether he be represented by a man or by a woman, since 'at the resurrection men and women do not marry' (Matt. 22:30)? But this text does not mean that the distinction between man and woman, insofar as it determines the identity proper to the person, is suppressed in the glorified state; what holds for us holds also for Christ . . . In Biblical Revelation this difference is the effect of God's will from the beginning: 'male and female he created them.' (Gen. 1:27)[8]

Adam/Eve, Jesus/Mary, Christ/the Church, man/woman have tended to function hierarchically in theological discourse so that the second term is understood as inferior to the first, but perhaps it is possible to reinterpret these pairings to suggest new relationships between them. What follows is not a comprehensive reinterpretation but an invitation to wander through a hall of mirrors, to confront strange images not as a way of saying 'this is!' but as a way of asking 'what if?' My purpose is not so much to endorse the Freudian viewpoint as to ask, if this is true how might it affect the way in which we interpret Christian symbolism as it relates to the resurrection.

Central to Freud's psychoanalytic theory is what he called the Oedipus complex, after the tragic figure of Greek mythology, Oedipus, who killed his father and married his mother. During infant development, the mother is the first object of the child's desire. The earliest memories of childhood, which are later repressed and assigned to the unconscious, originate in this pre-Oedipal stage of maternal desire. The child becomes aware of being in competition with the father for the mother's love, which leads to a wish to murder the father and marry the mother. Initially the pre-Oedipal child does not differentiate between the sexes, but in time the father's claim to the mother's body becomes associated with possession of the penis. The realization that the mother lacks a penis results in fear of castration in the male child as punishment for desiring her. He resolves the Oedipal stage by repressing his desire for the mother and identifying with the father as his means of entry into the social order, but also subliminally as an expression of the wish to kill the father and take his place. The resolution of the Oedipus complex entails the development of what Freud called the super-ego, the acquisition of the cultural and moral values which govern society, referred to by Freud as the Law of the Father.

However, the repressed desire to kill the father and marry the mother finds repeated expression by exerting a subliminal influence over conscious thought and actions.

Freud called female sexuality 'the dark continent' of psychoanalysis, with the stages of the Oedipus complex being less clearly resolved in girls. Believing themselves to be already castrated, girls develop penis-envy, repressing desire for the mother and identifying with the father in their wish to possess the penis, a wish which is ultimately satisfied by giving birth to a male child. All sexual identity, masculine and feminine, is therefore phallic, being ordered around possession or lack of the penis, with masculinity representing activity and presence, and femininity representing passivity and absence.

I want to imagine Freud's theory as a curved mirror in which to view the biblical story, standing in a position that reveals a different picture of Christianity from that described by Freud.[9] I begin my exploration not with the resurrection but with creation and the fall in the belief that, to quote Ricoeur again, 'Reflection must embrace both an archaeology and an eschatology.'[10]

There is a sense of pre-Oedipal innocence about the Yahwist account of the Garden of Eden. 'Now both of them were naked, the man and his wife, but they felt no shame in front of each other' (Gen. 2:25). The first sign of alienation between humanity and God is the severing of the relationship between male and female, who together reflected the image of God in creation: 'God created man in the image of himself, in the image of God he created him, male and female he created them' (Gen. 1:27). The moment of shame between Adam and Eve and their desire to conceal their nakedness reveals their disobedience to God: '"Who told you that you were naked?" he asked. "Have you been eating of the tree I forbade you to eat?"' (Gen. 3:11).

In pre-patriarchal symbolism associated with the goddess religions, the serpent and the tree of life were symbols of regeneration and fertility, and the serpent also represented wisdom and power.[11] In the Freudian world, women's libido is passive and dominated by the phallus, but if we accept the traditional belief that Eve was a virgin in Eden, it can be argued that the serpent represents Eve's active libido prior to any sexual intervention. (I use the word 'libido' loosely to suggest a sense of uninhibited pre-Oedipal desire experienced in and through the body but not focused on genitality alone.) 'The woman saw that the tree was good to eat and pleasing to the eye, and that it was desirable for the knowledge that it could give. So she took some of its fruit and ate it. She gave some also to her husband who was with her, and he ate it' (Gen. 3:6). The organization of the sexual drives around the phallus is a feature of the fallen psyche and it is difficult for us to imagine a state of libidinal fecundity innocent of all the connotations of our troubled sexuality.

The serpent symbolizes wisdom as well as fertility. So indoctrinated are we in our condemnation of Eve, that we rarely pause to consider the paradox that she poses. Wise Eve, confidante of the serpent, wanted that which we value above all else – she wanted the knowledge of good and evil from which springs all moral responsibility, freedom and choice. However, such knowledge represents temptation rather than wisdom in human existence. Our moral capacity is finite, unable to cope with the godlike nature of our knowledge. Hungering after the simplicity of Eden, weary of responsibility, confused by the pain of living, we long to return to a state of undifferentiated goodness. So we embark on a futile endeavour to separate good from evil, to locate the source of evil elsewhere than in our own existence. 'The man replied, "It was the woman you put with me; she gave me the fruit, and I ate it." Then Yahweh God asked the woman, "What is this you have done?" The woman replied, "The serpent tempted me and I ate"' (Gen. 3:12–13). After the fall, difference represents not the diverse goodness of creation but otherness and alienation marked by guilt and blame. Now, in order to live together we must have structures that contain our murderous desires and give expression to our need to blame, structures that divide between good and evil so that we can befriend those who are the same as us, and blame those who are other than us. Freud's Law of the Father makes coexistence possible in our state of alienation, but it does so by perpetuating that primal broken relationship when Adam pointed his finger at Eve. According to Freud, the complexity of the Oedipal stage in girls mars their personal development and affects the formation of their super-ego, so that they never become fully integrated into the social order. The structuring of the super-ego around the phallus makes women born losers in the system that governs our fallen world.

Genesis describes the serpent as 'the most subtle of all the wild beasts that Yahweh had made' (Gen. 3:1). Eve's yielding to temptation creates a change in her relationship to the serpent: 'I will make you enemies of each other: you and the woman, your offspring and her offspring. It will crush your head and you will strike its heel' (Gen. 3:15). Referring to the symbolism of dreams, Freud says, 'Male sexual symbols that are less easy to understand are certain *reptiles* and fishes: above all, the famous symbol of the *serpent*.'[12] The serpent, symbol of fertile wisdom, has become the phallus, symbol of painful yearning: 'I will multiply your pains in childbearing, you shall give birth to your children in pain. Your yearning shall be for your husband, yet he will lord it over you' (Gen. 3:16). The word 'yearning' evokes a sense of insatiable desire experienced as loss, representing in Oedipal terms the sacrifice of maternal desire in order to gain entry into the social order, and in biblical terms Eve's sacrifice of oneness with God, with Adam and with nature in order to gain moral knowledge. Eve's punishment brings into being the conflict between the Freudian drives of Eros and Thanatos, love and death, proliferation and annihilation, good and evil.

In introducing death as the inevitable corollary to birth and life, the curse of Genesis is a curse on fertility – on human fertility in the punishment borne by Eve, and on the earth's fertility in the punishment borne by Adam: 'Accursed be the soil because of you. With suffering shall you get your food from it every day of your life' (Gen. 3:17). Adam is alienated from the body in which his life originated, and is condemned to a futile struggle with the earth that will finally consume him. 'With sweat on your brow shall you eat your bread, until you return to the soil, as you were taken from it' (Gen. 3:19). The phallus symbolizes Adam's need to achieve domination over the body of Eve and over the body of the earth in order to survive, but he works in the presentiment of his own death, the death wish threatening to overwhelm his desire to live.

There is ambiguity in psychoanalytic theories about the relationship between the biological penis and the symbolic phallus, but the phallus has a power vested in language and the social order which is out of all proportion to the biological reality that it represents. There is, in other words, a severance between the word and the flesh. In an article entitled 'On Doing Body Theology', James Nelson writes:

We have genitalized so much of our masculine spirituality with the values of the phallus, the prized male erection, the quintessential symbol of manliness. Ideally, the phallus is big, hard and up. So we have accented those values in the divine. God, too, must be big, hard and up: sovereign in power, righteous in judgement, the transcendent Wholly Other . . . But, when we finally realize how one-sided this is, a new revelation comes. Genitally speaking, in fact, we men are *not* big, hard and up very much of the time – thank heavens. More of the time we are small, soft, and down.[13]

Yahweh says, 'The man has become like one of us, with his knowledge of good and evil' (Gen. 3:22). Cast out of Eden, Adam becomes like a god. Forgetting the nature of God and alienated from the woman with whom he might find the image of God restored, he begins to make god in his own image to serve as the repository of all his frustrated desires. Ultimately though, this Oedipal god becomes an idol, a symbol not of the primal goodness of creation but of the fall into murderous desire, repression and guilt, attesting to Adam's alienation and the futility of his struggle to defy death in his conquest of the earth. This is the god that, as Nelson suggests, eventually becomes a metaphysical erection towering over the failure of human existence.

Feminist analysis has revealed the extent to which women (and, I would add, 'womanly' men) have suffered and continue to suffer under phallic domination, to such an extent that the original goodness of sexual difference might seem irreparably damaged, and maleness eternally blighted in its potential to represent love and gentleness. If the risen body is glorified in Christ, it must be a body that is indeterminate in its sexuality and not one that glorifies maleness. But if God is to redeem the goodness of *all* creation, then the redemption of humanity as male and female is as central to the story of resurrection as it is to the story of creation. Our sexuality is not incidental to our humanity. It is the focus of our identity, and the source of our most intense desires and frustrations. To want to obliterate sexual difference is to suggest that our fallen sexuality is so painful that it can only be dealt with by an act of annihilation. But the symbols of incarnation and resurrection suggest another way, an order of redemption that does not forget our pain but that affirms our embodiment as sexual beings.

Why does the Word become male flesh? Is it because Eve, paradoxically cursed and blessed in childbirth, offers no symbol of femininity akin to the masculine phallus that represents the severance between word and flesh? It is Adam who experiences alienation from the earth and enters into battle with the material world, while Eve remains bound in her fertile but suffering body to the cycles and rhythms of nature. When the Word becomes flesh, Adam is reunited with the body he has denied, but in that reunification the power of the disembodied phallic symbol is disabled by the reality of the body's suffering, its softness and vulnerability. Christ took on the phallus in order to expose the 'big, hard, up' lie which sanctions male power and brutalizes the male body. 'God dealt with sin by sending his own Son in a body as physical as any sinful body, and in that body God condemned sin' (Rom. 8:3). If the social order is governed by the phallus, then women as well as men sin by their association with the phallic order, whether through aggressive participation or through passive collusion. When Christ becomes the sinful male body, he liberates women as well as men from the domination of the phallus.

The Freudian social order reserves its richest rewards for those manly men who are able to uphold its rules. The temptation in the wilderness symbolizes Christ's encounter with the privileges conferred by the god of this world. 'Next, taking him to a very high mountain, the devil showed him all the kingdoms of the world and their splendour. "I will give you all these" he said, "if you fall at my feet and worship me"' (Matt. 4:8–9). In rejecting Satan's offer, Christ steps outside the social order and embraces the values of otherness and difference, and when a man does this, he threatens to plunge the social order into chaos. The Law of the Father must be perpetuated in the Son or the edifice of power might crumble. Every religion and culture has its Law and its God which control our fallen desires by rewarding conformity and punishing difference. Until one day, a man comes claiming to be the Son of a different God, a God who puts love before the Law, who touches and heals, who communes with women and children, with lepers and outcasts, a God who seeks to topple the Freudian world from within.

The cross signifies the vengeance of the big, hard Phallus on this gentle and vulnerable God, but it also signifies the death of the phallic god in the rebirth of God into plurality and relationality. In the Trinity we are once again invited into a harmonious world of unity in difference. 'God wanted all perfection to be found in him and all things to be reconciled through him and for him, everything in heaven and everything on earth, when he made peace by his death on the cross' (Col. 1:19–20).

An image sometimes used to challenge patriarchal thinking is that of the Christa figure, in which the crucified body of Christ is female. While there is a certain iconoclastic value in such tactics, I think they are fraught with risk. The crucified woman's body affirms rather than subverts the social order, holding up an image that does not call into question the values of patriarchy but affirms those values in their most violent aspect. Christa perpetuates the violence done to woman by eternally inscribing the female body with the marks of her suffering. So what does the virgin body of Mary signify as the female symbol of redemption, given that in the Catholic tradition she shares in Christ's salvific suffering and prefigures with him our heavenly resurrection in the doctrine of the assumption?

Since the second century Mary has been known as the New Eve, and she has sometimes been identified with the feminine biblical figure of Wisdom. The conception of Jesus recalls Eve's association with fertility and wisdom outside the symbolic order of Freudian sexuality. In a moment of libidinal feminine desire, the Virgin Mary encounters the angel in the presence of God as once Eve encountered the serpent in the presence of God. 'Rejoice, so highly favoured! The Lord is with you' (Luke 1:28).

Mary's virginity represents the integrity of women before God in themselves, outside the defining roles of marriage and motherhood, and it is not reducible to its association with her motherhood. The traditional emphasis on Mary's spirituality has the power to subvert sexual hierarchies that associate men with spirituality and women with carnality. Perhaps this is why Mary's redemptive suffering constitutes a piercing of the soul (Luke 2:35), while her body remains inviolate. However, as mother Mary is also archetype of the Church and mother of all humanity, in a tradition that does not simply divide body from spirit. The celebration of the mother's body that is buried deep in the Freudian unconscious finds expression in the cult of Mary in art, music and devotion, in rich and sensual practices that overflow the restraints of the patriarchal Church.

In reuniting spirit and body, word and flesh, the incarnation represents not only the redemption of male and female sexuality, but also the healing of the damaged relationship between humanity and nature. In his conversation with Nicodemus with its imagery of new birth, Jesus says that 'the Son of Man must be lifted up as Moses lifted up the serpent in the desert, so that everyone who believes may have eternal life in him' (John 3:13–15). The biblical serpent is a symbol of healing as well as of curse, and paradoxically the serpent lifted up by Moses offered healing to those who had been bitten by serpents (cf. Num. 21:8–9). Mary as the New Eve makes possible the lifting up of the serpent in the desert, symbolizing the end of the curse on fertility, the healing power of love over barrenness and death. 'Let the wilderness and the dry-lands exult, let the wasteland rejoice and bloom' (Isa. 35:1). When man and woman are reconciled in the incarnation, the whole natural order is redeemed, as is suggested by St Augustine in his reflection on the Eucharist:

> In hesitation I turn to Christ, since I am herein seeking Himself; and I discovered how the earth may be worshipped without impiety. For he took upon him earth for earth; because flesh is from earth, and He received flesh from the flesh of Mary. And because He walked here in very flesh, and gave that very flesh to us to eat for our salvation.[14]

The incarnation restores to maleness the experience of loving self-giving expressed in and through the body, and to femaleness the experience of spirituality and joyful desire without violence or sexual possession, in sexual symbols that make possible once again the harmonious and loving difference that was shattered in Genesis. With this in mind, I turn now to the resurrection.

There are subtle resonances between John's account of the resurrection and the Genesis story. 'At the place where he had been crucified there was a garden, and in this garden a new tomb in which no one had yet been buried' (John 19:41). In Genesis, when Adam and Eve are cast out of the garden the earth itself is accursed and consumes Adam in spite of his efforts to master it. In the return to the garden in John, the new tomb suggests the earth's purity restored, a virginal womb that nurtures and gives birth to the new Adam in the risen Christ.

Christ appears first to Mary of Magdala, who was known as the apostle to the apostles in the early Church because she witnessed the resurrection. After the fall, God posted cherubs and a flaming sword 'to guard the way to the tree of life' (Gen. 3:24). When Mary of Magdala looks into the tomb, she sees 'two angels in white sitting where the body of Jesus had been' (John 20:12). The cherubs that barred access to the tree of life have become the angels that watch over the resurrection. In Mary's encounter with Christ, Eve at last eats of the fruit of the tree of life. Where Eve was cast out of the garden in suffering, Mary is sent out in the joy of the risen Christ.

Jesus tells Mary not to cling to him but to go and tell the brothers what she has seen, while Thomas is told to touch and believe. Woman, so long a symbol of silent embodiment, is invited by Christ to relinquish her fearful clinging to the body and to speak. Man, whose belief has become a product of language that has forgotten the feel of a body, is invited to touch the wounded body of Christ as the way to belief.

But by this stage in the story, the hall of mirrors has become a darkened room where we know the symbols we describe in terms of remembered images, intuitions and the most veiled of revelations. Mary does not recognize Christ by sight but only when he says her name. 'Jesus said, "Mary!" She knew him then' (John 20:16). The disciples on the road to Emmaus recognize him in the breaking of bread. Like these first disciples, we must learn to recognize the presence of the risen Christ through his association with other symbols, for we experience him only in indirect and shadowy forms that draw on the symbols of the past to open our imaginations to the promise of the future. The breaking of bread symbolizes the Eucharist, but does Christ's naming of Mary and her recognition of him symbolize baptismal rebirth? Perhaps the first Christian baptism entailed Christ naming a woman, in order that she might become the first apostle and the first member of the Church.

Paul suggests that belief in the resurrection is necessary to make sense of faith: 'If there is no resurrection of the dead, Christ himself cannot have been raised, and if Christ has not been raised then our preaching is useless and your believing it is useless' (1 Cor. 15:13–14). In its rejection of Gnostic tendencies to devalue the body the Catholic tradition has, perhaps in spite of itself, been led to an affirmation not just of bodily resurrection, but of the goodness of women's resurrected bodies. According to Augustine:

> Now the sex of the female derives not from a disorder, but from nature, a nature freed henceforth from the marriage union and from child-bearing. All the same, the female organism will survive, not indeed to serve its previous function, but enhanced with a new beauty, a beauty that will not excite concupiscence, which will have disappeared, but will serve to glorify the wisdom and mercy of God, who created what before did not exist, and who has freed from corruption that which He created.[15]

Augustine's ideas on sexuality and original sin make it unlikely that women reading the above will feel immediately reassured, but it is possible to read the quotation subversively to reveal a surprising affirmation of feminist values. At the resurrection, women will not be objects of exchange among men, valued only as wives, childbearers and sex objects. Women will exist purely for the joy of being, glorifying wisdom and mercy, beautiful in the eyes of God, with their sexuality affirmed as part of the goodness of creation and redemption.

In the Catholic tradition, the resurrection and ascension of Christ finds its sexual complement in the assumption of Mary, declared as dogma in 1950.[16] Mary, assumed into heaven body and soul at the end of her life, is the heavenly bride, queen, mother, daughter and virgin, loving transgressor of all the kinship systems that keep the Freudian world in place. In this world, our fallen sexuality must be controlled and repressed, but in the Kingdom of Heaven the fullness of loving is hinted at in the enigmatic relationship between Mary and the Godhead.

The book of Revelation tells us, 'Happy are those who are invited to the wedding feast of the Lamb' (Rev. 19:9). The symbolism of the wedding feast draws on the combined imagery of sexuality and food. I said earlier that the curse on fertility is represented by Eve's pain in childbirth and Adam's struggle for food. The greatest sufferings in this world revolve around sex and food, around lust and hunger, but alive within us, however embryonically, is an awareness of an alternative reality. Sexuality retains the goodness of creation in its potential to express delight and love far in excess of the procreative urge. Food represents feasting as communal and sacred celebration which achieves more than the satisfaction of physical hunger. We have never lost the capacity to share something of ourselves in ways that transcend the hierarchies of power and allow for fleeting but loving encounters that whisper to us of heaven.

The New Jerusalem symbolizes the fulfilment of the historical journey that began with Eve's desire to know good and evil, but it is not a simple return to Eden. Our journey has been too long and costly for that. The heavenly wedding feast begins with the wiping away of tears by a God whose hands are pierced and whose body has bled for love. However imperfectly we glimpse the promise of the resurrection, the combined images of consolation and celebration assure us that everything we are and have been, all our sufferings and our hopes, will be acknowledged and transformed. In this context, is there even significance in the fact that the eschaton is represented by a city rather than a garden? The city, symbol of all that we hold dehumanizing in this urban age but also symbol of humanity's greatest creative endeavour, will be caught up in the transformation that will make 'the whole of creation new' (Rev. 21:5).

Critics argue that such anticipations of heaven leads to a passive acceptance of earthly suffering, and that Christian eschatology translates into worldly indifference to injustice and inequality. This has led some theologians to reject the traditional symbols of resurrection in favour of a vision which they see to be more in harmony with contemporary concerns. According to Ruether, 'To the extent to which we have transcended egoism for relation to community, we can also accept death as the final relinquishment of individuated ego into the great matrix of being.'[17]

The problem with this is that theology itself has become disembodied from the symbols wherein it finds coherence. Christianity does not see the end purpose of creation as dissolution into the matrix of being – it might even be suggested that this represents the ultimate surrender to the Freudian death wish. At every stage of creation, God saw what he had made and it was very good. The resurrection of the body is a preposterous doctrine for the modern mind to accept, but it is also a powerful and coherent affirmation of the goodness of creation in all its wondrous diversity.

The challenge for Christians is not to change their symbols of redemption but to embody them in their own lives and institutions in such a way that they offer hope and new life to those who suffer under the phallic power of this world, under the curse of lust and hunger.

I have argued that the sexual/social condition diagnosed by Freud is a consequence of sin, but I have also affirmed the created goodness of sexual difference. This requires recognizing that many of our gender roles are socially constructed, while contending that our sexual identity is an essential aspect of our humanity. The mirrors of sexuality are the most distorting and sometimes the most perplexing of all our strange reflections, and that should caution us against imagining too simplistic a likeness between this-worldly and resurrected sexuality. To affirm sexual difference is not to impose a rigid definition of sexual stereotypes and identities. It is rather to celebrate the possibility of difference that is creative and good, a difference that finds loving union in relationship, in the other who is not like me. Together, male and female, we discover what it means to be lovers of God.

Notes

1. All biblical quotations are taken from *The Jerusalem Bible*.
2. Paul Ricoeur, 'The Hermeneutics of Symbols and Philosophical Reflection: I', trans. Denis Savage, in *The Conflict of Interpretations* (Evanston: Northwestern University Press, 1974), p. 299. Italics in this and all other quotations are as given.
3. To do justice to the relationship between psychoanalysis, feminism and theology would require a more substantial investigation than I can offer here. For a feminist appraisal of Freud, see Juliet Mitchell, *Psychoanalysis and Feminism* (London: Allen Lane, 1974). Readers familiar with the work of Luce Irigaray might recognize her influence in some of what follows.
4. Rosemary Radford Ruether, *Sexism & God-Talk* (London: SCM Press Ltd, 1992), p. 116.
5. Quoted in Elizabeth A. Johnson, 'Redeeming the Name of Christ', in *Freeing Theology – The Essentials of Theology in Feminist Perspective*, ed. Catherine Mowry LaCugna (San Francisco: Harper San Francisco, 1993), p. 119.
6. Ibid., p. 120.
7. Sandra M. Schneiders, *Women and the Word* (New York: Paulist Press,

1986), p. 54, quoted in Johnson, ibid., p. 129.

8. *Vatican Council II – More Post Conciliar Documents*, Vol. 2, ed. Austin Flannery O.P. (Collegeville, Minn.: The Liturgical Press, 1982), pp. 340–1.

9. For Freud's highly speculative account of the Oedipal origins of religion in general and Christianity in particular, see Sigmund Freud, *Totem and Taboo*, trans. James Strachey (London: Routledge & Kegan Paul, 1975).

10. Ricoeur, *The Conflict of Interpretations*, p. 333.

11. Cf. Marina Warner, *Alone of all Her Sex – the Myth and the Cult of the Virgin Mary* (London: Picador, 1990), pp. 268–9. See also Gerda Lerner, *The Creation of Patriarchy* (London and New York: Oxford University Press, 1986), Chapters 9 and 10. For an extensive discussion of symbolism see Paul Ricoeur, *The Symbolism of Evil*, trans. Emerson Buchanan (Boston: Beacon Press, 1969). Erin White's essay, 'Religion and the Hermeneutics of Gender: An Examination of the Work of Paul Ricoeur', in *Religion and Gender*, ed. Ursula King (Oxford UK and Cambridge USA: Blackwell, 1995), pp. 77–100, is an interesting feminist critique of Ricoeur's interpretation of the Genesis story. In referring to the symbolism of the goddess religions, I do not want to credit these cults with more virtue than the historical record can sustain but rather to unveil psychological interpretations that are preserved within the symbol, whatever the realities of its historical associations.

12. Sigmund Freud, *Introductory Lectures on Psycho-analysis*, trans. Joan Riviere (London: George Allen & Unwin, 1922), p. 130.

13. James B. Nelson, 'On Doing Body Theology', *Theology & Sexuality*, 2, March 1995, pp. 49–53.

14. Quoted in Monica Migliorino Miller, *Sexuality and Authority in the Catholic Church* (Scranton: University of Scranton Press; London and Toronto: Associated University Presses, 1995), pp. 154–5.

15. Quoted in Kari Elisabeth Børresen, *Subordination and Equivalence – the Nature and Role of Women in Augustine and Thomas Aquinas*, trans. Charles H. Talbot (Washington DC: University Press of America, 1981), p. 86.

16. For a history of the Assumption, see Warner, *Alone of all Her Sex*, Chapter Six.

17. Ruether, *Sexism & God-Talk*, pp. 257–8.

Chapter 10

THE RESURRECTION, THE HOLY SPIRIT AND
THE WORLD RELIGIONS

Gavin D'Costa

One might say that for St John the Evangelist, the
resurrection is Pentecost. John, as Raymond Brown puts
it well, should have logically 'joined the author of the
Epistle to the Hebrews in having Jesus go directly to the Father
from the cross, for the resurrection does not fit easily into John's
theology of the crucifixion'.[1] This ill fit has more to do with
John's profundity than with an ideological impatience or
demythologization (as Bultmann preferred to read it) of the
problematic details of the tomb, the nature of Jesus' risen body and
so on.[2] For John, the crucifixion, resurrection, ascension and
Pentecost are all part of the same event – Jesus' presence to his
disciples in the Spirit. In time, how can one deal with the eternity
of God's self-revelation except by narrative? Luke too sees this,
although in a quite different manner. Jesus, after the resurrection
and prior to his ascension, tells his disciples to 'stay in the city, until
you are clothed with power from on high' (Luke 24:49: RSV). Acts
1:8 makes it clear that this 'power' is that of the Holy Spirit. John's
grasp of the resurrection as the inauguration of a new community
and a new creation is yoked to the gift of the Holy Spirit. In this
sense, not only is the resurrection John's Pentecost, it is also the
beginning of the world – a new creation. The gospel ends where it
began, with the creation of the world.

When the risen Jesus appears to his disciples behind locked
doors, after his greeting of peace and commission, the account
continues: 'He breathed [emphysan] on them, and said to them,
"Receive the Holy Spirit"' (John 20:22). John's gospel began with
the theme of creation, and now at this point of decisive
signification, emphysan echoes the Septuagint version of Genesis
2:7, where the same Greek verb is used when God gives life to his
creation through his 'breath' of life, as is also the case in Wisdom
15:11, which rephrases this account as breathing 'a living spirit'.
John signals this dramatic trinitarian transaction earlier in his

narrative when he comments 'for as yet the Spirit had not been given because Jesus was not yet glorified' (7:49). In the resurrection, history and creation are turned inside out. Only after the story of Jesus is told (the hour of glory – 12:23), can the story of creation be properly narrated, a story that is still being enacted primarily in the community designated a 'new creation'. Quite literally, all creation revolves around this event from which it takes its meaning, an event which is made ever anew, or called to be, in the practice of the church. Hence, if we are to enquire about the resurrection in John, we must equally ask about the Spirit, and in John's logic, this is a question about the disciples who form the church – today's Christians. As I shall suggest later, John's seeming idealization of the church does not mitigate his ecclesiology, rather it puts a question to the reality of the church today.

What has all this to do with other religions? As a Roman Catholic, it is of immense significance to me that in Vatican II and since, there has been the claim that the Holy Spirit is present in the world religions. This claim can also be found in recent official church documents from a number of denominations and among differing theologians.[3] There is considerable dispute as to the meaning of such a claim. On the one hand, some have seen it as freeing Christian theology from the tyranny of a Christomonism whereby grace is exclusively related to faith in Jesus, but this view courts a rather free-floating Spirit theology that misreads the Orthodox opposition to the filioque clause.[4] On the other hand, some employ it as if it would make no difference at all if one equally said the Son or Father is present in the world religions, thereby obscuring the sense of this particular usage of 'Spirit' and its justification.

My purpose in this essay is to see whether John's account of the resurrection as the gift of the Holy Spirit can at all illuminate the claim that the Holy Spirit is present in the world religions. One could attempt to read the latter claim through different emphases within John's text, or via other gospels or later traditions. Hence, this is an extremely limited singular attempt to make sense of the claim that the Holy Spirit is present in the world religions and it requires correction and development in the light of wider intra-textual readings, as well as in the light of Christians' encounter with those from other faiths. One obvious objection to my strategy is that John was not concerned with non-Christian religions as such and that using John for this purpose is unlikely to be fruitful as he is so negative and dualistic regarding the 'world'. My response to this can only be unfolded in what follows, but is guided by the conviction that the logic of the gospel demands this type of reading strategy, and every reading is always an enactment.[5]

If a central theme of John's theology of resurrection is the resurrected Jesus breathing upon the disciples with the words 'Receive the Holy Spirit' (John 20:23), my question is: what is understood by the Holy Spirit, for this is key to the resurrection? One clue lies in the preceding chapters (the Farewell Discourse: John 13:31–17:26) where Jesus teaches his disciples about the Holy Spirit. Within this section there are four main Paraclete passages: 14:15–18, 14:25–7, 15:26–7, and 16:7–15 (the final one often being treated as two). As I am unable to enter into discussion of the disagreements over every verse I am citing, I draw the reader's attention to my main secondary materials.[6]

A major context for these four passages, which positions the Discourse text, is the new commandment to love one another *as Jesus has loved his disciples*, which is founded on the Father's love for his Son, which is God's love for the world (John 13:34). The commandment to love is therefore not an ideological egalitarian principle that can be translated without this particular narrative, in the way that liberal theology began to exegete its moral gospel in the nineteenth century. Rather it has both its source and shape in the 'person' of Jesus, God's gift to the world – apart from whom God's love is not known.[7] How, after Jesus' death, can the disciples enact such a commandment?

The section preceding John 14:15–18 suggests astoundingly that the disciples will continue Jesus' work, and even 'greater works than these' (v. 12), so that the reality of God's presence in the world is committed to a faithful community, whose witness to God's action is not to a past event, but a constant repetition, although a non-identical repetition, of this new life, this saving transformation. As John Milbank puts it:

> Christianity is not Platonism. It is not founded upon the vision of a transcendent original which we must imitate. Instead it makes affirmations about the real, and about 'meaning', through the constant *repetition* of a historically

emergent practice which has no real point of origination, but only acquires identity and relative stability *through* this repetition. And what is repeated is not an insight, not an idea (which is properly *imitated*), but a formal becoming, a structured transformation. The . . . forms of the gospel are therefore indispensable, not because they record and point us to a vision which is still available in its eternal 'presence', but rather because they enshrine and constitute the event of a transformation which is to be non-identically repeated, and therefore still made to happen.[8]

The first Paraclete passage throws light on the source of the awesome new creation promised: 'If you love me, you will keep my commandments. And I will pray the Father, and he will give you another Counsellor, to be with you for ever, even the Spirit of truth, whom the world cannot receive, because it neither sees him nor knows him; you know him, for he dwells with you, and will be in you' (14:15–18).

The theme of the Spirit's dwelling within the disciples is structured to parallel the indwelling of the Son and Father introduced at the beginning of the gospel (John 1:1,18), such that the Spirit's dwelling within the disciples will be their keeping the commandment of love, which requires their love of Jesus. The imitation of Christ is central to the meaning of the new church, for they cannot learn to love otherwise. And they cannot learn to learn to love without the Counsellor, the Spirit. Brown comments that in the phrase 'the Spirit *of* truth' the genitive is objective, indicating the relation of the Spirit to 'the' truth who *is* Jesus. Hence, the reading 'Spirit of truth' rather than the 'Spirit *is* truth'.[9] This is important, for the Spirit's role, as we will see, is as witness to 'the' truth of God's self-revelation inaugurated in Jesus. However, we shall also see that this is understood dynamically and personally, so that it does not simply mean identical repetition.

The second Paraclete passage develops this theme: 'These things I have spoken to you, while I am still with you. But the Counsellor, the Holy Spirit, whom the Father will send in my name, he will teach you all things, and bring to your remembrance all that I have said to you' (14:25–7). Compared to the first passage where the pronoun denoting the Spirit is neuter, we have here the personalization of the Spirit with *ekeinos* (he – v. 26), which is also used of the Spirit in 15:26, and 16:7, 8, 13 and 14. While one cannot simply read into this term later controversies regarding 'person' and 'nature', it can be said that God, who is love (1 John 4:8), cannot be other than personal. Indwelling relationships of love are central to this section, because they are central to the trinitarian God who lives. In predicating the presence of the Spirit one is speaking of a personal indwelling presence of God, which, in this passage, functions as teacher and rememberer.

Once more, the Spirit testifies to Jesus, so that the phrase 'he will teach you all things' contrasts with the opening section, 'These things I have spoken to you.' This is supported by 16:13, to which we will shortly turn, which certainly does not suggest that the contrast with 'all' things is to be understood as implying various new truths, or new revelations, but rather a deepening appreciation or a differing practice, or better, a non-identical repetition of the revelation which is given – and present in the Jesus-community's practice. Barrett rightly comments on 'remembrance': 'There is no independent revelation through the Paraclete, but only an application of the revelation in Jesus. The Paraclete recalls . . . and thereby recreates and perpetuates the situation of judgment and decision that marked the ministry of Jesus.'[10] Barrett's unfortunate phrasing tends to essentialize Jesus as a revelatory event, rather than seeing his person as the inauguration of a transforming revelatory practice entrusted to the church. If the Spirit's presence is predicated, it does not denote a new revelation, but rather indicates the power of God working to disclose, further deepen and enact the reality of his presence in the new creation inaugurated by Jesus's resurrection. This is deeply significant.

The third passage develops the theme of the Spirit as witness to Jesus in two related directions. First, in terms of strength and support in persecution (to be developed in John 16:7ff.). The passage comes immediately after a section (John 15:18–25) concerned with the hatred of the world towards Jesus, and the confirmation that if the world hates the disciples (who continue the new creation), it is because the world first hated Jesus. Second, witness is elaborated in terms of the Spirit's co-activity as witnessing to the new creation inaugurated in Jesus and unfolding within the church's practice. The third Paraclete passage reads as follows: 'But when the Counsellor comes, whom I shall send to you from the Father, even the Spirit of truth, who proceeds from the Father, he will bear witness to me; and you also are witnesses, because you have been with me from the beginning' (John 15:26–7).

The opposition to the world and the Spirit's function in forensically affirming the disciples against the world is usually rightly focused on, but sometimes at the cost of the simultaneously startling claim being made about the church. To a faithful church, a faithful witness, the Spirit co-constitutes this fidelity of witness, so that the structure of these two verses actually shows that the witness of the Spirit and that of the disciples 'are not two separate witnesses' – they are the same.[11] It is precisely because of this that John so daringly equates the persecution of Jesus and the persecution of the church. And if this is accepted, then the Spirit's testifying and teaching activity is to be understood as the enabling practice of the imitation of Christ's love in his risen body, the church. In his closing comments on verses 26 to 27, Brown confirms Barrett's remarks cited above regarding the Spirit as the exegesis of Jesus' revelation: 'Jesus is the supreme revelation of God to men: there can be no witness to the world other than the witness he bore. All other witness by the Paraclete through the disciples simply interprets that.'[12] Hence, in predicating the activity of the Spirit one is already predicating a transformative practice that is inaugurated in Jesus, that both witnesses to him and is an act of praise – and is therefore and must be a cause of both scandal and persecution. This scandal is because of Jesus' *inauguration* of the "political" practice of forgiveness; forgiveness as a mode of "government" and social being' and this in contrast to a 'world of violence and suffering in which human words and conventions – "the law" – are powerless over structures of human egotism and over physical death.'[13]

The final two sections of the last of our Paraclete passages, resume, develop and confirm these themes. The first section, verses 7 to 11, overturns the synoptic stress on the Spirit as advocate defending the disciples (e.g. Matt. 10:20: 'For it is not you who speak, but the Spirit of your Father'; and parallels Mark 13:11; Luke 21:15) into that of the Spirit prosecuting or convicting the world of its sin, in its obsession with dominating power and violence. It is, in Brown's words, a 'reversal of the trial of Jesus, the world is found guilty of *sin* in that it has not acknowledged the *justice* of God in the glorified Jesus'.[14] This inversion is typical of John's dramatic insight and timing. The passage reads:

Nevertheless I tell you the truth: it is to your advantage that I go away for if I do not go away, the Counsellor will not come to you; but if I go, I will send him to you. And when he comes, he will convince the world concerning sin and righteousness and judgment; concerning sin, because they do no believe in me; concerning righteousness, because I go to the Father, and you will see me no more; concerning judgment, because the ruler of this world is judged.[15]

Here the Spirit enables the continuing ministry of Jesus to be exercised in the non-identical repetition of his transformative love.

Those who find unacceptable in John an unrelenting opposition to the world are (or should be) profoundly questioned by the text. The commandment to love is unbearable, quite literally leading to the cross, the tearing apart of the fabric of civility, decency and self-righteousness that clothes our human projects, and unmasks them for what they are: saying no to God's 'power', to God's 'yes' to us in his invitation to self-abandonment and participation in his weak, defenceless, forgiving practice of love. The threefold structure of convicting the world of sin, righteousness and judgement are related to this body 'raised' and 'lifted up' (John 3:14), not only on the cross as a sign of the world's self-condemnation, but also as the 'raised' body of the risen Christ in his church, which must be the sign of the new redeemed creation. This is why the resurrected Jesus, after breathing upon his disciples and giving them the gift of the Spirit, adds: 'If you forgive the sins of any, they are forgiven; if you retain the sins of any, they are retained' (John 20:23). The Spirit, through women and men, continues the work of Jesus, and continues even 'greater works' (John 14:12). Any predication of the Spirit's presence thereby involves the presence both of the condemnation of the world's sin and unrighteousness and of the forgiving love that is greater than this violence and destruction. Atonement is a continuing event.

The second part of the passage returns to the teaching and guiding activity of the Spirit and reaches a crescendo in stating a key paradox: that Jesus brings us God's life in himself, but this life is not a past gift, but a present gift—invitation to die to ourselves, to live as if the future were assured – the madness of hope in the middle of tragedy, violence and destruction. This modality of Jesus' life is constitutive of the imitation of Christ, the non-identical repetition of forgiving practice. How this present gift is made, and how it reaches out into the future is for John through the power of the Spirit:

> I have yet many things to say to you, but you cannot bear them now. When the Spirit of truth comes, he will guide you into all the truth; for he will not speak on his own authority, but whatever he hears he will speak, and he will declare to you the things that are to come. He will glorify me, for he will take what is mine and declare it to you. All that the Father has is mine; therefore I said that he will take what is mine and declare it to you. (John 16:12–15)

The participation in the life of God and nothing less is promised to the disciples. Divinization through participation is a familiar theme in Orthodox theology, and here John indicates that the life of the disciples cannot therefore be anything other than a constant movement of dying into the new life to bring forth a new creation. This life is both a matter of practice and understanding. The Spirit, as in the previous passages, is entirely at the service of unfolding the 'glory' of Jesus. The Spirit's activity is not therefore a matter of disclosing new revelations, and as Brown says is 'more than a deeper intellectual understanding of what Jesus has said – it involves a way of life in conformity with Jesus' teaching'.[16] This is why the later church was to affirm as 'sacramental' the practices of love which conformed it to Christ: conversion (baptism), repentance and forgiveness (confession), a new sharing in God's life (eucharist), and so on. It recognized that in these practices, but not only in these, new life was made possible, for the Spirit of God is forgiveness and vulnerable love. And yet to freeze any set of practices without attention to context is to make non-identical repetition a matter of imitation, a mechanized, depersonalized, ineffective 'transmission' of grace.

Furthermore, and Bultmann saw this so well, the Spirit is the power of proclaiming Jesus' Word ever anew. In commenting on verse 14, he writes:

> This is an express statement that the Spirit's word does not displace or surpass the word of Jesus, as if it were something

new . . . The word of Jesus is not a collection of doctrines that is in need of supplementation, nor is it a developing principle that will only be unfolded in the history of ideas; as the Spirit's proclamation it always remains the word spoken into the world from beyond . . . the Spirit is not the 'inner light' that brings new knowledge on its own authority; it is the ever new power of Jesus' word; it retains the old in the continual newness that arises from the speaking of the word in the present.[17]

This is to say that all truth, goodness and grace can never in any sense contradict the reality of God's transformative life inaugurated in Jesus and that the many things that the disciples cannot bear now are only authentic if they maintain continuity, but not identical repetition, with what has been given as gift in Jesus.[18] Hence, to predicate the Spirit's presence is to invoke the sense in which the new life in Jesus is understood and practiced anew.

It may be possible to summarize some of the themes we have inspected by saying that in John the miracle of the resurrection is the beginning of a new creation, a new Pentecost, whereby Christ is made present in his disciples' practice of keeping Jesus' commandment through the Spirit. Crucifixion, resurrection, ascension and pentecost are the single 'hour' of glory. Almost in the same way that the Father, Son and Spirit indwell each other and the disciples, so is there an indwelling within these events which compels the church to celebrate liturgically after Easter, the feast of the Trinity, then in the Thursday after Trinity Sunday, the feast of the Body and Blood of Christ and the founding of the church. The trinitarian foundation of the church is profoundly developed and clarified in John. This is why one might say, in conclusion, that for John the resurrection is the disturbing gift of the Spirit, who in testimony and witness is always in the likeness of Jesus, both a bountiful gift of new life and a condemnation of sin, violence and greed. And for John, the Spirit's activity only takes place in indwelling those who follow Jesus' commandment to love as Jesus has loved.

Having briefly examined one of the main themes related to John's understanding of the resurrection, the Holy Spirit, we might now see if this bears any relation to the Roman Catholic pronouncements that the Holy Spirit is present in the world religions. But, before we proceed, there is a glaring problem with the exegesis offered above: the church falls desperately short of grand descriptions such as the body of Christ, a transformative atoning community, a new creation. And this dark and broken reality of ecclesial practice throughout history should always stand alarmingly before us lest we be seduced into the temptation to divinize the church and its practices. And despite the many teachings that try and account for and explain that this 'imperfection' is not in contradiction to the basic doctrines about the church – that it is a church of sinners, that we are saved by grace and not works, that we are but a pilgrim church – there is always the danger that these teachings, profound as they are, will obscure the reality of the unbearable darkness of the cross, the depths of our own sinfulness and stupidity, even though redeemed. Does all this negate John's ecclesiology? No, for in part, John's grammar is eschatological: this is what the church should be, but his context also allowed his writing to strike a deep and realistic contemporary note, for a persecuted church might often know more profoundly what it is called to be, than a church that has become part of the status quo.[19] Writing in the West, and from a tenured academic position, and in a society allegedly Christian, there is a temptation to think that John was somewhat extreme due to his experience of deep persecution, rather than to turn the tables round and ask whether it is my own complacent context of Christian practice that makes his church sound so idealized.

Hence, in now asking about *one* set of possible meanings of the claim that the Holy Spirit is present in the world religions, we might well start from the context of the community of Christians, so much in need of this Holy Spirit. One might turn the question round and say, what does it mean to the church to say that the Spirit is present outside itself – within the world religions, and more importantly, what prompts such an articulation? Put like this, I believe, John has much light to shed.[20]

John's own context would clearly have made it difficult if not impossible to attribute the presence of the Spirit to the communities that persecuted the church. Furthermore, it is clear from our exegesis that all talk of the Spirit is properly related to the experience of the church's discernment and practice of the new ways in which it can be, ever anew, an atoning community. This means that we must be extremely reticent about any abstract talk of the 'Spirit in other religions' for this bears little Johannine grammatical sense. If it is to bear any sense, then it can only be generated in the context of specific Christian encounters with non-Christians, for such speech can only be part of the church's discernment (not ownership) of the hidden depths of God's trinitarian history of love unfolding in creation. Hence, any claim about the Spirit in other religions should be taken neither as a phenomenological socio-historical description of a religion, nor as a claim that will necessarily be well-received by a non-Christian (although such usage will always be meant positively). Rather it constitutes a theological evaluation that must spring from and lead to new practice within the church, and is not introduced as part of any non-Christian theological discourse. Vatican II balances the theological ambiguity well: 'We are obliged to hold that the Holy Spirit offers everyone the possibility of sharing in the Paschal Mystery in a manner known to God.'[21]

Hence, John helps us to make clear from the outset that a bogus question has haunted much of the contemporary discussion on other religions.[22] For John, the resurrection means that the question of new, different and alternative 'revelations' is a non-question for it posits a false understanding of time and history. All creation, all time and history, all the irreducible particularity of each person, is now taken up into the new creation inaugurated by Jesus. This is why allegorical and typological readings of Israel's history were permissible in the church: this sacred history both pre-figured and participated in this single new creation in Christ. There was no question of an alternative revelatory history, although in this reading there lies the ever-present danger of repressing the other (the persecution of the Jews in this instance). However, by saying a priori there is no new revelation apart from Christ one is neither circumscribing nor restricting the reality of the Holy Spirit's activity or limiting it to previous practice and understanding as was seen in the preceding exegesis of John. It is simply to say (*without understanding* what this will mean in advance in both practice and theory) that all truth, in whatever form, will serve to make Christ known more fully to Christians. Milbank puts it well:

Jesus is perfectly identified only as the source, goal and context of all our lives: the *esse* of his personality is, in

Thomist terms, *esse ipsum*, or the infinite totality of actualised being which is 'eminently' contained in God. If this is the case, then it cannot be true that we have a metaphysically 'initial' perfect vision of Jesus . . . which we later approximate through our imitations. On the contrary, only through such imitations, and through observing the likeness of Jesus in others, will a full sense of Jesus's personality be approximated to.[23]

This 'observing' requires the Spirit in the act of discernment, and it is here that the possible use of 'Christ' language takes shape. The Spirit in the church allows for the possible (and extremely complex and difficult) discernment of Christ-like practice in the 'other', and in so much as Christ-like activity takes place, then this can also only be through the enabling power of the Spirit.[24] It is here that the distinction and relationship of Spirit and Son language takes on one possible meaning in the context of other religions. And it is here too that we see one sense in which saints are part of what resurrection constitutes in the church (making Christ-like disciples), as well as the significance of 'holy' non-Christian lives.[25] This never-ending process of non-identical repetition involves reading all creation in Christ, such that Milbank must add immediately: 'To some extent, the observation of *every* human "person" follows this pattern, but only in the case of Jesus does an accurate rendering of his personhood involve an ultimate attention to everyone, in so far as their "truth" lies in Christ.'[26] This brings out well the dynamic of John's theology and certainly precludes any triumphalist understanding of the Spirit's presence, for it does not elevate either the practice or understanding of the church, but points rather to the requirement placed upon the church to ever new transformative practice in 'his name', through the witnessing of the Spirit.

Hence, in the light of John, saying that the Spirit is present in the lives of non-Christians is both scandalous and joyous. It must be scandalous for John has told us that the Spirit's presence in bringing to form a new Christ-like creation is always a condemnation on the powers of darkness, 'the ruler of the world is judged' (John 16:11). For the church, it may be that through the actions of non-Christians it comes to recognize how it is itself ensnared by the powers of darkness. Through the witness that non-Christians give through their lives and teachings, Christians have often been called back to faithful discipleship. In this sense, it is also the source of great joy in this calling back, conversion, for the church enters more deeply into the new life it has been entrusted to live and proclaim. Charles Freer Andrews, at least in his early days, experienced precisely this in his meeting with Gandhi, as did Thomas Merton in his meetings with Buddhist monks.

This is certainly not to say that every event that prompts new practice of non-identical repetition is of the Spirit, for this would simply be an uncritical baptism with the Spirit of all creation and culture. Rather, it is to say that when a Christian encounter with non-Christians generates this type of language from the Christian (since it is a language that belongs within the Christian context), then we must remain radically open to its implications which are deeply ecclesiological and Christological. All examples are problematic here, but the presence of Buddhists and Hindus, for instance, involved in non-violent resistance to the use and proliferation of nuclear arms may remind Christians that their faith has not led them as it should have done to question and oppose the use of such unjust and indiscriminate power. Such 'power' is the very antithesis to the 'power' of the kingdom, ensnaring nations and communities in the logic of violence as a form of life. But while such Christ-like resistance may strike us deeply and the sense of the Spirit's presence might move us to speak of 'charity' and 'love', this is not to equate Buddhist notions of compassion for all living beings, the Hindu–Jain doctrine of ahimsā, and Christian forgiveness or forbearance. Ultimately, these forms of practice which we denote 'loving' in the non-Christian may or may not be such, and certainly their narrative context should create some disquiet about any easy correlation. This is one reason for the church's reticence in speaking about the modality of the work of the Spirit and Christ outside the church in any very specific terms.[27]

But John's theology of the resurrection drives us even further to explore any such affirmation of the Spirit's presence in other religions, for the new practice enjoined of the church in the making of such statements requires also the logic of indigenization and mission to be stated, although all too briefly. Each form of new enactment of Christ's atoning and forgiving life requires Christian communities to take up and transform God's creation into a new glorified creation. In the same way that Athanasius realized that what is not assumed is not healed was an expression of the fullness of the incarnation, the church as the body of Christ in its ever-different contexts must inculturate itself to discover the meaning of its designation as 'Catholic'.

Hence, inculturation or indigenization is always an act of continuity within a greater discontinuity; a taking up of what disciples from different cultures and religions may bring to the church, but in this taking up, this being raised, the configuration of new life that emerges can never be predicted or even fully assessed except retrospectively.[28] So while inculturation is always a process of transforming that which may have already been enlivened by the Spirit, it cannot but recreate this within the church's new practice. Vatican II expresses this precisely and starkly concerning growth in new indigenous churches: 'Whatever good is in the minds and hearts of men, whatever good lies latent in the religious practices and cultures of diverse peoples, is not only saved from destruction but is also healed, ennobled, and perfected unto the glory of God, the confusion of the devil, and the happiness of man.'[29]

That which is Christ-like by the power of the Spirit, outside the visible church, is called into a greater completion, its most profound fulfilment. 'Healed', 'ennobled' and 'perfected' all express this sense of the emergence of the new creation, but a creation that is only finally consummated eschatologically. Here the church is always in great danger of obscuring the cross from itself in any premature identification of consummation and fulfilment, for holding that the church is in any sense a 'fulfilment' must always be an enacted fulfilment, a new coming into being. Thus this is not a lesser coming to completion in an already greater, but a new creation taking shape in each practice of new authentic Catholicity, which cannot be predetermined or proscribed by any one community that forms the community of Catholic Christianity.

It is right and fitting that we end where Christ began, and from where John's theology of the resurrection unfolds – mission. The Holy Spirit given to the church is always a call to follow the commandment of love, as Jesus has loved us, with the love of the Father. And this is an invitation to a gift that is so freely given that nothing can contain it, neither the heavens nor the earth as Paul expressed it (Col. 1:20). It is nothing short of the gift of new life, participating in a love that never ends and a love that is powerful in its weakness and vulnerability, as on the cross. It is inconceivable that witnessing to the gospel can ever be less than the meaning of living this new creation, so that John reminds us that there can be no dialogue (as it is often called today) between religions, without mission, for Christians have nothing other to share with people than that which has been given so bountifully to them.

But I must attend to at least some final questions that the reader may entertain having read the above essay. Does not the designation (when it is 'correctly' made) that the Spirit is present in the world religions rob the 'other' of any genuine autonomy? Does it not finally render the non-Christian's life and practice as no more than an anticipation of Christ? Does it not imply a better reading of another's life than they may themselves have? John's theology of the resurrection presses us into having to question the assumptions that drive such questions – in the same way it pressed us to think of other religions not in terms of new revelations. For John, the only true freedom comes from discipleship, so that affirming the Spirit in other religions is actually the only way the church can really begin to take their 'otherness' seriously, for life in God is about dynamic loving relationality, not obliterating sameness, not identical imitation of an endless repetition. Hence, speaking of the Spirit in other religions, is always partly speaking and enacting our entry into a dark cloud of unknowing; a trusting in faith and hope that God's embrace and love for the other is always greater, more joyful and more surprising than we – or they – will ever know.

Notes

1. Raymond E. Brown, *The Gospel According to John. Introduction, Translation and Notes* (2 Vols, London: Geoffrey Chapman, 1966), 2, p. 1013.
2. See Rudolf Bultmann, *The Gospel of John. A Commentary* (Oxford: Basil Blackwell, 1971), especially pp. 681–99.
3. Roman Catholic statements can be found in Vatican II: *Gaudium et Spes*, 22, *Lumen Gentium*, 16, and Pope John Paul II who reflects and develops these themes in *Dominum et Vivificantem* (On the Holy Spirit in the Life of the Church), 1986, esp. paras. 53–4, and also *Redemptoris Missio* (1990), esp. paras. 21–30. For an ecumenical statement, see WCC 'Baar Statement' in *Current Dialogue*, 19, 1991, pp. 47–51 (pt. IV, p. 50); for an Orthodox viewpoint see Metropolitan George Khodr, 'Christianity in a

Pluralist World – the Economy of the Holy Spirit', in *Living Faiths and the Ecumenical Movement*, ed. S. J. Samartha (Geneva: WCC, 1971), pp. 131–42, and also 'An Orthodox perspective on Inter-Religious Dialogue', in *Current Dialogue*, 19, 1991, pp. 25–7.

4. Paul Knitter is partly guilty of this in Knitter, 'A New Pentecost?', *Current Dialogue*, 19, 1991, pp. 32–41 (esp. pp. 39–41). For a strong statement of the Orthodox insistence, see Vladmir Lossky, *The Mystical Theology of the Eastern Church* (London: James Clarke, 1957), chs. 7 & 8. See *Redemptoris Missio*, paras. 17–18 which are implicitly critical of Knitter's and like-minded positions.

5. In this I am sympathetic to the 'Yale school' in terms of hermeneutical strategy and for the notion of the performance of a text: see especially Hans W. Frei, *The Eclipse of Biblical Narrative* (New Haven: Yale U.P., 1974; Ronald F. Thiemann, *Revelation and Theology: The Gospel as Narrated Promise* (Notre Dame: Notre Dame U.P., 1985); George C. Lindbeck, *The Nature of Doctrine. Religion and Theology in a Postliberal Age* (London: SPCK, 1984); and Gerard Loughlin's masterly development of both these themes in *Telling God's Story: Bible, Church and Narrative Theology* (Cambridge: Cambridge University Press, Cambridge, 1996), and in his essay in this collection.

6. See Brown, *John*; Bultmann, *John*; C. K. Barrett, *The Gospel According to John*, 2nd edn. (London: SPCK, 1978); Barnabas Lindars, *The Gospel of John* (London: Oliphants, 1972); George Johnston, *The Spirit-Paraclete in the Gospel of John* (Cambridge: Cambridge University Press, 1970); C. F. D. Moule, *The Holy Spirit* (London: Mowbrays, 1978).

7. For a proper reading of 'person' as narrative relationship rather than enduring substance, see Bruce Marshall, *Christology in Conflict* (Oxford: Blackwell, 1987), pp. 176–89 and related notes.

8. See John Milbank's essay, 'The Name of Jesus: Incarnation, Atonement, Ecclesiology', *Modern Theology*, 7, 4, 1991, pp. 311–33 (p. 319). I am indebted to Milbank's articulation of an ecclesiological practice as the required site of revelation. Milbank, however, is in danger of playing down the problem of authority involved in such new practices.

9. Brown, *John*, p. 639; see also Bultmann, *John*, p. 615. I John v. 6/7 does use 'is', but the context there does not affect this reading.

10. Barrett, *John*, p. 467.

11. Brown, *John*, p. 700; also Bultmann, *John*, p. 554; Barrett, *John*, pp. 482–3.

12. Brown, *John*, p. 701.

13. Milbank, 'Name' p. 327, then p. 319.

14. Brown, *John*, p. 705.
15. See Pope John Paul II's excellent meditative exegesis on this passage in *Dominum*, Pt. II.
16. Brown, *John*, p. 715.
17. Bultmann, *John*, p. 576. See also Moule's illuminating comment about the Spirit in the New Testament as a whole: *Spirit*, p. 38.
18. See Lindars, *John*, p. 506.
19. See Raymond E. Brown, *The Community of the Beloved Disciple* (London: Geoffrey Chapman, 1979).
20. The early fathers saw this primarily in terms of a logos Christology. See C. Saldanha, *Divine Pedagogy: A Patristic View of non-Christian Religions* (Rome: LAS, 1984), regarding the logos spermaticus tradition; and J. Dupuis, *The Cosmic Christ* (Bangalore: Theological Publications in India, 1977), regarding the cosmic Christ tradition. I have touched on the way in which the Spirit might relate to this type of approach which is in great need of creative rehabilitation.
21. *Gaudium et Spes*, 22.
22. See my 'Revelation and "revelations": Beyond a Static Valuation of Other Religions', *Modern Theology*, 10, 2, 1994, pp. 165–84.
23. Milbank, 'Name', p. 325. He uses 'imitation' here in contrast to the earlier citation (note 8) to mean non-identical repetition as the imitation of Christ.
24. See *Redemptoris Missio*, esp. paras. 17–20; 28–30.
25. See the essay by David Matzko in this volume, and Jean Daniélou's beautiful treatment of pre-Christian saints: *Holy Pagans of the Old Testament* (London: Longman, Green & Co., 1957). All easy talk about saintly lives avoids the complex question of identifying saintliness, which is still one good reason for the cumbersome process of beatification employed by the Roman Catholic church. Countless unsung saints are also praised in the Roman Missal.
26. Milbank, 'Name', p. 325, my emphasis. Milbank's explicit view of the debate on other religions is not I believe incompatible with this use of his texts. See 'The End of Dialogue', in *Christian Uniqueness Reconsidered. The Myth of a Pluralist Theology of Religions*, ed. Gavin D'Costa (New York: Orbis, 1990), pp. 174–91.
27. See the documents cited, especially the stress on the 'inchoate' and 'incomplete' (*Redemptoris Missio*, para. 20) and 'unknown' manner (*Gaudium et Spes*, 22) in which God does act outside the church.
28. See further, Gavin D'Costa, 'Nostra Aetate – Telling God's Story in Asia', in *Vatican II and its Heritage*, eds. L. Kenis & M. Lamberigts (Leuven: Peeters Press, forthcoming), and 'Inculturation, India and Other Religions', *Studia Missionalia*, 1995, vol. 44, pp. 121–47.

29. *Lumen Gentium*, para. 17.

I am extremely grateful to Tina Beattie and Gerard Loughlin for their helpful criticisms on a draft of this chapter. Needless to say, this does not imply their agreement with its contents.

Chapter 11

THE RESURRECTION OF JESUS AND THE QUR'AN

David Marshall

*A*part from Christianity, Islam is the world religion which devotes most attention to Jesus, and Muslims often point out that they have a high regard for him as one of the greatest of God's prophets. Many studies have therefore been written on the place of Jesus in Christianity and Islam.[1] However, these studies have tended to give very little attention to the specific issue of the resurrection of Jesus. This neglect is quite understandable. Despite the important place of Jesus in Islam, his resurrection after his death by crucifixion does not form part of Islamic belief for the simple reason that the vast majority of Muslims deny that Jesus died on the Cross. Muslims generally believe that although there was an attempt to kill Jesus, God intervened before his death and raised him alive to himself. Thus it is not so much that Muslims reject the resurrection of Jesus from the dead as that the question is not discussed because of the logically prior denial of his death. Controversy and dialogue between Muslims and Christians about the end of Jesus' earthly mission have therefore naturally focused more on the question of his disputed death than on the Christian belief in his resurrection.

Thus a chapter entitled 'The Resurrection of Jesus and the Qur'an' might seem to be a misguided venture. On themes such as creation, prophethood, ethics and eschatology the possibility and the value of a comparative Christian–Islamic study would be more obvious. On other themes, such as the Trinity or the atonement, the Islamic critique of Christian theology is well known.[2] In all these cases there is clearly plenty to talk about, but what can this chapter hope to achieve beyond redirecting our attention away from its professed theme and back to the standing disagreement over whether or not Jesus died in the first place?

In response to this question, a justification for this study might run as follows. Admittedly, for Christian theology the resurrection of Jesus cannot be understood apart from his death, and in the context of Christian–Muslim discussion there is clearly a logical priority to the question of whether Jesus died at all. Nevertheless, there is value in focusing here specifically on the resurrection. Precisely because of the focus of past debates on the death (or otherwise) of Jesus, there has been comparatively little attempt by Christians to think about the resurrection in relation to Islam, a neglect which, while understandable, seriously truncates proper Christian engagement in theological discussion with Muslims.

Through a primary focus on scriptural material, the main aim of this study will therefore be to consider some of the theological implications of the resurrection of Jesus suggested by the New Testament alongside related Qur'anic concerns. I believe that this approach in fact illuminates both Scriptures, revealing not simply their more obvious divergences (in this case that the New Testament affirms the resurrection of Jesus from the dead and the Qur'an doesn't) but also aspects of their deeper logic.

Jesus in the Qur'an

Firstly, however, I shall outline the main features of the overall Qur'anic account of Jesus so that we can place in context the Qur'anic version of the events at the end of Jesus' earthly life.[3] The Qur'anic Jesus stands in the context of the Qur'an's distinctive understanding of the history of God's dealings with the world, an important aspect of which is God's sending of messengers to preach against idolatry and injustice. Muhammad, who is known as 'the Seal of the Prophets' (Qur'an 33:40),[4] is the last of these messengers, but the Qur'an devotes considerable attention to his predecessors, many of whom also appear in the Bible (e.g. Noah, Abraham and Moses).

Jesus is one of these messengers, and as such is portrayed positively. The Qur'an gives considerable attention to the circumstances of Jesus' birth (3:33–63; 19:2–36). Angels announce to his mother Mary that she will give birth to a son who is 'a word from Him [God], whose name is the Messiah, Jesus, son of Mary, illustrious in the world and the Hereafter' (3:45). Miraculous signs characterize the life of Jesus from the start; he is conceived directly by God's creative word without a human father (3:47), and his creation is thus comparable with that of Adam (3:59). The infant Jesus speaks from the cradle (19:30–3), and later performs other miraculous signs with God's permission (3:49). Jesus is also the bearer of 'the Gospel', a revealed message from God (3:48). He has disciples (3:52), and he preaches monotheism (3:51; 5:72). He points ahead to a messenger coming after him (61:6). At the end of Jesus' earthly mission he is the target of murderous plots by the Jews, but God outwits them and raises Jesus up to himself (3:54f.; 4:157f.). There is also a hint at one point that Jesus has a special connection with the eschatological 'hour' (43:61), a hint which subsequent Islamic tradition developed into a detailed account of Jesus' eschatological role.

These are the Qur'an's main positive affirmations about Jesus, but its portrayal of him also has a sharp polemical edge. The Qur'an attacks the ways in which Christians had distorted Jesus' true significance with their idea of his divine sonship; the related doctrine of the Trinity therefore comes under attack as well (4:171). The Qur'anic Jesus is portrayed as distancing himself from such errors (5:116f.). The Qur'an also implicitly rejects the notion of Jesus as a saviour. However, 'saviourship' is in fact scarcely a Qur'anic category at all – God sends messengers, not saviours – so it is perhaps more accurate to say that the Qur'an simply ignores the saviourship of Jesus, rather than directly attacking it. Thus although Jesus is referred to as 'Messiah' in the Qur'an, the title does not have any soteriological significance. This point should be kept in mind as we turn to the Qur'anic account of the events at the end of Jesus' earthly life.

The key to understanding this account is the repeated Qur'anic theme that God's messengers are rejected by unbelievers but vindicated by God. This had been the experience of messengers before Jesus, as in the narratives of *sura* (chapter) 11, describing the rejection and vindication of Noah, Abraham, Lot and Moses, as well as some pre-Islamic Arabian prophets, and we shall see that it was also the experience of Muhammad. This same pattern of rejection and vindication is played out in the case of Jesus: 'And . . . (the disbelievers) schemed, and Allah schemed (against them): and Allah is the best of schemers. (And remember) when Allah said: "O Jesus! Lo! I am gathering you and causing you to ascend unto Me"' (3:54f.). We see here how the scheming of the unbelievers against Jesus (which at 4:157 is specified as an attempt to crucify him) is outdone by God's scheming, his vindication of Jesus by raising him to himself. However, it is very important to note that these events have nothing to do with saviourship as understood in the New Testament. They are part of a Qur'anic pattern of rejection and vindication which culminates in Muhammad's own experience. It is significant that the phrase quoted above describing the scheming of the unbelievers and of God recurs at 8:30, where it relates to Muhammad's rejection and vindication, thus underlining that in the Qur'an the story of Jesus points ahead to the story of Muhammad. We should therefore read the Qur'anic account of the end of Jesus' ministry on the Qur'an's own terms, rather than in the light of the New Testament.

We have seen that in the Qur'an God's raising up of Jesus implies his vindication of a faithful messenger, but a further point must be made to give the full Qur'anic context of this event. According to mainstream Muslim interpretation the Qur'an states that Jesus did not die on the Cross. The Qur'an refers to the claims of the Jews to have killed Jesus, and responds: 'They slew him not nor crucified, but it appeared so unto them . . . But Allah took him up unto Himself.' (4:157f.). It should immediately be clarified that in context this is *not* a piece of anti-Christian polemic, even if it has subsequently been used as such; the Qur'an is here primarily concerned to reject the claim of the unbelieving Jews that they had been able to triumph over God's messenger. Nevertheless, for our present purposes we must note that on the accepted Muslim reading of this passage the Jesus whom God vindicated by raising him up had never died, and it is suggested that someone else died in his place.[5] God's raising up of Jesus would then be an ascension without a prior death or resurrection, reminiscent of the exaltation of Elijah (2 Kgs. 2:1–12).

In what follows in this study I shall work with the accepted Muslim reading of this passage, and will therefore speak of the absence of the resurrection of Jesus from the Qur'an. It should, however, be mentioned that some non-Muslim scholars argue that, despite its prima facie denial of the crucifixion, this passage is in fact only denying that it was the Jews who were ultimately responsible for this event, and that the Qur'an elsewhere implies that Jesus did die.[6] Even if this argument were accepted, however, it is clear that this sequence of genuine death followed by some kind of resurrection (scarcely expressed with great clarity) would still belong to the Qur'anic scheme of things; it would still be an instance of the specifically Qur'anic paradigm of rejection and vindication, rather than *the* central drama in God's saving activity for the whole of humanity.[7] Hence, from a Christian standpoint, it would still be accurate to speak of the absence of the resurrection of Jesus from the Qur'an.

Theological Consequences of the Resurrection of Jesus and some Qur'anic Parallels

In the sense which I have just explained, the Qur'an does not have a place for the resurrection of Jesus from the dead. However, we must press beyond this simple observation. The New Testament does not view the resurrection as an isolated fact, but rather as an event full of consequences for the human race, and indeed for God's creation as a whole. Even though the Qur'an does not have a place for the *event* of the resurrection, it does contain parallels to some of these *consequences* of the resurrection. In other words, some of the theological affirmations made by the New Testament on the basis of the resurrection of Jesus (e.g. that we also shall rise from the dead) are made also in the Qur'an, where they will obviously have a different basis. This study will now explore some examples of how consequences of the resurrection of Jesus (as understood in the New Testament) are paralleled in the Qur'an, though in each case on a characteristically Qur'anic basis. In the New Testament the resurrection is seen as having many different implications, for Jesus himself, for the human race and indeed for the whole of God's creation. I shall begin by considering what the resurrection has to say about Jesus himself.

The Resurrection as the Vindication of the One whom God has Sent

The New Testament conceives of the resurrection as God's vindication of Jesus. If the crucifixion represents the world's judgement on Jesus, its failure to recognize him as 'the Lord of Glory' (1 Cor. 2:8),[8] the resurrection represents God's verdict on Jesus, declaring his true identity as God's Son (Rom. 1:4), the Lord and Messiah (Acts 2:36). This contrast between the human rejection of Jesus in the crucifixion and God's vindication of him through the resurrection is also present in several other passages in Acts depicting the early preaching of the apostles (2:23f.; 3:14f., 4:10f.; 5:30f.).

Of course, the New Testament's convictions about the identity of Jesus differ crucially from the Qur'an's convictions about Muhammad, who is the messenger of God, but emphatically not the Lord of Glory. Nevertheless, this concern with God's vindication of the one whom he has sent but who is rejected by his people is certainly paralleled in the Qur'an. As already mentioned, it is a theme which recurs in the Qur'anic presentation of all the earlier messengers sent by God, including Jesus, but here I will focus on this pattern of rejection and vindication specifically in the life of Muhammad.

Just as Jesus' ministry unfolded in the context of 'opposition from sinners' (Heb. 12:3), so also Muhammad had long and bitter experience of rejection and ridicule at the hands of the unbelievers of Mecca, his native town. His claim to be sent by God was routinely mocked and he was rejected as a liar and as possessed (15:6; 34:8). Finally, after many years of opposition from his townspeople came to a potentially murderous climax, Muhammad left Mecca secretly and settled in Medina, the episode known as the Hijra (622 CE). The Hijra was in one sense a defiant act on Muhammad's part, a deliberate breaking-off of blood-ties in order to establish a new faith-based community in Medina.[9] Nevertheless, the Qur'an also views the Hijra as a blameworthy episode on the part of the Meccan unbelievers (22:39f.; 60:1). If seen in this light as the culmination of the Meccans' rejection of the one sent to them by God, the Hijra can be compared with the crucifixion of Jesus. What, then, is the Qur'anic equivalent to God's vindication of Jesus by the resurrection?

The answer that the Qur'an itself appears to supply to this question is that God vindicated his rejected messenger through the military victories which Muhammad won against his unbelieving opponents after the Hijra to Medina, especially at the first great battle of Badr (624 CE). The Qur'an's presentation of this first great victory (won very much against the odds) conceives of it as an act in which God was vindicating the truth of the message which he had revealed through Muhammad, and punishing the Meccans for their unbelief. At Badr: 'Allah willed that He should cause the Truth to triumph by His words, and cut the root of the disbelievers; that He might cause the Truth to triumph and bring vanity to naught, however much the guilty might oppose' (8:7f.). This idea that Badr is the moment of divine vindication in Muhammad's life is strengthened by parallels that the Qur'an draws between Badr and the Exodus.[10] Like his great predecessor Moses, Muhammad had been rejected, but was now triumphantly vindicated by God.[11] We should also note that Badr (much more than the Hijra) is a turning-point in the Qur'anic presentation of Muhammad. After this manifest act of divine vindication Muhammad's identity and authority as God's messenger are emphasized with increasing force.[12]

The obvious outward differences between the resurrection of Jesus and a military victory should not obscure the fact that these two events have logically equivalent roles in their respective Scriptures. There would thus appear to be a parallel between, on the one hand, the New Testament sequence of crucifixion and resurrection, and, on the other hand, the Qur'anic sequence of rejection (culminating in the Hijra) and military victory (especially at Badr). This point accounts for much in the contrasting visions of the New Testament and the Qur'an. Both Scriptures are concerned with how God vindicates his chosen servant in this world when that servant is rejected. If, as the Qur'an affirms (with ample precedent in the Old Testament), God vindicates him by leading him to military victory over his enemies, this, among other things, generates a certain attitude to the relationship between power and truth. God's truth is served by power, and achieves manifest victory in this world.[13] There are clear implications here for questions such as the religious basis of the state, but this would take us beyond the scope of this study.

In contrast, the vindication of Jesus by his resurrection lacks this quality of manifest victory in the world. Although I agree with the understanding of the resurrection as an event attested by an empty tomb, it is nevertheless an event characterized by a mysterious hiddenness. It is important that Christian discussion of the resurrection should not gloss over the point that only the disciples (rather than the public at large) were witnesses of God's vindication of Jesus.[14] It is striking, bearing Islam in mind, that the 'enemies' of Jesus (such as Caiaphas and Pilate) were to all outward appearances unaffected by his resurrection. Unlike the vindication of Muhammad, the vindication of Jesus had no immediate impact in the sphere of human *Realpolitik*. The New Testament affirms the resurrection as an event which bears on the life of the whole human race, but also knows that it is an 'open secret', still marked by a quality of hiddenness. To reapply a familiar phrase, the vindication of Jesus through the resurrection is 'in this world, but not of it'.

The Resurrection of Jesus and the Hope of Eternal Life

We turn now from what the resurrection implies about Jesus himself to consider its significance for the rest of humanity. Perhaps the most obvious of the consequences of the resurrection is that it provides a pledge to believers of their own future resurrection. This point naturally enough comes to clearest expression in a controversial context. In 1 Corinthians 15 Paul directly addresses the idea held by some in the Church at Corinth that there is no resurrection of the dead (v. 12). Although he does not make the point immediately, the key to Paul's response comes at verse 20: 'In fact, however, Christ has been raised from the dead, as the firstfruits of all who have fallen asleep.' The idea of the risen Jesus as 'the firstfruits' (cf. v. 23) is especially significant here. 'Because Christ has been raised from the dead, the resurrection of the rest of mankind (or at least of those who are in Christ . . .) is assured.'[15] In response to scepticism about the possibility of a future life, the heart of Paul's response is thus to argue from the past event of the resurrection of Jesus to the future event of our own resurrection. This basic insight, expressed here in the context of controversy, is present elsewhere in the New Testament in different contexts, sometimes explicitly, sometimes implicitly. Thus in passages such as 1 Corinthians 6:14, 1 Peter 1:3ff., John 11:25f. and 1 John 3:2 we find various expressions of the same basic conviction that the Christian expectation of life beyond death is bound up with the prior reality of the resurrection of Jesus. There are admittedly passages (such as Jesus' argument with the Sadducees in Mark 12:18–27) which argue for a general resurrection on other grounds. Taking the New Testament as a whole, however, there is a logical centrality to the resurrection of Jesus himself as the key factor in establishing the believer's hope of eternal life.

The reality of the afterlife is, if anything, more repeatedly and emphatically affirmed in the Qur'an than in the New Testament. As Andrae puts it, in the Qur'an 'The future life, with its judgment, underlies all other themes, like the deep bass of an organ.'[16] Many passages show that Muhammad was mocked for preaching about a resurrection which would lead to the eternal reward of the righteous and the eternal punishment of evildoers. The following verse illustrates well the scorn that Muhammad encountered: 'Those who disbelieve say: "Shall we show you a man [Muhammad] who will tell you (that) when you have become dispersed in dust with most complete dispersal, still, even then, you will be created anew?"' (34:7).

Our particular interest here is to ask how the Qur'an answers such scepticism. Three basic responses seem typical. Firstly, there are passages in which the unbelievers' scepticism is simply dismissed as evidence of their godless ignorance (e.g. 45:24; 79:10–14). Secondly, there are passages which point the unbelievers to the fact of their own creation, and in effect ask them whether or not the God who had originally made them out of nothing could not remake them after their death (e.g. 19:67; 36:78). Thirdly, there are passages that argue for the reality of the resurrection by pointing to 'the sign of the revival of dead land by the coming of rain, a sign peculiarly apt in Arabia, where the effect of rain is almost miraculous'.[17] The second and third responses are brought together in the following passage: 'O mankind! If you are in doubt concerning the Resurrection, then lo! We have created you from dust, then from a drop of seed . . . And you (Muhammad) see the earth barren, but when We send down water . . . it thrills and swells and puts forth every lovely kind (of growth). That is because Allah . . . quickens the dead' (22:5f.).

We have seen that both Scriptures affirm the reality of life after death, but we have also seen that, faced with the question 'How do we know that we will rise from the dead?', they give significantly different answers. The Qur'anic approach on this issue represents a kind of natural theology. The fact of our resurrection should be deduced from our experience of the world and from the wonder of our own creation, even if it is of course also confirmed by the revelation of the Qur'an. In contrast, the New Testament's answers to this question (especially where it is most fully treated in 1 Corinthians 15) do not depend on the observation of Nature or on appeals to general notions of the power of God, but rather are focused on the revelatory event of the resurrection of Jesus. Significantly, Paul's image of the growth of a seed into a plant (through its own death and resurrection) at 1 Corinthians 15:35–8 is not an argument in *defence* of the reality of the general resurrection; rather, *assuming* the truth of the resurrection, it serves as an illustration of how the body can die and then become something more glorious. It should also be noted that in the New Testament the risen Jesus does not only serve as an argument in favour of our own resurrection, but also as a model of our future glorified existence: 'We shall be like him' (1 John 3:2; cf. 1 Cor. 15:49). In contrast, the existence of the righteous in the Qur'anic Paradise is characterized by a more general understanding of human blessedness, involving both physical and spiritual fulfilment (76:11–22; 75:22f.), but without a focus parallel to the New Testament idea of becoming like Christ.

Thus we have seen how a conviction which is shared by both Scriptures ('We will rise from the dead') has, on closer inspection, a quite distinct character in each of them. To say that there is an afterlife, or that God vindicates his servant, leaves many questions still to be dealt with. The presence or absence of belief in the resurrection of Jesus clearly shapes the answering of them.

The Resurrection of Jesus and Christian Ethics

The consequences for others of the resurrection of Jesus are not, however, restricted to the expectation of a personal resurrection *after* this life. The resurrection also functions in the New Testament as a source of ethical motivation for the believer's life in this world. The union of believers with the risen Jesus is the basis for the risen life to which they themselves are called: 'Since you have been raised with Christ, set your hearts on things above' (Col. 3:1 (NIV); cf. Rom. 6:1–11).

The resurrection is of course not the only (nor even the most common) basis to which the New Testament explicitly appeals when expounding the ethical implications of Christian discipleship; for example, Paul's ethical exhortations at 2 Corinthians 5:9–10 and Philippians 2:1–11 are supported by references, respectively, to the final judgement and the humility of the crucified Christ. However, the resurrection is a central part of the whole action of God in Christ (including, for example, the Cross and the sending of the Spirit) which is at once the revelation of God's grace and of his call to a new life. Indeed, as the title of his work *Resurrection and Moral Order* succinctly conveys, Oliver O'Donovan argues that Christian ethics arise in particular from God's raising of Jesus from the dead.

O'Donovan suggests that within 'the richness of the New Testament's ethical appeal' it is appropriate 'to concentrate on the resurrection as our starting-point because it tells us of God's vindication of his creation, and of our created life'.[18] Whether or not we agree with this suggestion it is clear that the New Testament's ethical vision cannot be understood in isolation from the revelatory acts of God in Christ, among which the resurrection has a central part.

It hardly needs stating that the Qur'an shares the New Testament's concern with ethical renewal, but we need to reflect on the presuppositions of the Qur'an's ethical appeal to human beings. These presuppositions have been outlined by the Japanese scholar Toshihiko Izutsu, who writes that in the Qur'an 'God acts towards man in an ethical way, that is, as God of Justice and Goodness, and man, correspondingly, is expected to respond to this Divine initiative also in an ethical way.'[19] Ethical motivation in the Qur'an thus derives from the prior reality of the justice and goodness of God revealed in his actions. God's justice calls forth the human response of *taqwa* (the fear of God), and God's goodness calls forth *shukr* (gratitude).[20] There is thus a structural similarity in the ethical teaching of the New Testament and the Qur'an, in that both understand human ethics as a response to God's action. However, it is not enough simply to draw attention to this structural similarity. We must go on to ask what precisely in the Qur'an is the divine action that calls for the appropriate human ethical response.

As Izutsu points out, in the Qur'an God's action towards human beings is marked by the two essential qualities of goodness and justice. God's goodness, or mercy, is revealed in his acts of creation, both his creation of human beings and his bountiful provision for them through his gifts in nature. The goodness of God is also seen in his acts of revelation, his sending of messengers with divine Scriptures. It is significant that the Qur'anic passage traditionally taken as the first to be revealed to Muhammad (96:1–5) links God's generosity to these two activities of creation and revelation. God's justice, on the other hand, has been revealed in the repeated acts of punishment with which he destroyed successive generations of unbelievers and rescued the believers from among them. These divine actions in the past are frequently described in the Qur'an's many punishment-narratives, as in *suras* 7, 11 and 26. God's punishment of unbelievers and rewarding of believers is also an unavoidable future reality, to which the Qur'an constantly returns in its warnings about the Last Day.

These affirmations about God's actions of creation, revelation and judgement constitute the Qur'anic vision of the divine action in history (both past and future) which is the basis on which human beings are summoned to ethical renewal. It is worth noting that among the different component parts of this vision it is the Last Day, the eschatological judgement, which Izutsu sees as having the most decisive shaping influence on Qur'anic ethics. 'The fear of the Last Judgment and the Lord of the Day – that is the most fundamental motif of this new religion that underlies all its aspects and determines its basic mood. To believe in God means, briefly, to fear Him as the Lord of the Day.'[21] Rahbar's detailed analysis supports Izutsu on this point: 'In Qur'anic thought Fear of God becomes the *essential* motive-principle of virtuous conduct.'[22]

In this section we have seen that in both the Qur'an and the New Testament ethical motivation is generated by the understanding of how God has acted and will act in history. However, precisely because the Qur'an and the New Testament involve different 'histories' of the divine activity, their ethical visions are correspondingly differentiated. Limiting ourselves here to an observation about ethical *motivation*, rather than about specific ethical *ideals*, we should note simply that God's activity in the crucified and risen Jesus (with whom the believer lives in union) shapes ethical motivation in the New Testament in a way which is obviously alien to the Qur'an. Thus a broadbrush conclusion to this section might be that, faced with the question, 'What calls us to ethical renewal?', the Qur'an points us above all to the judgement of the Last Day, and the New Testament to the risen Jesus.

This observation is relevant to certain developments in the area of interreligious dialogue. Faced with the apparently insuperable doctrinal divisions between faith-communities, some writers have urged religious people to seek unity at an ethical level. Küng's support for a 'Global Ethic' is an example from within the Christian community,[23] while the late Muslim scholar Ismail al-Faruqi expressed the desire that the Muslim–Christian dialogue should leave 'the old questions regarding the nature of God' and 'turn to man, to his duties and responsibilities'.[24] The difficulty with such projects, laudable though their motives might be, is that they wrongly imply that the ethics of religious people can be detached from their underlying theological convictions. We have seen that in both the Qur'an and the New Testament ethical motivation is derived from their respective understandings of God's action in history, with the resurrection of Jesus in particular shaping the ethical vision of the New Testament. The same point of course applies to ethical ideals as well as to ethical motivation. Simply to call for a shift from theology to ethics ultimately does very little to further realistic interreligious understanding.[25]

Areas for Further Reflection

In addition to the three consequences of the resurrection of Jesus which have been discussed here alongside related Qur'anic concerns, it is possible to identify further avenues for exploration. The New Testament speaks of the risen Jesus as the great intercessor, providing grounds for confidence before God (Rom. 8:34; Heb. 7:25; 1 John 2:1). It would be valuable to consider Qur'anic parallels to this theme, and indeed post-Qur'anic developments in Islamic spirituality involving the intercession of Muhammad. The New Testament also speaks of a future regeneration of all things, which it implies is the final outworking of the resurrection of Jesus (1 Cor. 15:20–8).[26] This is a theme which it is harder to parallel in the Qur'an, where there is no obvious echo of Paul's hope that 'the whole creation itself might be freed from its slavery to corruption' (Rom. 8:21).

Finally, it might usefully illuminate the contrasting character of the two Scriptures to reflect on how the New Testament's witness to the resurrection of Jesus implies that an eschatological event has taken place in the present.[27] This aspect of the New Testament, to which there is no clear Qur'anic parallel, shapes it decisively, injecting into it distinctive tensions and paradoxes which are unfamiliar in the Qur'an. It is worth considering the extent to which Islamic criticisms of the New Testament are a reflection of this contrast.

Conclusion

The main aim of this study has been to show that in the Qur'an and the New Testament we find many parallel themes and concerns, but that these are located within contrasting overall theological patterns. Jomier puts this memorably by observing that with the same coloured stones one can design rather different mosaics.[28] Different readers will doubtless respond to this observation in different ways, some emphasizing the parallelism in general concerns, others the contrasting theological patterns. To the reader for whom either Islam or Christianity seems an utterly alien world it may be helpful to grasp the extent to which the Qur'an shares themes and concerns with the New Testament, while to the reader who is inclined to see all religious language as different ways of saying the same essential thing it is important to grasp the irreducible distinctiveness of each Scripture. In particular this study has shown how the presence or absence of belief in the resurrection of Jesus determines how crucial questions are dealt with in the two Scriptures.

I end on a personal note. To study the Scripture of another faith-community is a strange and enriching experience. Like a traveller abroad, one meets much that is new, but one also recognizes things that are familiar, signs of a shared humanity. Through the journey one also arrives at a fuller appreciation of where one comes from. The Christian travelling in the world of the Qur'an encounters, among other things, a Jesus who is honoured, but whose death and resurrection are at best obscured, and in effect unknown. The Qur'an's corrective redefinition of Jesus, and thus also of God and his ways, and much else, is very challenging. Paul's reflections on the foolishness and weakness of God (1 Cor. 1:25) acquire a vivid relevance, and one is forced to ask oneself more deeply whether one continues to believe that at the heart of all God's ways there stands the crucified and risen Jesus.

Notes

1. See especially Kenneth Cragg, *Jesus and the Muslim* (London: George Allen & Unwin, 1985); also Geoffrey Parrinder, *Jesus in the Qur'an* (Oxford: Oneworld Publications, 1995); Neal Robinson, *Christ in Islam and Christianity* (Albany: State University of New York Press, 1991).
2. For examples see Jean-Marie Gaudeul, *Encounters and Clashes: Islam and Christianity in History* (2 vols, Rome: Pontificio Istituto di Studi Arabi e Islamici, 1990).
3. Brief overviews of Jesus in the Qur'an are given by Robinson, *Christ in Islam and Christianity*, pp. 4–7; Cragg, *Jesus and the Muslim*, chapter 2; Jacques Jomier, *Bible et Coran* (Paris: Les Editions du Cerf, 1959),

chapter 12. For a fuller treatment see Parrinder, *Jesus in the Qur'an*.

4. Different translations of the Qur'an use different systems for numbering the verses; references here will be to Mohammed Marmaduke Pickthall, *The Meaning of the Glorious Qur'an* (London: Al-Furqan Publications, n.d.), a readily available version. I modernize some of Pickthall's more dated phraseology, and introduce single quotation marks to indicate where a speech begins and ends. Pickthall's glosses are in round brackets; additional glosses which I have added are indicated by square brackets. Henceforward scriptural references (of the type 33:40 above) apply to the Qur'an unless otherwise specified.

5. For details see Robinson, *Christ in Islam and Christianity*, chapters 12 and 13.

6. For example see Parrinder, *Jesus in the Qur'an*, p. 119.

7. See Jomier, *Bible et Coran*, pp. 115f., for some pertinent comments on this point.

8. Biblical quotations are from the New Jerusalem Bible, except in one case, where the New International Version (NIV) is used.

9. See Rudi Paret, *Mohammed und der Koran*, 3rd edn. (Stuttgart: Kohlhammer, 1972), p. 101.

10. See, for example, 8:52ff. and 3:11, and the description of Badr as 'the day of the *Furqan*' (8:41; cf. 2:53 and 21:48). Interestingly, there is a suggestion of a similar parallel in the New Testament at Luke 9:31, which refers to the '*exodos* which Jesus was about to accomplish in Jerusalem'.

11. See W. Montgomery Watt, *Muhammad at Medina* (Oxford: Oxford University Press, 1956), pp. 15f., 203.

12. See Alford T. Welch, 'Muhammad's Understanding of Himself: The Koranic Data', in *Islam's Understanding of Itself*, eds. Hovannisian and Vryonis (Malibu: Undena Publications, 1983), pp. 15–52.

13. An intriguing (if untypical) querying of this notion, from within the Islamic tradition, can be found in Kamel Hussein, *City of Wrong: a Friday in Jerusalem*, trans. Kenneth Cragg (Oxford: Oneworld Publications, 1994), an imaginative reconstruction of the events of Good Friday.

14. See Gerald O'Collins, *The Easter Jesus*, 2nd edn. (London: Darton, Longman & Todd, 1980), pp. 66f.

15. C. K. Barrett, *The First Epistle to the Corinthians*, 2nd edn. (London: A. & C. Black, 1971), pp. 350f.

16. Tor Andrae, *Mohammed: the Man and his Faith* (New York: Harper & Row, 1960), p. 60.

17. W. Montgomery Watt and R. Bell, *Introduction to the Qur'an* (Edinburgh: Edinburgh University Press, 1970), p. 123.

18. Oliver O'Donovan, *Resurrection and Moral Order: an Outline for*

Evangelical Ethics (Leicester: Inter-Varsity Press, 1986), p. 13.

19. Toshihiko Izutsu, *God and Man in the Koran* (Tokyo: Keio Institute of Cultural and Linguistic Studies, 1964), p. 230; cf. Toshihiko Izutsu, *Ethico-Religious Concepts in the Qur'an* (Montreal: McGill University Press, 1966), pp. 17f.

20. See Izutsu, *God and Man*, pp. 230–9; Izutsu, *Ethico-Religious Concepts*, pp. 195–202.

21. Izutsu, *Ethico-Religious Concepts*, p. 195.

22. Daud Rahbar, *God of Justice: a Study in the Ethical Doctrine of the Qur'an* (Leiden: E. J. Brill, 1960), p. 179 (his italics). For a different view see Fazlur Rahman, *Major Themes of the Qur'an* (Minneapolis: Bibliotheca Islamica, 1989), pp. 1–6.

23. See Hans Küng and Karl-Josef Kuschel (eds.), *A Global Ethic: The Declaration of the Parliament of the World's Religions* (London: SCM, 1993).

24. Ismail al-Faruqi, *Christian Ethics* (The Hague: Djambatan, 1967), p. 33.

25. For a warning against other fragile bridges intended to facilitate dialogue see an important article by Adolfo Gonzalez Montes, 'The challenge of Islamic Monotheism: a Christian View', *Concilium*, 1994/3, pp. 67–75.

26. 'In proclaiming the resurrection of Christ, the apostles proclaimed also the resurrection of mankind in Christ; and in proclaiming the resurrection of mankind, they proclaimed the renewal of all creation with him.' O'Donovan, *Resurrection and Moral Order*, p. 31.

27. Cf. O'Collins, *The Easter Jesus*, p. 31 (quoting Pannenberg).

28. Jomier, *Bible et Coran*, pp. 28f.

Chapter 12

THE RESURRECTION OF JESUS: A JEWISH VIEW

Dan Cohn-Sherbok

Some time ago my wife taught at King's School, Canterbury, and I used to go with her to the Sunday Matins service. When the school rose to say the Creed, I faced the right way but said nothing. But, reflecting on the contents of the Creed, I realized I could accept some of its tenets. 'You know,' I said to my wife, 'I believe a lot of the Creed.'

'Oh yes,' she said, 'Which parts?'

'How does it go?' I asked.

'Would you like me to recite it?' she asked.

'Please do.'

'It goes like this,' she said. 'I believe in God.'

'You see,' I said. 'I believe that. That's the central belief and I accept it. Belief in God – I believe in God!'

'The Father Almighty,' she continued.

'The Father Almighty!' I exclaimed. 'That's just what I believe. I think God is Father and that He is Almighty.'

'Maker of Heaven and Earth,' she went on.

'Yes. I can accept that,' I said. 'God is Father, and He has created the Universe.'

'And in Jesus Christ His only Son,' she continued.

'Well, that is where I start to have difficulties. I believe Jesus existed. And that he was a man. He could be regarded as God's son, just as we are all God's children. But I don't think he was God's only son. And I don't think he was the Messiah.'

'Our Lord,' she said.

'Now I can't accept that at all. The Incarnation and the Trinity are out.'

'Who was conceived by the Holy Ghost.'

'This is most unlikely. As a matter of fact, I think it's impossible. Joseph was Jesus' father.'

'Born of the Virgin Mary.'

'Out of the question,' I said.

'Suffered under Pontius Pilate.'

'That's OK. He did.'

'Was crucified, dead, and buried.'

'Yes, there's no trouble there.'

'He descended into Hell,' she continued.

'No, that isn't something I can agree with.'

'The third day he rose again from the dead.'

'I'm afraid that's out too.'

'He ascended into Heaven.'

'Unlikely,' I said.

'And sitteth at the right hand of God the Father Almighty.'

'That's a problem too. Is that it?'

'There's more,' she said, 'From thence he will come to judge the quick and the dead.'

'Well, I don't believe that either.'

'I believe in the Holy Ghost.'

'Yes,' I said, 'That's perfectly acceptable, as long as it's not understood as part of the Trinity.'

'The Holy Catholic Church.'

'I believe it exists.'

'The communion of saints.'

'Doubtful!'

'The forgiveness of sins.'

'That's all right.'

'The resurrection of the body.'

'No.'

'And the life everlasting.'

'Yes, I can accept that. Well, how did I do?' I asked.

'You got about fifty per cent,' she replied.

Fifty per cent is not bad. But the problem is that I don't believe in the right fifty per cent. What's missing are the central beliefs of the Christian tradition. And at the heart of my rejection of these Christian beliefs is my inability to accept the claim that Jesus rose from the dead. Traditionally this has been the linchpin of the entire Christian theological edifice. As Paul declared: 'If Christ be not raised, our faith is in vain' (1 Cor. 15:14). Jesus' resurrection was the first-fruit of things to come in the Messianic Kingdom.

I am aware, of course, that many so-called Christians find such a belief equally difficult to embrace. Indeed, even distinguished bishops in the Church of England have expressed reservations about Jesus' bodily resurrection. But there is no doubt in my mind that the Christian faith either falls or stands on this conviction. What I propose to explain in this chapter is why I find Jesus' alleged resurrection difficult to accept, even though the belief in the resurrection of the body is one of traditional Judaism's central tenets. Further, I want to consider whether theoretically I could be persuaded that Jesus was raised from the dead – could any event or series of events convince me of this occurrence?

Resurrection in Judaism

Do Jews believe in the resurrection of the dead? In the Hebrew Bible, there are a number of incidents in which those who died were revived. The first concerns a widow at Zerephath whom God told to feed the prophet Elijah during a famine. Despite her poverty she did so; subsequently the Lord provided her with meal and oil so that she, her son and Elijah had an adequate amount of food. I Kings 17:17–24 continues:

> After this the son of the woman, the mistress of the house, became ill; and his illness was so severe that there was no breath in him. And she said to Elijah, 'What have you against me, O man of God? You have come to me to bring my sin to remembrance, and to cause the death of my son!' And he said to her, 'Give me your son.' And he took him from her bosom, and carried him up into the upper chamber, where he lodged, and laid him upon his own bed. And he cried to the Lord, 'O Lord my God, hast thou brought calamity even upon the widow with whom I sojourn, by slaying her son?' Then he stretched himself upon the child three times, and cried to the Lord, 'O Lord my God, let this child's soul come into him again.' And the Lord hearkened to the voice of Elijah; and the soul of the child came into him again, and he revived. And Elijah took the child, and brought him down from the upper chamber into the house, and delivered him to his mother; and Elijah said, 'See, your son lives.' And the woman said to Elijah, 'Now I know that you are a man of God, and that the word of the Lord in your mouth is truth.'

The second instance concerns a rich woman living in Shunem who welcomed Elijah's successor, Elisha, into her home. In gratitude, Elisha predicted that she would have a son. Several years after his birth, the boy went out one day to his father among the reapers:

> And he said to his father, 'Oh, my head, my head!' The father said to his servant, 'Carry him to his mother.' And when he had lifted him, and brought him to his mother, the child sat on her lap till noon, and then he died. And she went up and laid him on the bed of the man of God, and shut the door upon him, and went out . . . When Elisha came into the house, he saw the child lying dead on his bed. So he went in and shut the door upon the two of them, and prayed to the Lord. Then he went up and lay upon the child, putting his mouth upon his mouth, his eyes upon his eyes, and his hands upon his hands; and as he stretched himself upon him, the flesh of the child became warm . . . the child sneezed seven times, and the child opened his eyes. Then he summoned Gehazi and said, 'Call this Shunammite.' So he called her. And when she came to him, he said, 'Take up your son.' She came and fell at his feet, bowing to the ground; then she took up her son and went out. (2 Kgs. 4:18–21, 32–7)

A third example concerns an unknown person whose corpse came into contact with Elisha's bones in the tomb:

> So Elisha died, and they buried him. Now bands of Moabites used to invade the land in the spring of the year. And as a man was being buried, lo, a marauding band was seen and the man was cast into the grave of Elisha; and as soon as the man touched the bones of Elisha, he revived and stood on his feet. (2 Kgs. 13:20–1)

In post-biblical literature, there are similar accounts of resuscitation. A midrash on Leviticus, for example, reports that

> Antonius the emperor . . . came to Rabbi; he met him as he was sitting with his disciples in front of him. Antonius said to him; 'Are those the ones of whom you speak so commendably?' He answered, 'Yes . . . the smallest among them is able to resurrect the dead.' After a few days a servant

of Antonius became sick unto death. He sent to Rabbi, 'Send me one of your disciples that he will make this dead man alive again.' He sent him one of his disciples . . . this one went and found the servant prostrate. He said to him: 'Why are you lying there prostrate while your master stands on his feet.' Right away he moved and rose. (Leviticus Rabba 19 (111d))

Again, the Talmud records that two rabbis, Rabba and Rabbi Sera, once became so drunk at the time of Purim that Rabba unintentionally killed his fellow rabbi. As soon as he was sober, he asked for God's forgiveness and Rabbi Sera was revived (Meg. 7b). In rabbinic literature the sages to whom such acts of resuscitation are attributed include Rabbi Shimon bar Yohai, Rabbi Hanina bar Hama, Rabbi Israel Baal Shem Tov and Rabbi Schmelke of Nikolsburg.

Despite such isolated instances of the resurrection of the dead found in biblical and rabbinic sources, it was not until the early rabbinic period that the doctrine of the general resurrection of the dead became a central feature of Jewish theology. All the Bible tells us about the hereafter is that the dead will continue to exist in a shadowy realm. This domain is referred to in various ways: in Psalms 28:1 and 88:5 it is described as a *bor* (pit); in Psalm 6:6 as well as in Job 28:22 and 30:23 the term *mavet* is used is a similar sense; in Psalms 22:16 the expression *afar mavet* denotes the dust of death; in Exodus 15:2 and Jonah 2:7 the earth (*eretz*) is described as swallowing up the dead, and in Ezekiel 31:14 the expression *eretz tachtit* refers to the nether parts of the earth where the dead dwell. Finally, the word *she'ol* is frequently used to depict the dwelling of the dead in the nether world. In addition, the words *ge ben hinnom*, *ge hinnom* and *ge* were used to refer to a cursed valley associated with fire and death where, according to Jeremiah, children were sacrificed as burnt offerings to Moloch and Baal (Jer. 7:31–2, 19:6, 32:35).

Although these passages point to a biblical conception of an afterlife where the dead exist in some bodily form, there is no indication of a clearly defined concept. It was only later in the Graeco-Roman world that such a notion began to take shape. The concept of a future world in which the righteous would be compensated for the ills they suffered in this life was prompted by a failure to justify the ways of God by any other means. According to biblical theodicy human beings are promised rewards for obeying God's law, and punishments are threatened for disobedience. Rewards include health, children, rainfall, a good harvest, peace and prosperity; punishments consist of disease, war, pestilence, failure of crops, poverty and slavery. As time passed, however, it became clear that life does not operate in accordance with such a tidy scheme. In response to this dilemma the rabbis developed the doctrine of the resurrection of the dead; such a belief helped Jews to cope with suffering in this life, and it also explained, if not the presence of evil in the world, then at least the worthwhileness of creation despite the world's ills.

Given that there is no explicit belief in eternal salvation in Scripture, the rabbis of the post-biblical period were faced with the difficulty of proving that the belief in resurrection is contained in the Bible. How did they do this? In order to prove that such a conception is found in Scripture, the sages employed certain principles of exegesis which are based on the assumption that every word in the five books of Moses was transmitted by God to Moses on Mount Sinai. Thus, for example, R. Eliezer, the son of R. Jose, claimed to have refuted the Sectarians who maintained that resurrection is not a biblical doctrine:

I said to them: You have falsified your Torah . . . For you maintain that resurrection is not a biblical doctrine, but it is written, 'Because he hath despised the word of the Lord, and hath broken his commandments, that soul shall utterly be cut off, his iniquity shall be upon him,' [Num. 15:31ff.]. Now, seeing that he shall utterly be cut off in this world, when shall his iniquity be upon him? Surely in the next world. (San. 906)

Again, R. Meir asked, 'Whence do we know resurrection from the Torah?' From the verse, 'Then shall Moses and the children of Israel sing this song unto the Lord' [Exod. 15:1]. Not 'sang', but 'sing' is written. Since Moses and the children of Israel did not sing a second time in this life, the text must mean that they will sing after resurrection. Likewise it is written, 'Then shall Joshua build an altar unto the Lord God of Israel' [Josh. 8:30]. Not 'build', but 'shall build' is stated. Thus resurrection is intimated in the Torah. Similarly, R. Joshua b. Levi said: 'Where is resurrection derived from the Torah? From the verse, "Blessed are they that dwell in thy house; they shall ever praise thee" [Ps. 84:5]. The text does not say "praised thee" but "shall praise thee". Thus we learn resurrection from the Torah.' (San. 916)

In the New Testament Jesus himself used a similar argument when confronted by the Sadducees. Thus Mark relates:

And the Sadducees came to him, who say that there is no resurrection; and they asked him a question saying, 'Teacher, Moses wrote for us that if a man's brother dies and leaves a wife, but leaves no child, the man must take the wife, and raise up children for his brother. There were seven brothers; the first took a wife, and when he died left no children; and the second took her, and died, leaving no children; and the third likewise; and the seven left no children. Last of all the woman also died. In the resurrection whose wife will she be? For the seven had her as wife.' Jesus said to them, 'Is not this why you are wrong, that you know neither the scriptures nor the power of God. For when they rise from the dead, they neither marry nor are given in marriage, but are like angels in heaven. And as for the dead being raised, have you not read in the book of Moses, in the passage about the bush, how God said to him, 'I am the God of Abraham, and the God of Isaac, and the God of Jacob'? He is not God of the dead, but of the living; you are quite wrong. (Mark 12:18–27)

We can see then that in the early rabbinic period the belief in resurrection of the dead became a central principle of the faith, and was fiercely defended by the rabbinic sages. With the destruction of the Temple by the Romans in 70 CE, this belief continued to serve as one of the major features of the Jewish tradition. As a result the mediaeval Jewish philosopher Moses Maimonides maintained in his presentation of the Thirteen Principles of the Jewish Faith that this belief is of fundamental importance, a view subsequently adopted by traditional Judaism. In the liturgy as well Jews express their conviction that the dead will be revived in a future age: three times a day, every pious Jew prays in the traditional Eighteen Benedictions:

> Thou, O Lord, art mighty for ever, thou revivest the dead . . . and keepest thy faith to them that sleep in the dust . . . who orderest death and restorest life, and causest salvation to spring forth. Yea, faithful art thou to revive the dead. Blessed art thou, O Lord, who revivest the dead.

Jews and Jesus

Given that the belief in resurrection is a central feature of traditional Jewish theology, there would be no logical inconsistency in accepting the account of Jesus' resurrection. For twenty centuries, however, Jews have steadfastly rejected the New Testament accounts of his survival after the crucifixion. No doubt this was largely due to the Jewish unwillingness to grant Jesus Messianic status. After all, Jesus did not fulfil the traditional role of the Messiah. On the basis of biblical teaching, the rabbis conceived of the Messiah as a human figure who would bring about the resurrection of the dead, the ingathering of the exiles to Zion, and a golden age of history. In rabbinic literature the order of Messianic redemption was presented as follows:

1. The signs of the Messiah.
2. The birth pangs of the Messiah.
3. The coming of Elijah.
4. The trumpet of the Messiah.
5. The ingathering of the Exiles.
6. The reception of proselytes.
7. The war with Gog and Magog.
8. The Days of the Messiah.
9. The renovation of the world.
10. The Day of Judgement.
11. The Resurrection of the dead.
12. The World to Come.

On the basis of their doctrine of the advent of the Messiah, Jews refuse to accept Jesus as their Messiah and Saviour because he did not fulfil these messianic expectations: he did not restore the kingdom of David to its former glory; nor did he gather in the dispersed ones of Israel and restore all the laws of the Torah that were in abeyance. Further, he did not compel all Israel to walk in the way of the Torah nor did he rebuild the Temple and usher in a new order in the world and nature. In other words, Jesus did not inaugurate a cataclysmic change in history. Universal peace, in which there is neither war nor competition, did not come about on earth. Thus for Jews Jesus did not fulfil the prophetic Messianic hope in a redeemer who would bring political and spiritual redemption as well as earthly blessings and moral perfection to the human race.

This, however, is not the sole reason why Jews have rejected Christian claims about Jesus. Another objection to Jesus concerns the assertion that he possesses a special relationship with God. This notion was repeatedly stated in the gospels. In Matthew, for example, we read: 'No one knows the son except the Father; and no one knows the Father, except the son' (Matt. 11:27). In John's gospel Jesus declares: 'I am the way, and the truth, and the life; no one comes to the Father but by me. If you had known me, you would have known my Father also; henceforth you have known him and have seen him' (John 14:6–7). This concept undermines the Jewish conviction that God is equally near to all.

Jews have also been disturbed by Jesus' attitude toward sin and sinners. The traditional task of the prophets was to castigate Israel for rejecting God's law, not to forgive sin. Jesus, however, took upon himself the power to do this. Thus he declared with regard to a paralytic: 'For which is easier, to say, "Your sins are forgiven" or to say, "Rise and walk"? But that you may know that the son of man has authority on earth to forgive sins' – he then said to the paralytic – 'Rise, take up your bed and go home' (Matt. 9:5–6). When Jesus said to a woman of ill-repute: 'Your sins are forgiven', his companions were shocked. 'Who is this, who even forgives sins?' they asked (Luke 7:48–9). It is not surprising that this was their reaction since such a usurpation of God's prerogative was without precedent. A similar objection applies to the gospel record that Jesus performed miracles on his own authority without making reference to God (John 5:18–21).

The rabbis sought to provide adequate social legislation, but Jesus had a view different from theirs. To him poverty was not a deprivation; on the contrary, he regarded it as meritorious. For example, Jesus told a potential disciple: 'If you would be perfect, go, sell what you possess and give to the poor, and you will have treasure in heaven; and come follow me' (Matt. 19:21). In the Sermon on the Mount, Jesus proclaimed: 'Blessed are you poor, for yours is the kingdom of God' (Luke 6:20). In Jewish eyes, however, poverty was an evil; the sages sought to alleviate it by enacting laws to tax the wealthy for the benefit of the poor.

A further objection to Jesus concerns his admonition to break all human ties: 'Whoever of you does not renounce all that he has cannot be my disciple, (Luke 14:33). Or again: 'Who is my mother? and who are my brothers? . . . Here are my mother and my brothers! For whoever does the will of my Father in heaven is my brother, and sister, and mother' (Matt. 12:48–50). Similarly, he declared: 'Call no man your father on earth, for you have one Father, who is in heaven' (Matt. 32:9). In contrast to these views, Judaism asserts that people cannot live full lives unless they are members of a family and are well integrated into the larger community. The renunciation of family bonds is regarded as a travesty of the created order.

Finally, Jesus' teaching is rejected by Jews because his interpretation of Jewish law is at variance with rabbinic tradition. Though at one point in the gospels, Jesus declared that no change should be made in the law (Matt. 5:16), he disregarded a number of important precepts. Several times on the Sabbath, for example, Jesus cured individuals who were not dangerously ill, in violation of the rabbinic precept that the Sabbath law can only be broken for the saving and preserving of life (Matt. 12:9–14, Luke 13:10–16, 14:3–6). Conversely, Jesus was more strict about the law of divorce than the Pharisees. Thus he stated:

It was also said, 'whoever divorces his wife, let him give her a certificate of divorce.' But I say to you that every one who divorces his wife, except on the ground of unchastity, makes her an adultress; and whoever marries a divorced woman commits adultery. (Matt. 5:31f.)

In a similar vein Jesus rejected the biblical and rabbinic teaching regarding dietary laws: 'Not that which entereth into the mouth defileth the man,' he stated, 'but what comes out of the mouth that defiles a man' (Matt. 15:11). Another serious divergence from traditional Jewish law was Jesus' view that the ritual washing of hands before meals was unimportant. In response to the Pharisees' criticism of his disciples for eating without first washing their hands, he rebuked the Pharisees for not keeping the ethical commandments: 'These are,' he stated, 'what defiles a man: but to eat with unwashed hands does not defile a man' (Matt. 15:20). Jesus also violated the laws regarding the fasts. The gospels record that when the Pharisees were fasting Jesus' disciples did not fast. When questioned about this, he replied: 'Can the wedding guests mourn as long as the bridegroom is with them? The days will come, when the bridegroom is taken away from them, and then they will fast' (Matt. 9:15). When the Pharisees criticized the disciples for plucking wheat on the Sabbath, Jesus proclaimed: 'The Son of man is lord of the Sabbath' (Matt. 12:8).

Could such a man have been resurrected? The Jewish answer has universally been 'No'. Through the ages, Jews have maintained that the Christian conviction that Jesus rose from the dead and sits at the right hand of the Father is totally misguided. For the Jews, the Messiah has not yet arrived, and they wait for his coming to redeem the world. Only at that time will the dead be resurrected to enter into a new life. The doctrine of resurrection is fundamental to traditional Judaism, but the Christian claim that Jesus' revival after death is the first-fruit of a new epoch is without justification. For the Jew, Jesus died and remained dead. Like all other human beings, his corpse rotted in the earth. He was buried in the dust and remained there despite Christian claims to the contrary.

Yet despite the universality of the Jewish rejection of Jesus' alleged resurrection, a distinguished Orthodox Jewish scholar has recently asserted that Jesus was brought back from the dead. In *The Resurrection of Jesus*, Pinchas Lapide maintains – in the face of Jesus' deviation from Jewish tradition and the fact that he did not fulfil the traditional expectations of the Messiah – that he was in fact resurrected for a divine purpose. In his view, the resurrection was a historical event that took place in the first century: its purpose was to bring about the formation of a religious community that would carry the central message of Judaism to the world. The experience of the resurrection 'as a foundation act of the Church was a means whereby faith in the God of Israel would be spread to the whole western world. The Easter event is thus part of God's providential plan. Quoting the mediaeval Jewish philosopher Moses Maimonides, he wrote:

All these matters which refer to Jesus of Nazareth . . . only served to make the way free for the King Messiah and to prepare the whole world for the worship of God with a united heart, as it is written: 'Yea, at that time I will change the speech of the peoples to a pure speech, that all of them may call on the name of the Lord and serve him with one accord' (Zeph. 3:9). In this way the messianic hope, the Torah, and the commandments have become a widespread heritage of faith – among the inhabitants of the far islands and among nations, uncircumcised in heart and flesh.[1]

Here then is a modern exception to previous Jewish teaching about Jesus' resurrection. Departing from generations of Jewish teaching about Jesus, Lapide sees in his death God's providential plan for humanity. Could he be correct? As we have seen Jews believe in the doctrine of the resurrection. There is no logical inconsistency in believing that Jesus could have been revived from the dead. But is such an idea plausible?

Was Jesus Resurrected?

As we have seen, throughout history Jews have steadfastly refused to embrace the Christian belief that Jesus was resurrected from the dead, even though the doctrine of the resurrection is embedded within traditional Jewish thought. Pinchas Lapide is a unique exception, and his views have been almost entirely ignored. But this is not the end of the matter. There is, I believe, an alternative approach to this question. Since the period of the Enlightenment, non-Orthodox Judaism has found it increasingly difficult to accept the concept of resurrection. Indeed, as early as 1869 the Reform movement in the United States decreed in its statement of principles that this belief should be abandoned in the light of modern scientific advance. Thus the Pittsburgh Platform asserts:

We reassert the doctrine of Judaism, that the soul of men is immortal, grounding this belief on the divine nature of the human spirit, which forever finds bliss in righteousness and misery in wickedness. We reject as ideas rooted in Judaism the belief both in bodily resurrection and in *Gehenna* and

Eden (Hell and Paradise) as abodes for everlasting punishment or reward.

Over the years, there has been a increasing disenchantment with the doctrine of bodily resurrection in the Jewish community generally. As the Jewish theologian Louis Jacobs has written:

> On the whole Jewish modernists have preferred the doctrine of the immorality of the soul to that of the resurrection of the dead. Accepting the thirteenth principle they have tended to limit it to immortality. There is no doubt that this is a departure from the traditional concept. But it is doubtful, to say the least, whether this warrants the slur that in the interests of a refined gentility it is preferred to give up the full-blooded doctrine of the resurrection in favour of the more 'refined' but less 'Jewish' doctrine of the immortality of the soul.[2]

According to Jacobs, there is no theological objection to such a notion – if God is omnipotent, he could bring about such an event. The objection is fundamentally philosophical:

> There are serious philosophical objections . . . in the way of acceptance of the doctrine of the resurrection. One of these is the difficulty of accounting for a body in the eternal life. If . . . eternity is outside time altogether, how can a body (which by definition must occupy space and time) exist for all eternity? There is a fundamental difference between the acceptance of the belief in immortality and that of resurrection. The only reason the devout Jew can have for accepting the belief in the resurrection is that tradition demands it.[3]

Jacobs is right in maintaining that resurrection is theoretically possible if God is all-powerful. Yet, like many other modern Jews, I find such an idea implausible because of the findings of contemporary science. If the dead were to be raised – including all those who died in the history of the human race – this would be a miraculous event of the most monumental proportions. It would not be impossible (assuming the existence of an omnipotent deity), but what evidence is there that it would happen? Certainly there is none from daily life.

The same conclusion applies to Jesus' death and resurrection as recorded in the gospels. What evidence is there that such an event occurred as a fact of history? We have only the conflicting records of the gospel writers, and as other essays in this book have demonstrated the picture presented there is riddled with difficulties. These reports of Jesus' death and resurrection were contrived by the faithful as the 'Good News', religious propaganda of the Graeco–Roman world designed to draw unbelievers to the true faith. Can such accounts be relied upon without corroborating evidence? Certainly I am not convinced by them. And why should I be? Biblical scholars have cast doubt on the historicity of the New Testament records, and over the last century we have witnessed an outpouring of scholarly attempts to capture the true words of Jesus.

It is well known that there is no universality of agreement, and if scholars cannot concur about such historical matters what credence can we give to the gospel accounts of the miraculous reappearance of Jesus to his disciples? And, even if we could substantiate (which we cannot) that Jesus' disciples really had some experience of the living Jesus after his death, this would not provide conclusive proof that he had been raised from the dead. It is after all possible, indeed likely, that those who encountered Jesus after his crucifixion had nothing more than a subjective psychological experience.

In short, the Gospels do not provide conclusive proof of Jesus' resurrection, nor do the personal religious experiences of Christians through the ages. Arguably, these personal encounters with Jesus are of a similar character to those subjective experiences of the early Christian community. They do not win me over, nor have they persuaded countless others. The difficulty with such evidence of Jesus' resurrection is that it is not sufficiently conclusive – if Jesus' resurrection is to be demonstrated, what is required is objective data.

In recent years, some Christians have argued that the Turin Shroud provides such proof. Before it was shown that the Shroud was a mediaeval forgery, a number of Christians contended that the image produced on the Shroud demonstrated that Jesus body must have risen from the dead. Yet, such a conclusion is misguided. Even if Jesus' body had been wrapped in the Shroud (which it was not), and even if no explanation could be given to account for the appearance of the image on the Shroud, this would not establish that Jesus rose from the dead. We would simply be presented with an inexplicable puzzle rather than conclusive proof of anything supernatural. In other words, there is a lack of sufficient objective evidence to draw the conclusion that Jesus' resurrection took place as a historical event, despite the claims of millions of Christians over the last twenty centuries. Does this mean that in theory nothing could persuade an unbeliever like me? On the contrary, I am open to persuasion! However, what I would require is solid, substantial, objective evidence.

As a Jew and a rabbi, I could be convinced of Jesus' resurrection, but I would set very high standards of what is required. It would not be enough to have a subjective experience of Jesus. If I heard voices or had a visionary experience of Jesus, this would not be enough. Let me sketch the kind of experience that would be necessary.

If Jesus appeared surrounded by hosts of angels trailing clouds of glory and announcing his Messiahship for all to see, this would certainly be compelling. But it would have to take place in the public domain. Such an event would have to be witnessed by multitudes, photographed, recorded on video cameras, shown on television, and announced in newspapers and magazines world-wide. Jesus' appearance would have to be a global event, televised on CNN and other forms of the world's media. Further, if as a consequence of his arrival, all the prophecies recorded in Scripture were fulfilled: the ingathering of the exiles, the rebuilding of the Temple, the resurrection of all those who have died, the advent of the Days of the Messiah, final judgement – I would without doubt embrace the Christian message and become a follower of the risen Christ.

Who wouldn't? This would be the long-awaited event, the cosmic fulfilment of human history as anticipated in the Jewish tradition. All human beings, regardless of their previous religious persuasion, would join together in a single religious community. This might prove embarrassing for the Chief Rabbi, the Dalai Lama and others . . . but what choice could there be other than to accept Jesus as Saviour. Yes, I could be persuaded of Jesus' resurrection and the truth of Christianity. I could become a willing convert, ardently seeking baptism to the one true faith. But what I would demand is concrete, objective, observable evidence of such a character. The Gospel stories are not sufficient, nor the myriad testimonies of Christians through the ages. Much more is needed than that.

It might be objected that such a hard-headed refusal to accept the risen Christ except under these conditions is totally misguided. Some modernist Christians would want to argue that I have totally missed the point. For these contemporary believers the story of Jesus death, resurrection and ascension is a myth of the deepest sort. Jesus' resurrection is not an historical event, but trans-historical in significance. Therefore, it makes no difference whether Jesus was physically resurrected. As a myth, the resurrection of Jesus provides a framework for true spirituality and moral living. The quest for objective evidence of Jesus' revivication is thus an unsophisticated misreading of the nature and significance of the Gospel stories.

Such a modernist interpretation is widespread across the Christian denominations. It is a form of spiritualizing the Gospel message, and it is reminiscent of the account of the Christian faith depicted by Evelyn Waugh in *Brideshead Revisited*. Rex – an unbeliever – is being instructed in the Catholic faith; here the priest complains about Rex's inability to understand the nature of the religion:

> The first day I wanted to find out what sort of religious life he had till now, so I asked him what he meant by prayer. He said, 'I don't mean anything. You tell me.' I tried to, in a few words, and he said: 'Right. So much for prayer. What's the next thing?' I gave him the catechism to take away. Yesterday I asked him whether Our Lord had more than one nature. He said: 'Just as many as you say, Father.'
>
> Then again I asked him: 'Supposing the Pope looked up and saw a cloud and said "It's going to rain", would that be bound to happen?'
>
> 'Oh, yes, Father.'
>
> 'But supposing it didn't?'
>
> He thought a moment and said, 'I suppose it would be sort of raining spiritually, only we were too sinful to see it.'

Those who defend Jesus' resurrection by denying its historicity while at the same time maintaining that it was a spiritual event are arguably as obtuse as this bewildered convert to Catholicism. Either

Jesus was physically resurrected or he wasn't. It's as simple as that. The Gospel account of the empty tomb and the disciples' recognition of the risen Christ point to such a historical conception of the resurrection event. To them it would make no sense that in some spiritual – as opposed to physical sense – Jesus' body was revivified. And such an idea should make no sense to us either, because it is a muddle. As a Jew, I am not persuaded that Jesus was revived after death and that he sits at the right hand of the Father. But I am capable of being persuaded. I wait for the evidence.

Notes

1. Moses Maimonides, *Mishneh Torah, Hilkhot Melakhim XI*, as quoted in *The Resurrection of Jesus* (London: SPCK, 1983), pp. 142–3.
2. Louis Jacobs, *Principles of the Jewish Faith* (Northvale, NJ: Jason Aronson, 1988), p. 413.
3. Ibid., p. 414.

Chapter 13

THE RESURRECTION AND BUDDHISM

Rupert Gethin

U nlike Judaism and Islam, Buddhism has no traditional attitudes to the Christian doctrine of the resurrection. There was probably no such thing as a Buddhist response to the idea of the resurrection prior to the late nineteenth century. The earliest explicit Buddhist response to the Christian doctrine of the resurrection that I have come across is one made in the course of a series of debates that took place in 1873 at Pānadura in Ceylon between the Buddhist monk, Mohoṭṭivatte Guṇānanda, and the Sinhalese Wesleyan minister, David de Silva.[1] On that occasion it is reported that Guṇānanda asked:

Why should Christians lay so much stress on the death of Christ . . . ? Besides, how unsatisfactory the evidence as to his bodily resurrection. The first witness they had to testify to this all-important event . . . was Mary Magdalene, who, they would remember, was a woman who had at one time been possessed of seven devils! What weight could be attached to the evidence of such a mad woman? The fact was that Christ's body was removed from the tomb by his disciples on the night when there were no guards, and how significant were the words in the Scriptures that even at that time it was rumoured that his body had been 'stolen' away. Well, if they were satisfied with this resurrection of Christ, they should believe it by all means![2]

So, although what follows may shed some light on the ways of thinking that give rise to such a response to the resurrection, this essay is neither a historical one, surveying the different responses Buddhists have made to the resurrection over the centuries, nor does it stand in an established tradition of responding to the resurrection. Instead the essay seeks to articulate certain questions and responses that the doctrine of the resurrection prompts for someone trying to make sense of the world in terms of the teachings of the Buddhist tradition. It does not aim to speak for the whole of the Buddhist tradition, and its only authority is a certain personal familiarity with aspects of the Buddhist tradition of thought and practice.

One of the first problems encountered by someone within one tradition trying to respond to the ideas and teachings of another tradition is that of reaching an understanding of those ideas that is acceptable and recognizable to that other tradition. There is a very real sense in which there is no such thing as *the* Christian doctrine of the resurrection; rather there is in its own right a tradition of Christian doctrines of the resurrection. The danger here is that one picks and chooses, and responds to one's own idea of what the Christian doctrine of the resurrection ought to be, rather than to a doctrine of the resurrection as actually formulated and held by Christians dead or alive. Thus the Buddhist ends up responding not to the Christian doctrine of the resurrection, but to a Buddhist doctrine of the resurrection. And yet the way one tradition understands or misunderstands the ideas of another tradition is in itself interesting and instructive for both traditions. Each tradition holds up a mirror for the other. But in any encounter between different traditions one might usefully take heed of King Aśoka's ancient advice not to try to present one's own tradition in a more favourable light by extolling it while disparaging another's, since this in fact ends in one's own tradition appearing in the unfavourable light and its standing decreasing; rather we should strive for concord and agreement.[3]

So with these preliminary remarks let me, as one with no expertise in Christian doctrinal history, state briefly what I take to be the principal constituents of the Christian doctrine of the resurrection. First of all, it would appear from modern historical scholarship that the New Testament writers themselves understood that Jesus, having died as a result of crucifixion, was three days later resurrected in a fleshly body that had a straightforward physical continuity with his body before his death. It would appear also that many early Christians and indeed many Christians over the centuries have understood the matter in this way. Of course, the doctrine of Jesus' resurrection for Christians has never been limited simply to this claim. Although the New Testament accounts seem to present Jesus' resurrected body as the same body as he had when he was alive, they also seem to suggest that it is in some sense a 'transformed' and 'glorified' body that is not quite like other bodies: it can dematerialize and rematerialize in different places (Luke 24:13–36; John 20:19–30); it is not going 'to die' again (it could not be crucified a second time); and, if we are to include Paul's experience on the Damascus road as a meeting with Jesus' resurrected body, it is also sometimes associated with blinding light (Acts 9). This brings us to what has been the more religiously significant aspect of Jesus's resurrection for Christians. A meeting with the resurrected Jesus is no ordinary experience; it has a profound effect. It results in an inner transformation, establishing in an individual an absolute faith in Jesus as the Son of God. But in what precisely does the transforming nature of this experience inhere? Does the transforming experience of faith in Jesus as the true son of God come about by the simple fact of the resurrection of a dead body – by the surprise of an encounter with someone believed to be crucified, dead and buried, but whom instead one suddenly finds in front of one still alive? Or should the transforming power of the encounter with the resurrected Jesus be attributed to something other than the mere fact that he has been raised from the dead?

It does not seem that the Christian tradition as a whole provides simple, straightforward answers to these questions. In fact what we find – at least when we observe from the outside – is a certain tension in the history of Christian thought between the presentation of Jesus' resurrection as an objective event, on the one hand, and a subjective inner experience on the other. Thus at times the Christian tradition seems to be suggesting that one should 'believe in' Christ precisely because of the resurrection: Jesus rose from the dead and this unique event of the resurrection reveals finally that Jesus was indeed the Son of God. Such a claim seems to rest on a more literal understanding of the resurrection as an objective event. Yet at other times, and certainly in more recent theological writings, the Christian tradition emphasizes the resurrection as a way of talking about an inner transforming experience in the context of which the objective event of a dead physical body actually coming back to life is ultimately irrelevant. From this perspective the New Testament writers' literalist understanding should be to a greater or lesser extent 'demythologized' in order to reveal the essential transforming and saving power of the 'resurrection'; the New Testament accounts of the encounters with the resurrected Jesus are then effectively read as a way of talking about and describing a profoundly transforming religious experience – an experience that the Christian tradition would still want to claim as in some theological sense unique. In what follows, at the invitation of a Christian theologian, I shall make some comments, drawing on the resources of the Buddhist tradition and my own experience and understanding of Buddhist practice, on both these dimensions of the Christian doctrine of the resurrection, namely, as a unique event that 'proves' Jesus' divinity, and as a transforming inner experience.

To any one coming across the bare Gospel story of the resurrection for the first time it must appear as a story of a wondrous and extraordinary event – men who are crucified, dead and buried do not as a rule come back to life. But other traditions too have their stories of wondrous and extraordinary happenings. If one turns to the writings of the Buddhist tradition one will find no lack of such happenings. This is true of every type of Buddhist literature of every age: the earliest discourses attributed to the Buddha himself known as Sutta, the systematic philosophical exposition of these known as Abhidhamma, the commentaries on these, the later summary manuals and textbooks, technical scholastic literature, popular stories and legends. All this literature takes for granted that wondrous and extraordinary events do, if rarely, certainly occur. Of course, in the twentieth century in Buddhist modernist circles, both in the West and in traditional Buddhist cultures, there has been a tendency to play down the tradition of the 'miraculous' in Buddhism and to see it as peripheral, but it is hard to treat this tendency as anything but revisionist. While there is no lack of wonderful and extraordinary happenings in Buddhist writings, such happenings tend not to become central doctrines of Buddhist thought. For example, the Buddha's conception appears to be presented in the ancient scriptural accounts as parthenogenic, yet probably few contemporary Buddhists register this, and there is no Buddhist 'doctrine of a virgin birth'.[4]

The Buddhist tradition's immediate response to accounts of wonderful and extraordinary happenings is to refer them to the general Indian yogic tradition which attributes a whole set of extraordinary feats beyond the capacity of ordinary men to 'holy men'. However, from the Indian cultural perspective such feats are not necessarily to be regarded as miracles in the technical sense of events that require the suspending of the laws of nature and some form of divine intervention.[5] According to the outlook of the Indian yogic tradition, whether it be Buddhist, Hindu or whatever, as a natural by-product of the cultivation of certain contemplative techniques and the attainment of what, for want of a better term, we may call altered states of consciousness, the 'yogin' or practitioner of meditation may develop certain abilities that the Buddhist tradition styles as 'beyond the capacity of ordinary people'. From the point of view of Buddhist spiritual practice, the prime aim of the contemplative techniques is to still and quiet the mind, but according to Buddhist psychological theory, the mind that has become still in certain states of 'concentration' (*samādhi*) can draw on resources and strengths that otherwise remain dormant and unused in order to cultivate various meditational powers. There is a stock list of these powers in the ancient literature: the yogin can produce 'mind-made' bodies, he can make himself invisible, he can pass through solid objects such as walls, he can go down into the earth as if it was water, he can walk on water as if it was solid earth, he can fly through the sky, he can touch the sun and the moon, he can visit different realms of the universe, he can have knowledge of distant sounds, knowledge of the state of others' minds, knowledge of his own and others' past lives.[6]

The only direct parallel here with the miracles attributed to Jesus is the ability to walk on water, although later commentaries do include an ability 'to make little much, and much little', which is illustrated by stories of making amounts of food less or more.[7] However, for one familiar with the Buddhist tradition certain aspects of the account of Jesus' resurrected body – its glorious and transformed nature – have resonances with the Buddhist understanding of 'mind-produced' bodies. It is noteworthy that the ability to cure disfiguring diseases and to rise from the dead are not generally included in the lists of yogins' abilities. However, that great spiritual teachers possess a certain healing power is not alien to the tradition; when the mother of the future Buddha conceived we are told how the blind saw and the deaf heard.[8] The exorcism of 'devils' or 'demons' of some sort also has parallels within Indian tradition, and certainly the Buddhist tradition has made use of the metaphor of healing, presenting the Buddha as a 'physician'; but it is the diseases of the mind that he cures rather than the diseases of the body.[9] While there are to my knowledge no stories of yogins who have died coming back to life in the Buddhist tradition, or of yogins bringing others who have died back to life, there are certainly examples of monks being taken for dead by others while sitting in still and silent meditation, and it is probably fair to say that an ability to appear dead for a period of time could be regarded as one of the accomplishments of the Indian yogin, though it is not one that is very apparent in the tradition.

While certain Buddhist modernists might wish to deny this tradition of meditational powers a significant place within Buddhism, and despite the fact that these powers are not precisely those attributed to Jesus, the natural tendency for one whose outlook is moulded by the general Indian yogic tradition must be to see Jesus as presented in the New Testament as a kind of yogin. That is to say, Jesus was a wandering, celibate religious and spiritual teacher who gathered around him a group of followers. Such people are in Indian cultural terms 'wanderers', 'renouncers' or 'yogins'; furthermore it is the norm for such people to have certain powers and abilities beyond the capacity of ordinary people. So, for example, the Sri Lankan Buddhist monk, Hammalava Saddhatissa, in his book *The Buddha's Way*, straightforwardly takes the view that Jesus and his miracles are to be understood in these terms.[10]

It is perhaps worth trying to indicate the way in which the Buddhist tradition might be tempted to explain the resurrection as an example of a yogin's meditational powers. In the first place I think it would have to be suggested that Jesus was not in fact dead when he was brought down from the cross, rather he was in some sort of meditational state in which he appeared dead. As I have suggested a circumstance of this nature is not particularly alien to the general Indian yogic tradition; the control over certain bodily functions (such as the breathing) implying the slowing of metabolic processes is generally accepted. In the second place, from the perspective of the Buddhist tradition at least some of the Gospel accounts of Jesus' resurrection appearances might be interpreted in terms of a yogin's abilities to make himself disappear in one place and appear in another, and to manifest glorified and radiant bodies. Someone might wish to ask why on earth a great religious teacher might wish to do such things. The response that the Buddhist tradition would make is that the performance of such wonders is normal in the case of holy men; indeed, as witnessed by various stories, it is just one of the many techniques a Buddha or any accomplished religious teacher will employ in order to teach, according to circumstance and what is judged helpful.[11]

To the Buddhist tradition Jesus' resurrection will naturally appear then as one more example of a holy man's yogic powers. Of course, the Christian tradition must protest that a yogic feat is exactly what the resurrection is not; what the resurrection shows is God acting decisively and finally in history in order to redeem the human race. But I must emphasize here that to see the resurrection in terms of a holy man's yogic powers is not some underhand device for explaining away the resurrection, it is merely that if the New Testament accounts of Jesus' resurrection are to be taken more or less literally, then this is how such a story inevitably appears to the Buddhist tradition.

So, drawing on its own resources, the Buddhist tradition has a number of potential ways of making sense of the basic facts of the story of the resurrection. All these Buddhist ways of making sense of the story revolve around seeing Jesus as basically an accomplished yogin. Of course, all these ways of understanding the apparent phenomenon of Jesus' resurrection may appear far-fetched and fantastic to us in the modern world, but the question is whether for most people they are any more far-fetched and fantastic than the suggestion that what we in fact have is a case of God resurrecting the dead body of Jesus. With this question in mind I would like to explore a little further the place occupied by such yogic powers in Buddhist thought and practice. This should clarify the Buddhist attitude to a resurrection viewed as an objective event.

Leaving aside what I have styled the Buddhist modernist attitude to miraculous powers, as I have already indicated, such powers and abilities are for the most part seen as the natural by-product of the development of certain kinds of contemplative technique. These powers are not to be confused with the goal of the Buddhist spiritual path, and indeed certain contemporary teachers will emphasize that there is a danger that one may become fascinated by them and that they may become a distraction that hinders one's progress towards the goal.[12] On the other hand, the mastery of these contemplative techniques that is involved in developing these abilities is certainly regarded as in the main conducive to the spiritual path, and, as I indicated above, there are stories of their being employed by the Buddha and Buddhist saints in order to teach and help others in their spiritual practice. While there is certainly a tradition of these miraculous powers being seen as proving a yogin's or holy man's credentials, the Buddhist attitude to the display of such powers is well illustrated by a conversation that is presented in early Buddhist literature as taking place between the Buddha and the layman Kevaddha.[13] One day, it seems, Kevaddha requested that the Buddha invite some accomplished monk to undertake a display of miraculous power in order that people with faith in the Buddha's teaching might be inspired with confidence. The Buddha refuses. The reason he gives for refusing is that, although someone with faith in the Buddha and his teaching might well be inspired by the display of a miracle, when he or she subsequently runs off and enthusiastically relates the wonder just witnessed to someone lacking in faith, the latter might remain singularly unimpressed, merely responding that it is by means of some trickery that a monk displays these wonders.[14]

I have noted elsewhere how the reaction to the paranormal in the twentieth century parallels rather closely the scenario envisaged by the Buddha here.[15] Any actual examples of the 'paranormal' in fact only serve to confirm people in their prejudices: the faithful tend to point to various people and incidents as evidence inexplicable except as examples of the 'paranormal', while the sceptics, maintaining that trickery or self-deceit has been involved, doggedly seek out rational 'scientific' explanations. Thus if one really believes in these things no amount of evidence to the contrary is going to convince one that they cannot happen (though I grant that one may be persuaded that particular examples are 'tricks'). Likewise, if one is a convinced sceptic one will always suggest that there is some form of rational 'scientific' explanation for what has occurred or what someone has experienced.

The relevance of this kind of thinking to an understanding of Jesus' resurrection as an objective event that somehow proves Jesus' divinity might be stated thus. It would always be impossible to prove to a sceptic's satisfaction that the resurrection represents a wondrous or miraculous event. That is, even if one could gather historical evidence to show conclusively, which of course one could not, that the Jesus who was crucified and put in the tomb subsequently was seen walking about as real flesh and blood, it would still be impossible to demonstrate to the sceptic that this was the resurrection, since it is impossible to see what could count as real historical evidence that Jesus was really dead when he was put in the tomb. That is, if the 'objective' historian concerned to establish hard facts is presented with evidence that suggests that someone who was assumed dead was subsequently found to be alive, then he is bound to conclude that there must have been some mistake: either this person was not really dead in the first place or he was not really alive. For what kind of 'objective' or 'scientific' *historical* evidence could suggest that we are in fact dealing with a case of resurrection from the dead?

The conclusion that I would suggest follows from this is that although for the most part the Buddhist tradition has been quite sympathetic to the idea of wondrous and miraculous occurrences, it sees these as the norm for the realized and accomplished spiritual teacher. Moreover miracles and wonders prove nothing to the convinced sceptic. And since this is so, they cannot be regarded as proving or guaranteeing the profound truth of the Buddha's teaching. The tradition does in fact record that there is a miracle that no other religious teacher or yogin but a Buddha can perform. This is 'the miracle of the pairs', so-called because it culminates with the spectacular issuing of double streams of fire and water from every pore of the Buddha's body.[16] But it is not the performance of this extraordinary and unique feat that finally reveals the Buddha to be the Buddha. Indeed, no mere miracle, however wondrous and unprecedented in history, could usefully demonstrate to the satisfaction of the convinced sceptic that the ascetic Gotama who lived in the fifth century BCE in the north of India was a Buddha. What makes a Buddha a Buddha is not his ability to perform miracles, but his accomplishments with regard to four truths about the world: suffering, its cause, its cessation and the path leading to its cessation. It is in the presentation of these four things that the teachings of Buddhas are said to be special. Thus the Buddha has understood fully the ultimate nature of suffering; he has completely eradicated in himself the causes of suffering (craving for objects of the senses, craving for existence and craving for non-existence), he has experienced directly the cessation of suffering, namely the transcendent nirvāṇa, and this has been achieved by his cultivation in all its various aspects of the path that leads to the cessation of suffering. Moreover, what truly makes a Buddha a

Buddha is his accomplishments as a teacher – his ability to lead others to knowledge of these four truths, both as a historical teacher and as founder of a Buddha's 'dispensation' (*sāsana*), the Buddhist tradition of thought and practice. Thus in his conversation with Kevaddha the Buddha concludes by pointing out that the greatest wonder is 'the miracle of instruction' (*anusasānī-pāṭihāriya*). So to see Jesus's importance and indeed the 'truth' or 'falsity' of Christian teaching and practice as somehow hinging on a unique miraculous event in the history of the world, namely the objective and literal fact of the bodily resurrection of Jesus, is puzzling and indeed makes little sense, it seems to me, to the Buddhist tradition.

There is a further dimension to the way in which an objective bodily resurrection of Jesus fails to make good sense to the Buddhist. If focusing on a wondrous event as the proof of Jesus' divinity is puzzling, then focusing on a wondrous event that apparently denies the universality of human death is deeply perplexing. The language of 'immortality' is certainly not alien to the Buddhist tradition. Thus soon after his awakening the Buddha can declare that 'for those who have ears, the doors of the deathless have been opened'.[17] And certainly it is understood that the path taught by the Buddha leads to 'the deathless' (*amata*). But this 'deathless' is never understood in terms of a literal immortality. Buddhist Nirvāṇa is understood as 'the deathless' in that it transcends the conditions of both birth and death. It is a fundamental axiom – indeed perhaps *the* fundamental axiom – of Buddhist thought that whatever is born must die. Thus although there is an old Buddhist tradition that the Buddha's meditational accomplishments could have enabled him to prolong his life somewhat, there is not the suggestion that he could simply have avoided death, that he could have lived on for ever.[18] In a very deep sense it is upon this that the whole of Buddhist teaching pivots. One might go so far as to say that it is precisely his own death that constitutes the Buddha's profoundest teaching: whoever one is, whatever one does, one cannot avoid death, this is the nature of the world. Thus the Buddha informs one of his closest disciples:

I am now grown old, Ānanda, and full of years; my journey is done and I have reached my sum of days; I am turning eighty years of age. And just as a worn out cart is kept going with the help of repairs, so it seems is the Tathāgata's [that is, the Buddha's] body kept going with repairs.[19]

And as the Buddha lay dying between two blossoming sāl trees, it is related how the monk Ānanda, who unlike many of his other disciples had not achieved the state of the *arahat* or Buddhist saint, lent against a door and wept. Then the Buddha sent for him:

> Enough, Ānanda, do not sorrow, do not lament. Have I not formerly explained that it is the nature of things that we must be divided, separated, and parted from all that is beloved and dear? How could it be, Ānanda, that what has been born and come into being, that what is compounded and subject to decay, should not decay? It is not possible.[20]

The Buddhist attitude to death is simply and exactly illustrated by an extremely well-known story.[21] It happened, we are told, that the young child of a woman called Kisā Gotamī died. Distraught with grief she wandered about pleading for medicine to cure her child. Eventually she was sent to the Buddha who declared that he did indeed know the medicine she needed. The Buddha advised her to collect white mustard seed, but from a house in which no son or daughter, nor any other person, had ever died. Of course, she found white mustard seed, but at every house she was told how someone had died there. Yet although her search was in vain, in its course she realized the foolishness of thinking herself the only mother who had ever lost a young child.

Let me sum up what I have suggested so far concerning the Buddhist attitude to the resurrection as an objective event. First, it is natural for the Buddhist tradition to see the resurrection in terms of yogic powers. It is natural in that such an understanding of Jesus' resurrection makes much more sense to the Buddhist tradition than an understanding of the resurrection as some sign or 'proof' of Jesus' divinity, since from the Buddhist perspective the claim that Jesus was the Son of God makes little if any sense, as the concept of 'God' as an omnipotent, loving creator is a priori problematic. From the Buddhist perspective the universe, rather than being created by any God, simply *is*. Furthermore, the universe comprises innumerable 'world systems' that pass through vast cycles of expansion and contraction across incalculable periods of time. It is quite meaningless to think of a God acting decisively and uniquely in the 'history' of such a universe. In such a universe there is nothing for God to do; no purpose could be served by a single, unique incarnation and resurrection. Essentially the same point as I am making here was made by Ninian Smart some thirty years ago when, writing as an academic theologian, he suggested that, given the presuppositions of belief in a personal God and a view about the importance of history, then the events of the Bible may fall into place, but without them they hardly have the great significance claimed for them.[22] Thus that Jesus's resurrection might possibly be a sign of his divinity – a sign of the incarnation – would not begin to occur to the Buddhist tradition, but that it was a sign that he was indeed an accomplished yogin and great religious teacher might. However, as the Buddha warns Kevaddha, even miracles only serve to impress those who are already convinced. Moreover the Christian claim that the body of Jesus was resurrected and somehow transcended death must also seem to the Buddhist to be at odds with the Buddhist understanding of the very nature of human suffering, almost a denial of the reality of suffering – all bodies are impermanent, we cannot escape death. If the Christian were to counter that the bodily resurrection of Jesus thus precisely showed his divinity, the Buddhist must reply that the world just is not like that. As long as we are attached to the idea of being human beings with bodies we will never overcome death, for death – the dying of the body – is precisely the condition of having a physical human body: for the Buddha, for Jesus, for everyone. What is illustrated by this then are the very different assumptions from which the Buddhist and Christian traditions are working. Thus Buddhist theory might certainly accommodate the objective event of Jesus' resurrection, but in doing so it would largely deprive it of the religious significance the Christian tradition imparts to it.

At this point I would like to turn briefly to the question of the resurrection as a subjective, inner experience of transformation. If the Buddhist tradition must see the resurrection as an objective event in terms of its own understanding of a yogin's ability to perform extraordinary and miraculous feats, then it must interpret the resurrection as a subjective experience in terms of its own understanding of what I called above 'altered states of consciousness'. Such an expression is a rather vain attempt at a neutral expression for the variety of religious experience recognized by the Buddhist tradition. In fact the detailing and classification of a whole range of 'altered states of consciousness' is one of the hallmarks of Buddhist psychology. According to this scheme of classification such experiences fall into two main classes: experiences of the 'divine' (*brahma*) and experiences of the 'transcendent' (*lokuttara*). This requires some explanation. Buddhist psychology distinguishes a range of meditation attainments known as *jhānas* which are regarded as experiences of different levels of existence associated with various kinds of divine being collectively known as *brahmās*. Such divine or, perhaps better, angelic beings possess great power and compassion, and they may live for many aeons, but nevertheless they are still regarded as mortal. They are most definitely not personal creator Gods – although from the perspective of the Buddhist tradition they are sometimes mistaken as such or even mistake themselves as such.[23] By the cultivation of the appropriate techniques the yogin can develop in himself a state of consciousness that has the essential qualities of these divine beings. Furthermore, according to the Buddhist understanding of things, the yogin who does so will eventually be reborn as one of these divine beings. The characteristic state of mind of such a being is one of great happiness and tranquillity, marred only by its temporary and ultimately unstable nature.

This experience of the divine contrasts with the experience of the transcendent. The experience of the transcendent is equivalent to a direct experience of Nirvāṇa, and such an experience constitutes 'enlightenment' or 'awakening' (*bodhi*). For Buddhism this is the transforming experience par excellence; it is the experience of the transcendent that radically transforms the individual, cutting off the defilements of greed, hatred and delusion such that the being who has fully experienced Nirvāṇa can but thence act only from non-attachment, compassion and wisdom. In whatever manner the nature of the transcendent or Nirvāṇa is to be understood, the Buddhist tradition is clear that it should not be understood in terms of a single omnipotent, personal being regarded as the creator.

To attempt to pronounce on which of these two Buddhist categories of religious experience the Christian experience of the resurrection might be regarded as falling into is not my intention.

To do so would be to fall foul of the complex and subtle issues that mark the debate over comparative mystical and religious experience during the last thirty years, issues surrounding the question of pure, unadulterated experience and its relationship to conceptual content and interpretation.[24] Yet it is worth suggesting the kinds of question the Buddhist tradition would ask of any religious or mystical experience that presents itself as a candidate for a transforming religious experience. It seems to me that the Buddhist tradition is here less concerned with the conceptual content of that experience than with its practical consequences and effects. That is, for the Buddhist tradition the significant question is whether or not an experience permanently cuts off or eradicates greed, hatred and delusion, and leaves a person established in non-attachment, compassion and wisdom. Of course, it may seem easier to establish a common understanding of the nature of greed/non-attachment and hatred/compassion than of delusion/wisdom; to talk of delusion and wisdom apart from conceptual and intellectual content is not a straightforward matter. Thus to isolate the effects of an experience from its conceptual content may prove in itself problematic. But just as understanding the objective event of the resurrection as a yogic feat deprives it of its Christian significance, so too does understanding the subjective experience of the resurrection as a kind of meditation experience. Christians and Buddhists are talking different languages here, and while mutual understanding may not be impossible, so much is lost in translation that what has been translated is rendered unrecognizable.

In all this the Christian might with some justification claim that instead of responding to the Christian doctrine of the resurrection I have distorted it beyond all recognition. The Jesus of my essay is not the Son of God who was crucified, dead and buried, and who on the third day rose again, but rather a yogic trickster, a mere wonder worker. Yet in a sense this is my point. The doctrine of the resurrection can only make sense within its own 'mythic' or – if one prefers – 'theological' or doctrinal context. The Christian claim that Jesus's resurrection somehow demonstrates the uniqueness of Christianity only makes sense when preaching to the converted. The Buddhist tradition is *bound* to make sense of the resurrection in its own terms, since not to do so would be to allow its own self-understanding to be radically undermined. And although the Christian might wish to suggest that this is precisely the challenge of the resurrection, the Buddhist will continue to be puzzled as to why this one event of all events, wondrous though it may have been, should count as sufficient reason to question the accumulated wisdom of a tradition that traces itself back to a living Buddha.

Notes

1. See K. Malalgoda, *Buddhism in Sinhalese Society 1750–1900: A Study of Religious Revival and Change* (Berkeley: University of California Press, 1976), pp. 220–31.
2. Pranith Abhayasundara (ed.), *Controversy at Pānadura or Pānadura Vādaya* (Colombo: State Printing Corporation, 1990), pp. 161–2.
3. Twelfth Major Rock Edict; see for example R. Thapar, *Aśoka and the Decline of the Mauryas* (Delhi: Oxford University Press, 1973), p. 255.
4. T. W. & C. A. F. Rhys Davids (trans.), *Dialogues of the Buddha*, 3 vols. (London: Pali Text Society, 1899–1959), II, 10.
5. Cf. Rhys Davids, *Dialogues of the Buddha*, I, 272.
6. Rhys Davids, *Dialogues of the Buddha*, I, 87–92; Ñāṇamoli (trans.), *The Path of Purification* (Colombo: Semage, 1964), pp. 409–78; some of this material can also be found in E. Conze, *Buddhist Scriptures* (Harmondsworth: Penguin Books, 1959), pp. 121–33.
7. Ñāṇamoli, *The Path of Purification*, p. 441; Conze, *Buddhist Scriptures*, p. 128.
8. See N. A. Jayawickrama (trans.), *The Story of Gotama Buddha: The Nidānakathā of the Jātakaṭṭhakathā* (Oxford: Pali Text Society, 1990), p. 68.
9. Cf. C. A. F. Rhys Davids & F. L. Woodward (trans.), *The Book of Kindred Sayings*, 5 vols. (London: Pali Text Society, 1917–30), III, 1–5.
10. H. Saddhatissa, *The Buddha's Way* (London: George Allen & Unwin, 1971), pp. 79–80.
11. Cf. Ñāṇamoli, *The Path of Purification*, pp. 424–30; Conze, *Buddhist Scriptures*, pp. 122–7; L. O. Gomez, 'The Bodhisattva as Wonder Worker' in *Prajñāpāramitā and Related Systems: Buddhist Studies in Honor of Edward Conze*, ed. L. Lancaster (Berkeley: University of California Press, 1977), pp. 221–61.
12. Cf. J. Kornfield (ed.), *Living Buddhist Masters* (Santa Cruz: University Press, 1977).
13. *Kevaddha Sutta*; see Rhys Davids, *Dialogues of the Buddha* I, 276–84.
14. R. M. L. Gethin, *The Buddhist Path to Awakening: A Study of the Bodhi-Pakkhiyā Dhammā* (Leiden: E. J. Brill, 1992), pp. 97–101.
15. Ibid., p. 100, n. 85.
16. E. W. Burlingame (trans.), *Buddhist Legends Translated from the Original*

Pali Text of the Dhammapada Commentary, 3 vols (London: Pali Text Society, 1969), III, 35–56.

17. I. B. Horner (trans.), *The Middle Length Sayings*, 3 vols (London: Pali Text Society, 1954–9), I, 213.

18. See Rhys Davids, *Dialogues of the Buddha*, II, 110; Gethin, *The Buddhist Path to Awakening*, pp. 94–7.

19. Translation adapted from Rhys Davids, *Dialogues of the Buddha*, II, 107.

20. Ibid., pp. 158–9.

21. Burlingame, *Buddhist Legends*, II, 257–60.

22. N. Smart, 'Christianity and the Other Great Religions' in *Soundings: Essays Concerning Christian Understanding*, ed. A. R. Vidler (Cambridge: Cambridge University Press, 1966), pp. 103–21, particularly pp. 110–11, 117.

23. Rhys Davids, *Dialogues of the Buddha*, I, 30–2.

24. See especially S. T. Katz (ed.), *Mysticism and Philosophical Analysis* (London: Sheldon Press, 1978).

List of Contributors

Dr John M. G. Barclay is a Lecturer in the Department of Biblical Studies at the University of Glasgow. He previously studied at Cambridge (MA, Ph.D.). He has published *Obeying the Truth: A Study of Paul's Ethics in Galatians* (1988) and several articles on Paul and early Christianity. He has just completed a historical monograph on Jews in the Mediterranean Diaspora.

Tina Beattie is doing doctoral research in the Department of Theology and Religious Studies at the University of Bristol on sexuality and the cult of the Virgin Mary. She lectures in feminist and liberation theology, and is the author of *Rediscovering Mary – Insights from the Gospels* (1995).

Dan Cohn-Sherbok was ordained a Reform rabbi at the Hebrew Union College, received a doctorate from Cambridge University, and has served congregations in the United States, Australia, England and South Africa. Since 1975 he has taught Jewish theology at the University of Kent, and is currently a Visiting Professor at the Universities of Middlesex, Wales at Lampeter, and St Andrews. He has been a Visiting Professor at the University of Essex, a Visiting Fellow at Wolfson College, Cambridge, and a Visiting Scholar at Mansfield College, Oxford and the Oxford Centre for Hebrew and Jewish Studies. He is the author and editor of over forty books including *Jewish Mysticism: An Anthology* (1995), as well as *A Short History of Judaism* (1994) and *A Short Reader in Judaism* (1996) with Lavinia Cohn-Sherbok.

Gavin D'Costa is an Indian Roman Catholic, born in Kenya, educated in England (at the Universities of Birmingham and Cambridge) and is currently Senior Lecturer in the Department of Theology and Religious Studies at the University of Bristol. He has written *Theology and Religious Pluralism* (1986) and edited *Christian Uniqueness Reconsidered: The Myth of a Pluralistic Theology of Religions* (1990). He is an adviser to the Anglican Board of Mission and the Roman Catholic Committee for Other Faiths (England and Wales). He is currently writing a book on the trinity and religious pluralism.

Rupert Gethin is Lecturer in Indian Religions in the Department of Theology and Religious Studies at the University of Bristol. His principal research interests are in the area of Theravāda Buddhist thought, especially the psychology and philosophy of the Abhidhamma, and Buddhist meditation theory. His publications include *The Buddhist Path to Awakening: A Study of the Bodhi-Pakkhiyā Dhammā* (1992) and '*Bhavaṅga* and Rebirth According to the Abhidhamma' in *The Buddhist Forum*, vol. III, eds. T. Skorupski and U. Pagel (1994). He has been a member of the Samatha Association for the some fifteen years.

Michael Goulder was educated at Eton, Cambridge (Classics) and Oxford (Theology, with Austin Farrer). In 1951 he was ordained to the Anglican ministry in Hong Kong, and served parishes in Salford and Manchester, returning to Hong Kong as Principal of Union Theological College. From 1966 to 1994 he worked as Tutor in Theology in the Extramural Department at the University of Birmingham. He resigned his Orders in 1981, having ceased to believe in God. He was Speaker's Lecturer at Oxford and D D (Oxon, 1975), and was made Professor of Biblical Studies at Birmingham in 1991. He has written nine books, mostly on the gospels and psalms, and thirty-nine articles.

Gareth Jones is Lecturer in Systematic Theology at the University of Birmingham. He has published two books: *Bultmann: Towards a Critical Theology* (1991); and *Critical Theology: Questions of Truth and Method* (1995). He edits the journal *Reviews in Religion and Theology* and is currently writing a book on theology and social theory.

Dr Gerard Loughlin is a Lecturer in the Department of Religious Studies at the University of Newcastle-upon-Tyne, where he teaches Christian theology, ethics and philosophy of religion. He has published articles and reviews in a number of leading journals, including *Modern Theology*, *Theology*, *Heythrop Journal* and *New Blackfriars*, and is the author of *Telling God's Story: Bible, Church and Narrative Theology* (1996).

David Marshall has studied Theology at Oxford and Islamics at the Centre for the Study of Islam and Christian–Muslim Relations at

Selly Oak, Birmingham, where he is writing his doctoral thesis. He and his wife Helen are both priests in the Church of England. David has recently become Chaplain of Exeter College, Oxford.

David McCarthy Matzko is Assistant Professor of Religious Studies at the College of St Rose in Albany, NY. Among his publications, he has written another essay on saints which is pertinent to his chapter in this volume, 'Postmodernism, Saints and Scoundrels', *Modern Theology 9* (1993).

Jürgen Moltmann was born in Hamburg and is a member of the German Reformed Church. He studied at the University of Göttingen and is now Professor of Systematic Theology at Tübingen University. Moltmann is Chairman of the Society for Evangelical Theology and has published extensively, with many of his books translated into English, including *The Theology of Hope* (1967), *The Crucified God* (1974), *The Church in the Power of the Spirit* (1977), *The Trinity and the Kingdom of God* (1981), *God in the Creation* (1985), *The Way of Jesus Christ: Christology in Messianic Dimensions* (1990), and *Jesus Christ for Today's World* (1994).

Wolfhart Pannenberg studied philosophy and theology in Berlin, Göttingen, Basel and Heidelberg. He is Professor of Systematic Theology at the Institute of Ecumenical Theology (which he founded) at the University of Munich. He has published widely in Christology, Christian anthropology, the theoretical foundations of theology, and the philosophy of science. Especially well known to the English-speaking world, among his many works, are *Jesus – God and Man* (1966), *Theology and the Philosophy of Science* (1976), and the first two of his three volumes of systematic theology.

Rowan Williams is Bishop of Monmouth, formerly Lady Margaret Professor of Divinity at the University of Oxford, and has taught theology for seventeen years. He has written on various topics in the history of theology and spirituality (most recently *Teresa of Avila*, 1991), and in 1982 published a brief theological meditation on *Resurrection: Interpreting the Easter Gospel*. He is currently working on a book on trinitarian doctrine, and on Russian religious thought in the twentieth century.

Index

Abraham, and sainthood 113, 114
absence and presence, in empty tomb
  tradition 95–100
accessibility, and bodily resurrection
  40–1
Alsup, J. E. 88
altarity 44
analogy, and history 14, 64, 78, 84,
  121–2
anastasis (resurrection), meaning 18
Andrae, Tor 175
Andrews, Charles Freer 162
angels, in empty tomb tradition 19, 88,
  90–1, 145
Anselm, St 126
Anthony of Padua, St 110, 115
anthropology: of Bultmann 33–4, 36,
  37; of Rahner 36–7
apocalypsis: in Paul 76; and presence of
  Christ 76
apologetics, and New Testament
  scholarship 13–14
appearances of Christ: in 1 Cor. 15 14,
  16–17, 19, 24, 48, 66–7, 74–5; as
  collective delusions 25–6, 52–5, 58,
  197–8; as conversion visions 25–6,
  48–52, 74–6; as early tradition 24, 48,
  95; gospel accounts 17, 18, 24, 66,
  68, 74, 107–8; historicity 20, 23–6,
  199–200; location 16, 24, 25, 57; and
  non-recognition theme 91, 98; and
  the Pauline church 94; to 500 16, 24,
  53, 74; to the apostles 53, 74; to
  James 16, 94; to Paul 16, 17, 49–52,
  66–7, 74–5, 203; to Peter 16, 17, 25,
  50–2, 67, 74, 94; to women 16, 17,
  24, 60 n.18, 74–5, 145, 201; and
  yogic powers 206
Aquinas, St Thomas, and existence 36
ark of the covenant, as throne of God
  90, 99
Aśoka, King 202
Athanasius, St 136, 163
Atkins, Susan 48–9, 50, 51, 58
atonement, as continuous 156, 159, 162
Augustine of Hippo, St 144, 146
authority, institutional 94–8

Baba Mezia 7
Badr, battle of 173–4
Balthasar, Hans Urs von 122, 123–4

baptism: as entry into story of Jesus 129,
  157; naming as symbol of 145; in Paul
  106
Barclay, John M. G. 9, 13–28, 217
Barrett, C. K. 90, 154, 155
Barrow, J. D. 133 n.5
Barth, Karl 33, 35, 38, 44, 81
Beattie, Tina 10, 135–48, 167, 217
Beker, J. C. 52
bereavement, and visions 25, 51–2
bible: and positivism 8–9; *see also* New
  Testament; Old Testament
body: and grace 102, 106–9, 116; and
  incarnation 102–3; 'mind-produced'
  205; in Paul 17, 24, 27, 67, 85,
  103–7; spiritual 17–19, 67–8, 104;
  theft of Jesus' body 14, 19, 69, 201;
  and wholeness of being 68, 84–5
Boff, Leonardo 42
Bonhoeffer, Dietrich 35, 39
Brown, Raymond E. 150, 153, 155, 157
Buddha: and compassion 162; and death
  210–11; and Kevaddha 208, 210, 212;
  and miracle 209–10, 212
Buddhism: and afterlife 210; and miracle
  204–10, 212; and resurrection 8, 11,
  201–15; and transformative
  experience 204–5, 212–14
Bultmann, Rudolf 9, 31–5, 44, 45–6,
  89, 150: Christology 32–3, 36; and
  the Holy Spirit 157–8; and nature and
  grace 34–5, 37, 39; and Rahner 36,
  38, 40
burial of Jesus: in common grave 21, 87;
  historicity 23, 87

Campenhausen, Hans von 69
Camus, Albert 73
Catherine of Siena, St 111, 115
Celsus, and appearances of Christ 25
Cephas *see* Peter
Chareas and Callirhöe 88
cherubim, and the ark 90, 99
Christa figure 143
Christians, Jewish, and spiritual
  resurrection 55, 58
Christology: in Bultmann 32–3, 36;
  ecological 82; feminist 87–8; logos
  166 n.20; in Rahner 36
church: as body of Christ 93, 102–7,
  155, 159, 163; as context 10, 118–32;

221